Llama Drama
by Anna McNuff

Llama Drama

Copyright © 2020 by Anna McNuff

All rights reserved.

No part of this book may be reproduced in any form by any electronic or mechanical means, including information storage and retrieval systems, without written permission from the author, except for the use of brief quotations in a book review.

For Faye, thanks for sharing your Cheesy Poofs with me.

Contents

Part II

Epilogue

Faye and Anna's Route

Faye   Anna

La Paz

Salar de Uyuni

Mendoza

Santiago

Puerto Montt

Ushuaia

"THE END OF THE WORLD"

Prologue

'Waaaaa! Anna! Anna! I've been stung…!'

I looked up from the bike and over to where Faye was standing. Poised like the Karate Kid, she was balanced on one leg in the sand, holding her left foot up in the air. Dangling from her second toe was a tan-coloured scorpion. 'Ahhhh! It's a scorpion,' she yelped, waggling her foot and catapulting the venomous blighter back onto the sand.

'Oh, it hurts, oh my god it hurts. I don't know what to do!' she screamed, hopping around on her other leg. It was at that point I realised I didn't know what to do either. I was still processing the fact that there even were scorpions in Bolivia, which was news to me. A wave of panic threatened to take a hold. I pushed it away.

Right. You're the non-stung one here, Anna. You need to step up to the plate, I thought. *Time for some hero stuff. Think now. What do you do when your friend gets stung by a scorpion?* Hours spent immersed in *Dr. Quinn, Medicine Woman* now seemed like hours wasted. I had also watched the popular UK dramas *Casualty* and *Holby City* as a kid, but no one got stung by a scorpion in those. I wracked my brain. Do I pee on it?! I thought, before remembering that was definitely for jellyfish stings and not scorpions. I *had* once read something about sucking out poison… I looked at Faye's toe and shuddered. No, not that. *Think logically, McNuff, think logically... Come on...*

'Oh. Owwwww. Owwwww. It REALLY hurts,' Faye yelled, pressurising me to find a solution, and fast.

We were still close to the town of Llica, probably only 10 miles away. I hadn't checked the previous night whether we'd had any phone signal, but as I flipped my phone off airplane mode – hallelujah!! One bar! We were just in range of the town's 3G mobile tower. So naturally the only thing I could think to say next was:

'Hang on, Faye, I've got signal. I'm going to google it.'

'Okay, okay, and pass me my first aid kit?' pleaded Faye. I moved over to her and, with my left hand googling, began rummaging for it in her pannier with my right hand. Somehow, I managed to successfully make headway in both tasks. Faye pulled some after-bite out from one of the pouches and decided that applying it was worth a shot – anything to ease the pain, after all. 'It's empty!' she whimpered, shaking the tube before throwing it on the ground. (Note to self: check all items before packing them into the first aid kit.)

After-bite being no use, I forged on with my google plan and typed 'Bolivia. Scorpion... death?' into the search bar.

'Oww... Owww... My toe's gone hard! It's really hard! Is that normal?!' Faye shouted.

'I don't know, hang on...' I deleted my search and started again, inputting: 'Bolivia. Scorpion. Hard toe. Death?'

2

I was scrolling as fast as I could through the search results and then… 'Oh no!' I shouted, staring at the screen in disbelief.

'What is it?! Is it bad? Am I going to die?' wailed Faye.

'No, but I've lost 3G connection,' I replied.

'Ohhh, Anna! Hurry up!' she whimpered.

'Okay, hang on!' The 3G kicked back into life and after a few clicks I found an article online from 2012 which seemed to indicate that the outcome of a scorpion sting in Bolivia might only be mild. Phew. Although I couldn't be sure. That was a long time ago, and scorpions might have upped their venom game since then. I pressed onwards for a more recent information source, and found an article from the current year. I scanned it as quickly as I could.

'Ahh… I think it's okay, Faye,' I said, before reading aloud from the page: 'Only twenty-five to forty species of scorpions out of the four hundred in existence cause fatalities. And most fatalities are in elderly people or young children. And often in North America, where the sting is from a large, black scorpion. The small, tan scorpion will likely just cause severe pain around the bite area, but not end in fatality.'

Faye exhaled. 'Oh good' she said, letting her legs collapse and slumping down onto her pannier in the sand. She looked exhausted.

'The pain's easing off too,' she continued.

'Are you sure you're alright?' I asked.

'Yeah… I think I'm fine. God, that was the most painful thing ever,' she said, and I could hear the relief in her voice. Mostly because I felt that relief too. How many other creepy crawlies were there in South America that could pump their poison into our unsuspecting body parts? I wondered. I hoped we wouldn't have to find out.

PART I

La Paz to San Pedro de Atacama

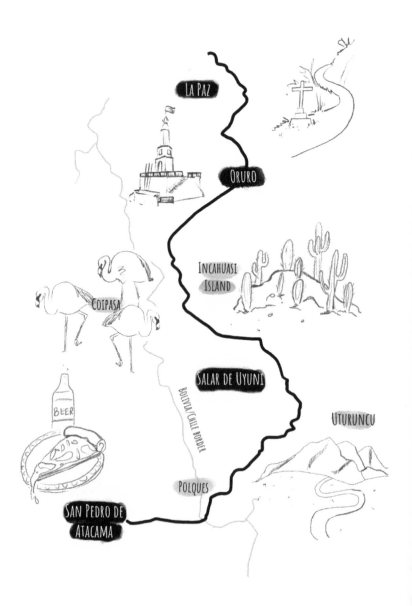

La Paz

Oruro

Incahuasi Island

Coipasa

Salar de Uyuni

BOLIVIA/CHILE BORDER

Uturuncu

BEER

Polques

San Pedro de Atacama

1

The First Plan Isn't Always the Best Plan

Distance cycled: 0 miles
Metres ascended: 0

The phone rang three times before a familiar voice came on the line.

'Hello, McNuff, how are you?'

'I'm good thanks, really good. What's happening down there in Cornwall?' I asked.

'Oh, you know, not much. I've done some tip runs with the trailer and just taken the dogs out for a stroll on the beach.'

'Sounds like you're living the Cornish dream…'

'I am indeed.'

'Faye… I've got something to ask you,' I said, getting straight to the point.

'Go on.'

'I'm going to scoot the length of South America.'

'You're what?!'

'South America. On a scooter.'

7

'What, like a Vespa? She asked.

'No, not one with a motor. A kick-scooter. You know, those things that kids ride to school, only an adult version – they do adult versions you know.'

'Do they?!' Faye laughed. 'Only you would know that.'

'Anyway, what I wanted to ask is… Do you fancy coming with me?' I paused for a moment. 'I think it'll take around six months and we could start sometime in the autumn?'

'Okay. Let me get this straight. You're asking me if I want to spend six months in South America, with you?'

'Yes.'

'On a giant kids' scooter?'

'Yes.'

'Why me?' she asked.

'Err, well… for a start, I think I could spend six months with you. Secondly, you're hard as nails and I know you won't give up. And really… honestly, I don't know anyone else crazy enough to say yes.'

There was a long silence now. I couldn't see Faye's face but I knew deep down that she wanted to jump in feet first. I knew that she'd recently been made redundant and wasn't particularly excited about the prospect of finding a new job. I knew that, like me, she craved adventure. Then again, I couldn't be so arrogant as to assume that I could just waltz into her life and ask her to put it on hold for six months to join me on a jolly.

'Faye… are you still there?' I asked.

'Yes, I'm still here.' She took a deep breath. 'Alright, Mc-Nuff, I'm in.'

Faye Shepherd of Cornwall-shire has the most wonderful auburn hair, the likes of which I have never seen on another human head. It is a blend of fiery terracotta and sunset red with just a few streaks of golden yellow, cascading all the way down to the middle of her back. I am convinced that if Faye and I were ever to appear in a sci-fi movie (one of those ones where we are in a race against time to save the world) then we would soon discover that the power of all the universe is contained within Faye's hair, such is its majesty. Couple her auburn locks with the fact that Faye is 6 ft 1 in. tall, has blue eyes and skin that turns golden in the summer months, and she has all the makings of a world-protecting superhero.

I first met Faye (and her hair) when she appeared at a roadside on the North Island of New Zealand in 2015. I was midway through a mission to run the 2,000-mile Te Araroa Trail and Faye was on a Kiwi adventure of her own, cycling the length of the country. Despite us being complete strangers, she tracked me down to say hello and, in the process, turned what was a miserable day into one that ended with laughter, wine and ice cream. It's no surprise that we've been friends ever since.

Having been home from New Zealand for a while, the adventure cogs in my mind were beginning to turn again. They creaked and groaned into motion after months of gathering dust. Months in which I'd restocked my hideously deplet-ed bank balance, moved out of London to make a home in Gloucester with the new love of my life, one Mr Jamie Mc-Donald, and launched my first book into the world. Come the start of 2016, I was feeling ready for the road again.

With dreams of a long-distance scooter adventure in mind, I pondered where I might take it. South America had always intrigued me. A mass of wonky teardrop-shaped land way down there, dangling from North America. Clinging on by… well, Panama. I had often wondered what went on down *there* – a place full of desolate sweeping mountain passes, dense jungles, wild and winding rivers and home to the driest place on earth, the Atacama Desert. Yes, there were drug lords (or so the news told me) but there were also vibrant cities, bottles of delicious wine and many, many llamas. Plus, pop sensation of the early noughties, Shakira, hailed from South America. She and her hips that didn't lie had helped me navigate some turbulent teenage years, so that sealed the deal. South Amer-ica it would be.

***

After the initial phone call with Faye, I decided to seek out some expert advice on the terrain that we'd be facing in South America. I met cycle-touring experts and South American whizz kids Neil and Harriet Pike (aka Pikes on Bikes) in a cafe in their home town of Bristol one Wednesday evening in early spring. As a couple who have spent years exploring large areas of the Andean mountains, by bike and on foot (and written many books on the subject), they were the perfect people to share my bonkers scooter idea with.

Over a few beers, the Pikes listened patiently as I explained the plan. They managed to keep a straight face throughout the meeting, even when my answers to *all* their logical questions were; 'I don't know yet.'

'How far can you go in a day on a scooter?' Harriet said.

'Umm... I don't know yet,' I replied.

'Okay, probably best to work that one out. And how do you plan to carry enough water across the Atacama Desert?' Neil asked.

'Well, we'll just... umm... Oh. I don't know yet,' I said.

'Will it go over rough terrain?' asked Neil.

'Maybe. Possibly. I don't know yet.'

'Hang on... these giant scooter things, do they go uphill?' Harriet interrupted.

'Yes, of course they do! Oh no, wait, actually – I don't know yet,' I replied.

'What is my favourite colour?' said Harriet. Okay that wasn't one of their questions but, if it had been, I would have taken a Monty Python-esque guess.

After an hour of discussion, I left my meeting with the Pikes feeling more determined than ever to make a journey through South America work. I felt so lucky to have them as a sounding board. How wonderful it was to have people in my life who didn't try to shoot me down, no matter how bizarre the idea. Granted, there were a few 'details' to iron out, but all in all – I was ready to book six months out in my life-calendar, buy a plane ticket and immerse myself in app-based Spanish lessons.

A few weeks after my meeting with the Pikes and in a bid to iron out some of those 'details', Faye and I decided to go on a tester trip. We hired two adult scooters for the weekend, strapped them to the back of the car and hauled our asses to Wales. Why Wales? Because, according to the Pikes on Bikes, the forestry roads around the Dolgoch Wilderness hostel in mid Wales were about as close as we could get to the roads in South America. Who knew? I can see the Visit Wales slogan now: *Sod South America, come to Dolgoch instead.*

For two days we zoomed along the tracks of the Tywi Forest and by Jove it was fun. The sun was shining, the birds were a-singin' and the scooters were just about the most fun you could have on two wheels. However, that's not to say that everything went *entirely* to plan.

We had been so hung up on testing out whether the standing platforms on the scooters would be high enough to make it over rocks on the rough roads that we had failed to consider one other potential showstopper. After leaving the hostel on the first morning, we scooted merrily down a gravel track before hitting a small incline. We started to slow down and the expression on our faces changed from joy to quiet contemplation. When my speed dropped to a painful creep, I got off the scooter and began walking alongside it, pushing it up the incline. Faye followed suit. We walked for thirty seconds in silence.

'Faye…' I said.

'Yes, mate?' she replied.

'These scooters don't go uphill, do they?'

'No, they don't.'

'And there are hills in South America, aren't there?'

'I think they're called the Andes,' she smiled.

'Faye?'

'Yes, mate.'

'We're not going scooting in South America, are we?'

'I don't think so,' she sighed.

With that one small incline, the original plan was dashed. They say that it is better to have tried and failed than to not have tried at all. And our plan had failed, spectacularly. We were gutted. But it wasn't the end of the world. We would simply return to the drawing board, put some Polyfilla in the giant crack in our plan and work out which parts of it were salvageable.

***

Over the weeks that followed, Faye and I revised our journey. The more we chatted, the more it became apparent that we both had our hearts set on South America. If the trip to Wales had driven anything home, it was that we both adored mountains. It was, therefore, decided that we would go to South America, but on plain old bicycles instead of scooters. We also decided that we would go up as many peaks and passes of the mighty Andes as we could, setting ourselves the goal of making over 100,000 metres of ascent over the course of the journey. After all, why would you take the flattest most direct route through life, when you could take the wiggliest, most mountainous one possible?

One April afternoon, Faye and I met for a planning session, part way between our home cities, at a cafe in Bristol. I'd recently bought a paper map of South America and I couldn't wait to spread it out and discuss route options.

Thirty minutes into the plan-a-thon, we had decided that we would begin the journey in La Paz, Bolivia. Largely because we knew nothing about Bolivia, and also because we had recently learned (courtesy of Google) that La Paz is the highest capital city in the world, situated 3,640 metres above sea level. As we traced a line south from La Paz, we were drawn to the mystique of the Atacama Desert, the vineyards of central Argentina, and the wild, untamed landscapes of Patagonia. So it made sense to begin in La Paz and pedal our way roughly 5,500 miles south, criss-crossing the border between Chile and Argentina, zigzagging across the Andes until we reached the last chunk of land before Antarctica, and a place called

Ushuaia.

I sat back from the table and stared at the line we'd just drawn on the map. In that moment, I realised that I'd been holding back. Since our first plan had failed, I hadn't yet let myself believe that we were going on this adventure. But now, the excitement surged like a Patagonian river. It thundered through my veins and, by the time it made it to my heart, I was ecstatic! We were off to South America!

As the months rolled by, Faye and I spoke often about equipment, budget and flight options. I also completed the pre-adventure prep by getting a new bike. Boudica, the beautiful pink beast that I had pedalled through the 50 states of America, wasn't suitable for the kind of off-road rocky terrain we'd be facing in the Andes. I needed a bike that could cope with everything South America would throw at it… a bike with chunky tyres and a hardy frame… I needed Bernard. Bernard was lovingly crafted at a British company called Oxford Bike Works. He was steel-framed, teal blue and just about perfect. Bernard was also the name of my late grandad. He died when I was 13, and he really loved cycling – so I decided that I would take my grandad with me on a pedal through the Andes, in spirit at least. Faye followed suit with a new bike of her own and lovingly christened it Gustavo. I don't think Faye had any relatives called Gustavo, she just liked the name.

Beyond the bike purchases, we often sent one another pictures of wiggly roads that we hoped to cycle on, or fascinating facts that we'd read online.

'Do you know that there's this thing in Bolivia called Death Road?' I said.

'No, I didn't. But did you know that Lake Titicaca is the highest navigable lake in the world?' Faye replied.

'Woah! I don't know what 'navigable' means, but let's go there. I bet there'll be llamas there.'

'I've always wanted to meet a llama,' said Faye.

'Me too. Did you know that they're related to camels? They're like their long-lost cousins or something,' I said.

'No way!' said Faye.

'Yes way. Also, I just found a picture of this mental road near Santiago with forty switchback bends… we should go down it,' I said. And so it went on…

The planning of the journey was turning out to be even more exciting than usual. Over those months, I realised that excitement – like many of the other great emotions in the universe – is not halved in the presence of another person. It is, in fact, doubled. Like gas in a hot-air balloon, it expands to fill the space that you create for it between the two of you, and it allows you to float together above the clouds. Faye and I were floating alright – we were actually sharing a spot, somewhere on cloud nine. During every discussion we had about the adventure, whether it was on the phone, in person or via message, our shared excitement grew. It grew so much that soon I could think of little else in daily life, except South America.

***

On a long car journey with Faye down to Cornwall one weekend, I decided that it was time for a team chat. Despite excitement levels being at an all-time high, I could tell that she was nervous about certain elements of the adventure, and I was worried, with all my planning excitement, that I was bulldozing her, shoving my ideas upon her and dragging her along for the ride.

When we hit a traffic jam on the A303, just outside Stone-henge, I prepared myself to ask Faye a few questions.

'So, Faye…' I said from the passenger seat.

'Yes, McNuff.'

'Your three greatest fears about the trip, what are they?'

There was a long pause, during which I wondered whether Faye was genuinely coming up with things she was scared of or whether she was just deciding if she could be completely honest with me.

'Okay, so the first one… is that I'll hold you up. I'll be slower and unfit and won't be able to keep up with you.'

'Okay. So that's one of them… number two?' I asked. I was keen to listen to all the fears before trying to do anything to appease them. Because fears are fragile things – they need space to be heard, and to breathe.

'And the second one is that we might come to some kind of harm… you know, get mugged or something. I have no idea whether or not it's safe to camp alone as two women in South America,' said Faye.

'Okay. That's understandable,' I said.

'And the third is whether or not I've chosen the right kit. I've never done a long bike trip before and I'm worried that I'm going to pack all the wrong things.'

'Is that all of them?' I asked.

'Yeah, I think so,' she said.

'Well, I'm not sure I can offer much advice on the second two, but most importantly, I can tell you that you don't need to worry about you holding me up. This is *our* adventure. I know that the idea started with me, but this isn't Anna's adventure with Faye in tow. It's ours. So we go as fast or as slow as is right for the both of us. Deal?'

'Okay, deal. Thank you. That makes me feel better,' Faye said as she let out a sigh, and she now seemed happier. There was a silence.

'Okay, come on then, your turn – what are your three fears?' Faye asked. It was then that I realised I hadn't thought about my own. I bit my lip.

'Okay, we share one fear – that we'll wind up in some kind of harm out there. Maybe through dodgy people, but maybe up a mountain and we run out of food and water or something.'

'Well, it's good we're both worried about that,' said Faye.

'Number two is that I'll let you down and you won't enjoy it.'

'What?! Of course I'm going to enjoy it! It's got to be better than a day in the office, right?'

'That's a fair point. I'll try to remember to always make it better than the office,' I smiled.

'Good. And number three?' Faye asked.

'Number three is that I'll miss Jamie too much, or put such a strain on our relationship by being away that I mess it up, and I don't want to lose him, you know?'

Faye nodded. I hadn't let on until then, but I was most nervous about that third fear. In both my previous big adventures, I'd left the UK as a singleton. But things were very different this time around: I was loved up. I'd been with Jamie for just over a year, and we were still in the honeymoon period of our relationship. I had fallen in love, and it had been going so well that I was terrified it was all going to be taken away from me. Do you ever have moments in life when you are so happy that you struggle to enjoy it because you're scared that the happiness won't last? That was me as I prepared to leave for South America.

In hindsight, the conversation we had in the car that day was invaluable. It served to bond us tightly from the start and, more importantly, it set the bar for open and honest discussions about things that we might be thinking but not saying.

I was as nervous as ever in the weeks that led up to getting on the plane, but I was used to those feelings by now. And the closer the Andes adventure got, the more I remembered why I did these journeys. Despite all the discomfort, the sleepless nights and an overwhelming feeling that I was in way over my head, the very thought of an adventure made my stomach turn in somersaults. Out *there*, on a lone mountain pass, covered in dust from the road, arms slightly tanned and grinning through a dirt-encrusted face, I would feel more alive, more often than I ever would at home. I would learn more, I would see more, and I would grow. And this time, I would grow with someone else.

2

La Paz and the Elastic Band

Distance cycled: 0 miles
Metres ascended: 0

At 4.30 a.m. one October morning, after ten hours of cruising through the air from London Heathrow, our plane skidded onto the tarmac at La Paz airport. In between enjoying the airplane food and watching back-to-back Disney movies, I had spent a large chunk of the flight playing with my new toy: a watch with an altimeter. It didn't seem to work while we were in flight (which was disappointing) but, as we touched down, I inspected it with a renewed sense of hope. After the seatbelt sign was switched off and the passengers made a bid for the doors, it finally displayed what I'd been waiting for.

'Faye! Look!' I said, pointing at the altimeter which now read 4,001 metres.

Faye gave a thumbs up and an excited grin. 'We're living the high life now, McNuff. There's no way back,' she said, and she was right.

I sat back in my seat and inhaled deeply. *So, this is what being at 4,000 metres above sea level feels like*, I thought. I held the breath in for a moment before letting it go, then looked down at my hands and forearms, watching my body closely for signs of change. What would happen next? I wondered. Was I going to struggle to breathe? Would I spontaneously combust? Would my eyes pop out of my head just like in the movie *Total Recall*, when Arnold Schwarzenegger found himself oxygen-starved on the plains of Mars? After a few minutes of nothing dramatic happening to my body, I concluded that life at 4,000 metres seemed very much the same as life at sea level.

Once off the plane, we mooched through to passport control, taking the time to chat to a couple of Bolivian immigration policemen in the arrivals building.

'*Buenos días, Señoritas,*' said one policeman, as we approached the immigration desk. It seemed like the perfect opportunity to give my limited app-learned Spanish a go. I grinned and rambled off some version of 'Hello. We don't speak much Spanish, but I like your uniform.'

'*No hay problema. Gracias,*' said the policeman, seemingly satisfied with the fashion-related compliment. He then looked at Faye, who hadn't done quite as much Spanish prep as I had.

'Errrr… *Pingüino!*' she said, offering up one of the three random Spanish words she knew. The policeman looked confused.

'¡*Policía!*' I said, pointing at his arm.

'*Sí,*' said the policeman. He seemed rather less interested at the confirmation that he was, indeed, a policeman.

Two steps out of passport control and there was our

luggage on the single baggage belt at La Paz airport, right in front of us. Marvellous. We spotted two tattered cardboard boxes which contained Bernard and Gustavo and went over to take them off the belt. It was during my attempt to remove the bike from the belt that I realised the altitude was affecting me after all. The simple task of picking up the box and putting it onto a baggage trolley felt like I was 20 miles into a marathon. Huffing and puffing my way through the task, I looked down the belt at Faye and noted that she was struggling just as much as I was. She looked up and we both burst into fits of giggles. I wasn't sure what Faye was laughing at, but I was laughing at the fact that we were about to cycle up mountains in South America, to explore our physical potential, to push our bodies to their limit and so far we seemed to have met our limit at baggage reclaim.

Regaining some composure, we managed to wheel our bikes through to the arrivals lounge, where we were met by our La Paz host, Sergio. Sergio was a member of the cycle-touring network *warmshowers.org* and often hosted cycle tourists in La Paz. We'd never met him before, and had only ever exchanged messages, but he'd gotten himself out of bed at 3.30 a.m. to collect us from the *aeropuerto* – an act which I thought was above and beyond the call of hosting duty. I told him, in broken Spanish, that my mum was very grateful that we had someone meeting us and Sergio chuckled as we shuffled slowly behind him to the car.

'What now, Sergio?!' I asked, as we loaded the bikes onto the top of his 4x4 and hopped inside.

'Oh, we do some things today. Today I am your La Paz tour guide for the whole day.' He grinned. GREAT! I thought. We'd get a chance to see a little bit of the city before we crawled gleefully into sleeping bags at Sergio's apartment.

Fast forward eight hours to 5.30 p.m. and we had witnessed a car plough into the side of a building (apparently handbrakes are important on the steep roads of La Paz); been treated to an empanada breakfast (empanadas are little pastry parcels filled with meat and cheese); and met Sergio's uncle, his step-mum and half-sister at various locations around the city. We had swung by his Dad's old house in a beautiful area called Valle de la Luna (Moon Valley), before collecting his friend Carolina and her son for a three-course lunch. Full of local fare, we had pressed on through the afternoon, visiting a local outdoor climbing wall, a bike shop and some nearby parks (where Sergio encouraged us to get out of the car to do 'exercises' to help us acclimatise). As the sun went down, we were treated to the *pièce de résistance* of the day, as Sergio took us on an off-road tour in the 4x4, down steep dirt tracks through the backstreets of the city, all the while with the bikes still on the roof. When we finally got back to his apartment we had driven 50 miles around the streets of La Paz and been awake for 43 hours since leaving London. We were pooped.

***

After recovering from our first day of sightseeing, we settled into life in La Paz. The plan was to spend a full week in the city, acclimatising to the altitude, getting all the supplies we still needed for the journey and to ready ourselves for the road ahead. Sergio's apartment was centrally located and a great base to explore the city from. We slept on our camping mats in a bare room and met a few other cycle tourists who were staying there too. We got on particularly well with a fellow Brit called Campbell, who showed us where to get delicious pastries (always a bonus) and offered advice on the best GPS app we could load onto our phones for navigation.

Despite being aware that we didn't blend in seamlessly with the locals, I felt at ease in La Paz. Set in a deep basin, it's surrounded by the grey-blue volcanic peaks of the Cordillera Real. The largest mountain, Illimani, is visible to the southeast and often dusted with snow. The city itself is a sea of oranges, yellows, reds and browns, rooftops and steeples, all coated in a thick haze from the throng of cars, which jostle for position on the downtown streets. Weaving its way through the centre of the chaos is the muddy brown Río Irpavi, which snakes down the valley and out of sight.

The 800,000 city dwellers live in houses that span everything from ornate villas to slum-style shacks. The real estate in La Paz is topsy-turvy in relation to other cities around the world, where those who can afford it live high up in the hills and enjoy stunning views and fresh air. Instead, in La Paz, the wealthy live as far into the basin as they can – at the lower altitude of 3,500 metres – and it's why the most opulent and impressive buildings are in the city centre. Going upwards and outwards, towards the surrounding mountains, the roads become dirt tracks, as the homes get more shack-like and those living there endure the harsher, thinner air.

La Paz straddles the divide between the developed and developing worlds. It has many modern twists – like an infrastructure of cable cars to help commuters get up and down the city – but in other ways, it's a topsy-turvy place. For example, in the centre of town, there was a posh sports clothing store, run by a global brand, selling a pair of shorts for 435 bolivianos (£50). Sitting just outside the shop was a grandmother in traditional Bolivian dress, selling phone chargers from a ragged blanket for nine bolivianos (£1). These two things sat unapologetically side by side. Much as I tried, there seemed to be no way to compare La Paz with anywhere else.

One of the things that I was nervous about before starting the journey had been my Spanish or lack of it. Until this point, my adventures had seen me travel to English-speaking countries like the USA and New Zealand. I had promised myself that I would take some Spanish lessons and at least be able to say a few basic things before I arrived in La Paz. Yes, yes, I would take Spanish lessons at home, that's what I would do. Did I take those Spanish lessons? Did I hell. But wait, I had several good excuses. Number one: I didn't make the time. Number two: I got so nervous thinking about learning Spanish that it was better to not learn Spanish (so that I didn't have to think about it). And number three: Life got in the way. Faye was in the same linguistically challenged boat as I was, although she had at least been realistic and accepted that she wouldn't learn any Spanish until she made it to Bolivia. And so, while our bodies were acclimatising to life at 3,600 metres above sea level, we signed up for three days of intense Spanish classes. For the princely sum of 315 bolivianos (about £37), we scored a few hours each day of private lessons with Milka the Spanish teacher. Much to my disappointment, she was not the actual Milka cow of alpine chocolate fame but, instead, a local teacher from the nearby town of El Alto with dark hair, kind eyes and an even kinder smile.

Each morning we studied for three hours, and once we had the basics mastered, Milka started to teach us phrases like: 'Does this hotel have a pool?', 'Is there an en-suite bathroom?' and 'Which way to the bus station?' With limited learning-time on our hands and very little chance of us catching a bus to a swanky hotel with a pool over the following six months, we repeatedly railroaded Milka into teaching us some more ad-venture-related things like: 'Can we camp here?', 'My bike is broken', 'I like chocolate', 'Where is the bike shop?' and 'We prefer to travel by bicycle.' Come the final lesson, we were sad to leave Milka. In a city where we knew no one, she had been like a *mamá* to us. Faye even asked her (in Spanish) which one of us she preferred. Of course, like any mother, she couldn't choose between her children.

***

Even though, outwardly, things in La Paz were progressing well, in the evenings and in my mind, I was struggling. I had forgotten how uncomfortable the first 10 days of an adventure always were. I thought it would be easier this time around. That the confidence gained from previous journeys and the excitement of being in South America would overrule everything else, but it didn't. I was still questioning whether leaving home and, more specifically, leaving Jamie, for six months was the right thing to do. I had finally found the person that I wanted to spend the rest of my life with and now I had upped sticks and left him at home alone. What was I doing?

I recognised this set of thoughts and likened it to an elastic band. I realised that, in the first week of an adventure (or indeed of any great change in life), you are stretching yourself away from normality but you are still bound to it by a giant elastic band. Every fibre in your being wants to just let go, to give up the fight for forward motion and snap you right back to normality. To comfort, to knowing, to safety, to certainty. The further you move from what is familiar, the greater the resistance of the elastic band. It's a test: how badly do you really want to be there? What are you willing to put up with in order to carry on?

In a bid to find some distraction from the uncomfortable thoughts, I turned my attention to the 'tester rides' that lay ahead. These were a couple of short trips we would do from La Paz, to get our minds and bodies used to the altitude and to test our kit. The main items under scrutiny were power-bank batteries (to hold charge for our phones and GPS safety trackers), dyno-hubs (which would charge the batteries when the wheels of our bikes were moving at a decent speed), and water bottles with inbuilt filtration systems to keep out the nasties.

The first tester ride was to a nearby ski station called Chacaltaya and it didn't quite go to plan. We were aiming to make it to 5,200 metres and back again in a day, but we fell short. Somewhere around the 4,200-metre marker, we had our first llama sighting, an event which caused both of us to squeal in delight and bring the bikes to a halt. It was the first time either of us had seen a llama 'in the flesh'. Thirty-three years of life without so much as a whiff of one, and then there were five of them at the side of the road, just goin' about their daily llama business. We were off the bikes and midway through conversing with the llamas (which may have been a one-way conversation) when I began to feel nauseous and lightheaded. Sitting down on a mound of nearby earth, I announced to Faye that I felt a bit funny.

To keep an eye on how we were coping with life way above sea level, we'd been using an oxygen saturation monitor that you slip over the end of your finger to measure the level of oxygen in your blood. A normal, healthy adult should have a saturation level (or sats) between 98–100%. Under usual circumstances and in a country at sea level, sats lower than 95% would mean a trip to hospital. Our sats had been running at around 90% (sometimes lower), but this was to be expected in our first week at high altitude. On our tester ride to Chacaltaya, however, the oxygen percentage in my blood had dropped to 74%, so we decided to turn around and head back to the city.

A few days later, with my sats back at 90%, we left La Paz again, this time on a longer four-day return trip to Copacabana, on the shores of Lake Titicaca. We waved goodbye to

Sergio (having used up more than enough of his hospitality) and set off on the two-hour climb out of town. I say 'set off' – really, we wobbled off. In my wisdom, I'd decided that I would heavily load my front handlebar bag to ease the weight in the panniers over my back wheel. What I didn't think about is that the handlebar bag had a high centre of gravity and, when heavily loaded, made the steering uncontrollable. Imagine the scene: I pedal 100 metres from the apartment. I puff and wheeze as we start up a steep hill and zigzag all over the road. Faye looks back, laughing, and I know she is thinking the same thing I am: how are we ever going to do six months of *this*?

***

Over the days that followed, slowly but surely my body began to cope with the strain of cycling at altitude. I was less breathless than I had been when we arrived in La Paz and my appetite was beginning to creep up too. Since arriving in Bolivia, I had barely been able to eat anything. I would usually buy a burrito for breakfast, chop it into four pieces, and if I had managed to eat three out of the four pieces by the end of the day, it was a triumph. On the final day of our journey back from Copacabana, something felt different. In the city of El Alto (just above La Paz), I noticed a strange sensation in my stomach. I was starving.

'Faye!' I yelled above the smog and the noise of the El Alto streets.

'Yeah?' she hollered back.

'I'm keen for something to eat. Can we stop?'

'Sure! I could eat,' she replied.

A few minutes later, we'd located a suitable-looking eatery at the side of the road. We parked our bikes up outside and wandered in to find two women in traditional Bolivian dress. It was a relaxed place: red plastic chairs, pictures of greasy meals on the walls and whole chickens turning on a chest-height rotisserie out the front. Next to the rotisserie were what looked like small brains in jars – blobs of mangled pink suspended in oil or perhaps vinegar. I had no idea what they were, but I decided not to ask in case the waitress mistook my query for a side order of brain. Instead, we used our limited Spanish to say that we would love to order some chicken and chips. The Spanglish seemed to work and the waitress nodded, although I wasn't sure if I'd just ordered us two whole chickens.

Sitting outside the cafe in a couple of red chairs, we watched the bustle of the El Alto markets go on around us and waited patiently for the plates of food to arrive. Fifteen minutes later, the waitress appeared. She smiled and handed over two meals. I was relieved to see that we'd been given chicken, rice, some form of undercooked potatoes (chips would be pushing it) and a pile of sauce. The sauce looked like a mild salsa verde but, in fact, turned out to be the spiciest chilli concoction known to humankind. I'm pleased to say that Faye took one for the team when she spooned a dollop of red-hot sauce onto her undercooked chips and took a big bite. She almost choked to death, tears streaming down her cheeks and a look of panic on her face. Faye really doesn't 'do' spicy food and so, as any good friend would, I wet myself laughing.

That afternoon, covered in soot from the road and with half a chicken and some undercooked potatoes inside me, I felt something give way. I wasn't nervous anymore. I wasn't questioning whether I should be anywhere else, whether I should have stayed at home or whether this adventure was a terrible idea. In that moment, I realised that I didn't want to be anywhere else. The elastic band of normality had been stretched and stretched until finally, after 10 days in Bolivia, it had snapped. It had let me go, releasing me into the adventure and into a world of unknowns. There were no thoughts taking me back to my old life now. There was just me, Faye, Bernard and Gustavo on a journey to the end of the world.

3

Now THAT Is the Andes!

Distance cycled: 140 miles
Metres ascended: 4,926

In a hotel on the cobbled backstreets of downtown La Paz, I sat on my bed and looked at Faye's ashen face. Since returning from Copacabana the previous day, Faye had taken a turn for the worse. In fact, her stomach had taken several turns for the worse and had now progressed to full-on somersaults. In one of the rare moments that Faye wasn't making friends with the en-suite toilet, I broached the subject of our planned ride out of La Paz.

'Faye… we don't have to go today, you know? We've still got almost six months to make it to Ushuaia, there's no rush,' I said, as she lay on her bed, clutching her tummy.

'I know,' she sighed.

'Well… take an hour or so to think about it,' I replied, realising that I had lost my leaving-the-city mojo too. I would quite happily slump back into the crisp white linen sheets, put my head on the fluffy pillow and start this whole leaving-the-city shebang the following day. There was a logical reason to stay too. If Faye was ill, it was practical to stay in a nice hotel, rather than her having to deal with gut acrobatics in a tent, halfway up a mountain.

At this early stage in the journey together, I was still learning when to push Faye and when to let her be. Ultimately, whether or not she was well enough to leave was her decision, so I decided to let her be. An hour later, Faye emerged again from the en-suite toilet.

'Okay, McNuff, I'm good to go.'

'Are you sure?' I asked, closely studying her face for signs of faux bravery.

'Yeah. I'll be fine. I'm sure once we get going and I get some fresh air, I'll perk up.'

'Alright… if you're sure?' I pressed.

'I am,' she said.

'Then let's do it.'

It was gone 1 p.m. when we began the long climb out on the north-eastern side of the city. Despite having left La Paz twice before on our 'tester rides', we were now headed in a different direction. That day, we planned to snake our way from the depths of downtown, up and over La Cumbre Pass at 4,650 metres, and into an area of northern Bolivia called the Yungas. Being late October, it was the end of spring in the southern hemisphere, so we had a good five hours of daylight left to make the 15-mile ride to the top of the pass and find somewhere to camp on the other side.

Faye was quieter than usual for the first hour of the climb, but I attributed that to her having ejected most of yesterday's food intake out of a hole that wasn't her mouth. I tried not to worry, but as the second hour slipped by and Faye slipped further and further behind, it became apparent that she really was in no fit state to be on a bike. I was a few hundred metres ahead of her, so I stopped to wait while she caught up. Why hadn't she just played it safe and stayed in the hotel? I thought. Then again, if I were in Faye's shoes, I would have told my unwell body to pipe down and get on the bike too. We were similar in that respect; we would both push ourselves past where our bodies wanted to go. By the time Faye made it to where I was, I had moved beyond questioning her decision and to a point of understanding. I was back in full supportive-friend mode.

'How you doing?' I asked, watching her slump over the handlebars of her bike. Her face was now as white as it had been after one of the hotel-room toilet trips.

'Not good, mate,' she sighed, shaking her head.

'Oh, Faye-bomb,' I said softly.

If there was any chance of us making it over that pass by nightfall, we needed a new plan. After some discussion, we decided to carry on upwards but put Faye up the front so that she could dictate the pace. We also agreed to stop regularly for something to eat. Trying to get energy into Faye was a top priority.

Together, we continued to inch up the mountain, following a road which contoured around it. Everything up there was grey and dusty. Grey road, grey skies, grey rubble. All grey. The metres of ascent ticked by, and by 4,400 metres, Faye was a mess – she was barely moving the pedals around and weaving all over the road on the bike. Soon after, things tipped from the mad to the downright ridiculous. While huddled behind a rock at one of our rest stops, I was watching Faye try to force-feed herself a cereal bar when it started to snow. There was a moment of silence as the first few flakes fell on our arms and cheeks. Then we looked at one another and burst out laughing.

'Oh, my goodness!' said Faye.

'This is ridiculous!' I said, shaking my head.

Our first day, our glorious exit from the city, our first foray into the Andes proper, and Faye was at death's door and we were being snowed on. Brilliant. We stayed crouched behind the rock to pull on a few more clothes and I did some on-the-spot maths.

'Okay, Faye, we've got two hundred and fifty metres of ascent left to make over three miles, and ninety minutes until the sun goes down.'

'Are we going to make it?' Faye asked, shivering.

'Honestly, I'm not sure. Let's just keep going and see. We can always camp on this side of the mountain tonight,' I replied.

Faye stared at the ground and her expression changed.

Her eyes flickered, and there was a fire in her belly. She looked up.

'Stuff it. Let's just go hard,' she said through gritted teeth.

'What? But you're struggling. You're weaving all over the place and I—'

'I know, but I think I've got about another two hours left in me before I conk out completely, so we might as well try to make it down the other side in that time. Just go faster, and I'll try to keep up.'

'Are you sure?'

'I'm sure. The top or bust,' she replied.

'The top or bust,' I affirmed. Faye Shepherd – what a trooper.

Off we went, this time with our eyes firmly fixed on the top-of-the-mountain prize. I did my best to keep my pace steady, adding speed very slowly like turning a screw. I also appointed myself chief cheerleader for the final section of the ascent and shouted at Faye each time we ascended another 50 metres, just to let her know that she was doing AMAZING. Which was true.

'A hundred metres left to the top!!!' I yelled over the wind. It was still snowing, and despite pushing hard, we were both now wearing our thick down jackets. The landscape around us had changed from grey-brown to a yellowish green. It reminded me of Exmoor National Park back home. Wild and windswept, harsh and open. Even though the incline softened towards the top of the pass, my energy level started to wane. While I had been so concerned about Faye, I had neglected to realise that pedalling to a height of 4,650 metres was going to be a challenge for me too.

'Fifty metres to go!' I hollered, as a bit of dribble escaped from my mouth onto the handlebars. I had given up trying to control any facial expressions in the wind up there.

'That's the top!' rasped Faye from behind me, just as a grey stone house on the summit came into view.

'Rarrrrrrr!' I yelled. 'We are WARRIIOORRS!!'

'WARRRIIIOOORS!!!' Faye screamed back, before we both fell silent, gritted our teeth and made a final bid for that stone house and the top, at last.

Our stop at the top was brief, and we wasted no time in whizzing along a flat section of open moorland, before rounding a bend to begin the descent. We should have been gathering speed by that point but, instead, my pedals had slowed. I pulled on my brakes to bring the bike to a halt and stood stock-still with my mouth wide open. Faye appeared beside me, and she was silent too.

'Oh. My. Goodness,' I whispered.

'Wow,' said Faye.

We were standing at the top of a huge valley, sandwiched between two dark grey mountains. On the lower slopes, small patches of straw-coloured tussock were doing their best to grow, with wild, punk rocker-style hair swept to one side or the other, depending on which direction the wind had ravaged them from. The colours were dull, ugly even, but all along the slopes were fragments of shale, scattered like shards of a broken mirror. I stood and watched as a ray of evening sun managed to sneak through the low-hanging cloud and catch one of those jagged pieces of shale, making it sparkle like a diamond in the rough. Everything about the mountains was sharp. I was sure that if I reached out towards one of the peaks, I would prick my finger on it and sleep for a thousand years.

It was an intimidating sight, but I felt no fear, only awe. From where we were standing, I could see three dusty grey roads. One plunged to the valley floor, another snaked back and forth along a steep slope opposite, and a third, the highest road, contoured around the mountain to the left of us until it disappeared into a wall of cloud. That third road was the one we were on. We would be riding into the clouds, and into the unknown. A wave of excitement welled up inside me.

'Now THAT is the Andes!' I yelled at the top of my lungs, grinning at Faye. Faye half-smiled back. The adrenaline rush of having made the top had swiftly worn off, and she had begun to look terrible again.

'I think it might rain,' she said quietly.

I looked up at the sky above our heads. She was right. In all my excitement at the view, I hadn't noticed the slow creep of ominous black cloud.

'Okay, let's get down the mountain and find somewhere to camp,' I said, and Faye nodded.

We swung our legs over the bikes and pushed off to begin the descent. We began whooshing along the mountain's edge, swooping around bends, through one wall of cloud and into the next – down, down, down we went. Within 10 minutes it had started to rain, and after 20 minutes, it was pouring. Big blobs of icy rain dropped onto our down jackets and threatened to soak through. I briefly considered stopping to pull on a rain jacket, but we expected to find a camp spot any minute now.

'You alright?' I shouted at Faye, as she appeared beside me. It had been 45 minutes since we'd left the top and I was getting worried about her.

'I really need to stop soon,' she said, and I could hear the desperation in her voice.

The wind had picked up and it dawned on me that the rain was more than a passing shower – we were riding into a full-blown storm. A moment later, a fork of lightning shot from the clouds up ahead, the sky flashed with purple and the thunder boomed. At last we spotted a small road off to the right of the main one.

'Faye!! Over there!' I shouted, pointing to the track as another rumble of thunder threatened to drown out my call.

We followed it downwards for a few hundred metres, knowing that we would have to cycle back up in the morning, but at that point we didn't care. Throwing the bikes down in haste, we both began pulling items out of our panniers. Faye looked awful and was unsteady on her feet, so I went into drill-sergeant mode. Priority one was to get her warm and dry. Together, we quickly put up Faye's tent and, as soon as it was vaguely shelter-shaped, I unzipped the door for her to get in.

After Faye's tent was secure, I picked up my own tent and began to remove it from its bag. Again, the lightning flashed and the thunder boomed. Then it started to rain even harder.

'Oh. Sod that!' I said out loud, stuffing my tent back in the bag and running over to Faye's.

'Faye! I'm coming into your tent, okay?!' I yelled.

'Come in!' she shouted back.

I crawled inside to see Faye clutching her legs to her chest. She was shivering, her red hair was plastered to her still white face but, despite all of that, she looked a darn sight better than she had done five minutes earlier.

After managing to wriggle out of wet clothes and into dry ones, we cooked up a modest noodle dinner in the porch of the tent. While slurping down steaming noodles, I thought back over the events of that day: watching Faye dig deep into her well of self-belief, being dumbstruck by the misty mountain vista and managing to get our simple shelter up in a beast of storm.

I felt a swell of pride. We had travelled out of the city, and up and over La Cumbre Pass under testing circumstances. It was towards the end of basking in post-challenge glow that I remembered I should let the outside world – namely, my mum – know that I was safe and well. Mum was used to getting

GPS messages from me in far-flung places. Over the years, I had learned that when you are a wayward daughter, a check in once a day can help to stave off sleepless nights of motherly worry. It was the least I could do for Mum's lifetime of sacrifice. That night, I was excited to share with my mum what had been a day of triumphs. I fired up the GPS and tapped out a message:

'Hi Mum! All okay here. Faye not well. Made it over a 4,650m pass. Storm going on but cooking up dinner now. Safe and dry! xxx'

A reply came back swiftly.

'Anna, get yourself down from that mountain and get hydrated right away! xxx'

Mothers. God love 'em.

4

Death Road

Distance cycled: 315 miles

Metres ascended: 5,955

Death Road is one of Bolivia's greatest tourist attractions. Originally built by prisoners of the Paraguay-Bolivia war in the 1930s, it was once the only way for motorised traffic to move between La Paz and the town of Coroico, on the very edge of the Amazon basin. The road itself is narrow and winding, cut sharply into the dense green mountainside, with a perilous drop to the valley floor off one side. In years gone by, drivers would head up or down the road, hoping that they didn't meet another vehicle at a dodgy point along it (and there are lots). Hope was an insufficient strategy and accidents were inevitable. As drivers tried to pass one another in buses and cars, the road would crumble, or one driver would make a wrong move and slip off the edge of the road, into the abyss. You only need count the number of crosses along Death Road to see just how frequently people made that mistake.

In 2006, a new, wider, safer tarmac road was built to Coroico, and the old rubble road became redundant, to motorised traffic at least. In place of the local cars and buses, it began to attract thrill-seeking cycle tourists. Now, thousands of visitors each year flock to its location in the North Yungas to ride mountain bikes from the small town of Pongo, at 3,500 metres, down to the valley floor. While the number of deaths on the road each year has fallen dramatically (from hundreds to just a few) it's still a very dangerous road.

Death, in itself, isn't an attraction, of course, but Death's best mate, Danger, now he's a real draw. We humans love danger. Well… all humans except me. In a pre-trip discussion about Death Road and whether or not we should ride down it, I wasn't so sure. What with all the chat about 'perilous precipices', the Death Road tourist board had done such a great job at creating global hype that I had actually questioned whether it was something I really needed to 'do'. Other examples of this include: sky diving (no, thanks); bungee jumping (done it once, don't need to do it again); snowboarding down black runs (I'd rather stay on the blue slope and stop for a hot chocolate); and, lastly, downhill mountain biking (no way, José). I knows what I likes and my overactive imagination likes feeling in control.

'Come on, mate… it can't be that bad,' pleaded Faye during one of our phone calls.

'Okay, okay, but you know I hate riding down hills fast. If we get there and it's all death-like and crumbly, then I'm taking the main road.'

'Deal,' said Faye.

If Faye was the adrenaline-loving Danger Mouse (which

she is) then I would be Penfold the Mole. All milk-bottle glasses and safety first.

***

The morning after the thunderstorm, I'd woken up in my own tent. The storm had continued around us for a couple of hours, but by 10 p.m. it was calm enough for me to put up a second tent. So I'd decided against spooning Faye for the night and made a move to sleep in my own pop-up palace, just next door. Over a breakfast of cardboard-tasting cereal bars, Faye assured me that she was feeling better than the previous day. This wasn't to say that she was on tip-top form, but any improvement in her health was a major positive. And besides, that day was all about riding down the mountain rather than up it. That day was about riding Death Road.

Rounding the bend and catching a glimpse of the road for the first time, it was easy to forget about the rumoured dangers – the view was spectacular. Having now begun a descent into the Yungas region, the landscape had changed dramatically from the day before. Everything was softer-looking there; each part of the mountain was covered in lush trees. Death Road itself was a thin ribbon of whitish grey, parading around the mountain and dissolving into the sky in the distance. The road hugged the steep cliffs so tightly that from afar you couldn't tell if it was a road at all. Winding and weaving, rising and falling, but mostly falling, tumbling out of sight all the way to the valley floor. Now that I had seen the road, its allure outweighed any trepidation still lurking at the back of my mind. I simply had to ride it. I smiled at Faye. Faye smiled at me. Then she mouthed, 'Awesome.' And off we went.

I began the descent by staying as close as possible to the mountain wall, taking care to steady the bike as it juddered over the rocky ground. Making sure that I didn't pick up too much speed in a physical sense was mirrored by trying to make sure that my imagination didn't gather too much speed as well. I didn't want either to become a runaway train.

To my right was a solid wall of rock, and to the left, just 3 metres away, was a 2,000-metre drop. No barricades, no… nothing. Well, except the metal crosses – they were dotted along the edge of the cliff, commemorating the people who had lost their lives to it over the years. We'd already passed dozens of them. Faye seemed less nervous than I was. She didn't feel the need to hug the mountain wall and was cycling in the middle of the road.

After the first 30 minutes on the road, I got used to having such a big drop to the left of me. Slowly but surely, my emotions progressed through mild fear to quiet delight and eventually arrived at sheer joy. I grew in confidence and began to look up and around as I cycled.

The weather had perked up since the previous day and what was once a yawning expanse filled with grey cloud was now a picturesque backdrop of blue, with white wisps of mist rolling over the peaks and clinging to the sides of the mountain. It was like a scene from a movie – *King Kong*, *Avatar*, even

– one of those Hollywood blockbusters in which you follow a plane swooping through a cloud forest. After an hour of descending, I began to hear the rush of water from Río Santa Elena, which was weaving its way along the valley floor. We pedalled on, along the rubble road, passing under small cascades and swooping around hairpin bends. All the while, the air got warmer and the temperature rose just a fraction every hour.

Eating and drinking on the bike was tricky, so every now and then we'd take a break, tucking ourselves into the wall of the mountain near one of the waterfalls. On one of those breaks, I watched a butterfly hover above my panniers before settling onto one of them. I'd seen a few butterflies that morning but none as bold as this one, which had jet-black wings with bright patches of royal blue and orange. I watched as it slowly strutted the length of the pannier, pausing to flick its wings every now and then, seemingly knowing just how fabulous it appeared in the midday sun. Above our heads, a small flock of black birds were busying themselves in intricately constructed nests, which hung like sacks off the ends of slim tree branches clinging to the rock. Each bird had a shock of yellow on its side and I later learned that they were golden-winged caiques. What was life like with gold on your wings?, I wondered.

I would love to tell you that we were alone out there that day, that the serenity and calm of a three-hour descent into the Bolivian Yungas were broken only by the sound of twittering birds, our squeaky breaks and whoops of delight at the surrounding landscape. But that would be a lie. Every 10 minutes, a 20-strong group of riders would whizz by on rented mountain bikes. Sometimes they looked frightened, sometimes they looked 'radical', but each and every one, without a doubt, was going substantially faster than we were.

Thanks to our steady speed, the punctures, the rough and rocky terrain, and stopping repeatedly to take photos, it took us four hours to make the bottom of the valley. There, we passed many of the tourists again. They were now sitting outside a ramshackle cafe in the tiny town of Yolosa, enjoying beers before clambering into a bus for a ride back home. We too were now ready for the ride out of the valley, although it would be 5 miles by our own pedal power. We paused briefly by a small bridge over Río Yolosa and I inhaled deeply.

'Jeez, it feels good to be able to breathe!' I said to Faye, lapping up the oxygen at 1,200 metres above sea level, the lowest we'd been since arriving in Bolivia three weeks earlier. Faye took a deep breath too.

'Oh yes!' she sighed. 'Although it's pretty hot down here,' she continued, and I agreed. I checked my watch and the temperature on it read 35°C. Yikes. That was hot. In all the cruising downwards, we hadn't noticed how much the temperature had crept up and, now that the clouds had well and truly moved away, the afternoon sun was beating down. We slapped on some sun cream, took a few big swigs from our water bottles and set off up the hill, bound for Coroico and deeper into the Yungas Jungle.

***

Everybody knows that there are laws in the Jungle, and the Yungas was no different. There are two laws that apply in the Yungas: the law of the up and the law of the down. There is no along. Along is a luxury reserved for other areas of Bolivia and something we could only ever dream of while in the Yungas. In fact, beyond Coroico, I began to wonder whether the concept of riding along a flat plain was something we'd imagined, such was the relentlessness of the ups and downs.

If you looked at a bird's eye view of that area of Bolivia, it would appear as if a giant had scooped up the earth in his palm and crumpled it like a piece of paper. It was all peaks and valleys, highs and lows, deep troughs and gentle summits. Everything in the landscape was green: deep, dark, and almost black in places. The only breaks in the green were the rubble roads, either a yellowish brown or a dark grey, rising and falling, disappearing around bends, flowing onwards into the horizon and mirroring the path of the dark green rivers, which weaved along the valley floor, way down below. If it was a hot, dry day then those roads coated us in dust, every spare particle of it clinging to our glistening skin or sweat-sodden clothing. If it was a rainy day, as happened often in the Yungas, the roads would grow thick muddy fingers and take a hold of our tyres, sucking our bikes into the earth, clawing as we passed and slowing progress from a few miles an hour to not much at all.

Each morning, we would sit outside our tents, watching and listening to the jungle come to life around us. Sometimes we'd be joined by a solitary beetle, shuffling slowly through the camp, and one day a slim-beaked hummingbird hovered by, its blue-green body shimmering in the dawn light. I knew I shouldn't really have favourites when it came to wildlife, but I did: I always looked forward to seeing one particular little black bird with a tinge of green running through its coat. I liked that little fella the most because he had a patch of red feathers on his head, which looked like he'd put a hat on just before leaving the nest that day.

In between bird 'n' beetle watching, and usually over a breakfast of crackers and cheese, Faye would call over to me.

'How many metres are we in for today, McNuff?' To which my reply was usually a number between 1,500 and 3,500. Those metres were split between two or three big climbs, with some hair-raising descents in between, so Faye would get a briefing on the full scope of the ups and downs ahead. We rarely spoke about distance. Distance became irrelevant in the Yungas – the Land of No Along.

Going downhill was just a case of clinging on for as long as we could before our hands tired from gripping the brakes. But we soon came up with a more specific strategy to break up the long climbs and decided to stop for a short break each time we ascended 100 metres. A 100-metre upwards stint would usually take us 20 minutes of cycling, which doesn't sound like much, but when it was 35–38°C, with a blanket of humidity wrapped around us, and we were grappling for balance on a rocky road, then it was long enough. We found that we could just about bear the heat and exertion for those 20 minutes, before needing to flop into the shade at the side of the road and throw as much water down our necks as we could. After a short rest, word would have spread to all horseflies in the area that there was an opportunity for two easy meals sprawled on the roadside, so they would begin to swarm, at which point, we would leap back on our bikes and resume our journey up the hill. The 20:20 rest-to-ride ratio was a painfully slow way to make progress, but it was all we could do to keep going in the suffocating heat.

***

The morning we left our camp spot in the hills above the town of Arapata, our tyres jostled for position on an especially uneven and loose road surface. Riding Bernard and Gustavo downhill was like clinging on to a pneumatic drill: our hands juddered on the handlebars, our arms shook, all of our wobbly bits jiggled, and if we didn't clamp our teeth tightly together, they would chatter on the way down too. It was on these long downhills, which sometimes lasted up to 90 minutes, that I wondered whether I perhaps preferred slogging uphill. But on the ups I wished to go down and on the downs I wished to go up. It was modern life all over – the grass was always greener on the other side of the hill in the Yungas.

At the bottom of the valley, I had just about regained some feeling in my hands and eased off on the brakes when I noticed a strong smell in the air.

'Faye… can you smell that?' I sniffed.

'Smell what?' she said.

'I'm not sure… It smells like home brew? Like rotting fruit?' I replied, now looking off to the side of the road and into the trees. Faye spotted them before I did.

'MANGOOOOSSS!' she hollered at the top of her lungs.

'MANGOOOSSSS!!' I hollered back.

And there they were: hundreds of mango trees lining the roadside, laid out in rows with big juicy green teardrop-shaped things dripping from every branch. Now, I'd never been anywhere mangos grew before, and what with them being in my top three favourite fruits of all time (the mighty banana will never be beaten and the blueberry sneaks a close second), I was overcome with excitement. It was like meeting a pop star for the first time. I'd been a big fan of mangos and their work in my local supermarket for many years now, but to see them in the flesh, on their home turf, hanging around naturally in the trees – well, that was fabulous. I inhaled a long, deep breath and let the hot mango-tinged air hit the back of my throat.

We pedalled on, riding along the valley floor in dappled sunlight. Soon we passed some modest terracotta-coloured homes, where I watched the residents picking the fruit and piling it into large orange crates. I liked being able to see what they did in that town. These were the mango people and everyone had a job. While the pickers picked, others shovelled unripe fruit under large green plastic sheets to warm in the sun. One man who was standing next to a rusty blue 4x4 truck, handed his two young kids crates of mangos, before driving off with both the children and the fruit piled precariously on the open back.

On the outskirts of the mango town, I could bear it no longer. Pulling over at the side of the road, I spotted some trees that didn't look like they were part of anyone's orchard. I laid Bernard gently down on the ground and darted up the bank. After plucking two ripe-looking mangos from a tree, I returned to Faye and handed her one of them.

'Care for a mango, m' lady Faye?' I offered in a faux posh voice.

'Oooo. Why, thank you. Don't mind if I do,' she replied.

Our grubby little fingers couldn't peel back the skin fast enough and, after several agonising moments, I plunged the whole thing into my gob. As I sucked the orange flesh from around the stone, mango juice dribbled down my chin and onto my hands. It was sweet, it was sticky and it was deeee-li-cious.

As is the rule with sweet, sticky and delicious things, one mango leads to two mangos, leads to three mangos, and more. Twenty minutes later we were still in the vice-like grip of the mango grove, repeatedly scrambling up the banks and gobbling from the trees like wild animals. I pulled out my phone and took a video, to make sure I would never forget the moment I ate my first wild mango:

'We cannot leave the mango area!' I shouted. 'I have mango stuck in my teeth, it's all over my hands. I have mango on my face. We are Mango Happy!'

Eventually, we managed to drag ourselves away from the mango groves and continue down the valley. By that point it was approaching midday and the temperature had started to soar. Now coated in a mix of mango juice, sweat and dust, we looked an absolute state. As we crossed a small river, I glanced down at the clear rushing water. It looked so cool and fresh, tumbling over rocks and whooshing under the small wooden bridge beneath our wheels. I looked at Faye, then back to the river. We didn't even need to exchange words; she knew exactly what I was thinking. I followed as she turned right down a small track to the river's edge. We hopped off the bikes and waded straight into the river, fully clothed. I let out a little yelp as the icy water hit my ankles, then calves, thighs and then, that no-going-back moment, the crotch. Soon I was in for a full-body dunk. Oh, the relief! After a minute or so in the water, I headed back to my bike to grab my camera. When I turned back around, Faye was sitting waist deep in the water, just on the edge of the river. She was looking out upstream with a huge grin on her face. I took a photo of her through the blades of long green grass that lined the bank. She was easily visible in her blue T-shirt against a backdrop of green, smiling from ear to ear. Despite the mango gorging, I noticed how her face was gaunt, far slimmer than it had been when we arrived in La Paz a few weeks earlier. She looked so happy there – her auburn hair plastered to her cheeks, waist deep in an icy stream in the middle of the Bolivian jungle.

Soon, I rejoined Faye in the river. Sitting beside her with the water rushing over my legs, I took in a deep breath and exhaled. Despite the hardships, the slow progress, the stifling heat and the new addition of biting bugs, the Yungas had begun to enchant me. I had never been anywhere like it, let alone had the privilege to ride a bike through somewhere like that.

The landscape was so dense. It was packed with vegetation, birds and bugs. With each mile that passed, it felt as if the thick layers of bush had parted to allow us through, and then closed up behind us, like a magic maze. In the Yungas, we were not looking out on the landscape, we were in it. We were riding through it, entangled in the branches of its trees and swept along by its meandering rivers until such a time came that it wanted to release us back into the real world.

5

Welcome to the Jungle

Distance cycled: 365 miles

Metres ascended: 11,003

Had you looked at our route for the first week of our journey through the Yungas, you would have been forgiven for thinking that someone had let a child loose with an Etch a Sketch. It zigged and it zagged, and then it zagged some more, making its way through the small villages of Coscoma, Coripata, Ass-key-sa-man-ya, Parani,

Match-a-ca-marca and Las Anguilas, each with a population of no more than 100 people, and often less. As we passed through the villages, we were chased by dogs, cheered on by children playing in the street and swerved around brave, wild chickens (that *were* actually trying to cross the road).

These villages served as neat little markers to break up what were long and hot days in the saddle. Each small pocket of civilisation was different from the last, and we never knew what we would find. Many were just a few streets wide, with small concrete houses and tin roofs, the walls left grey and unpainted. Others were larger, with plazas surrounded by houses with white-washed walls. Whatever the size of the village, and however many people lived in it, there was always, without fail, a football pitch. Some of them were just barren patches of scrubland marked out with a faint white line and rusting goalposts, but others (where the locals had decided to really invest in the pitch) were perfect carpets of green grass, short and well kept, looking completely out of place in the middle of the unruly jungle that surrounded them.

The plazas were my favourite places to take a rest. When I struggled on the bike, I looked forward to each one, collecting them and the people who lived around them like trinkets. Some plazas would boast grand statues, lines of trees, flowerbeds, pagodas with vines and varnished wooden benches. Others were more modest – empty, dusty squares with concrete benches around the edge and an open gazebo at one end, offering respite from the midday sun. Whatever the size, plazas were always an explosion of activity, of colour, of noise. Street corners filled with the giggles of teenage girls, who were dressed in jeans and bright T-shirts, with jet-black hair running down their backs. Younger kids kicked footballs around, shrieking with delight. I'd catch wafts of boiled meat and potatoes escaping from the houses, swiftly followed by the whiff of a nearby pile of rubbish, which had been left out in the sun on the curb just that little bit too long. These plazas were a window to a secret world and they epitomised what we had come to know about Bolivia. Vast stretches of nothingness on a harsh dusty road and then, just around the bend, there everybody was.

As the days wore on in the Yungas, and as we creaked and

groaned our way deeper into the jungle, the towns became our lifelines. Much as we both loved the solitude on the roads in between them, I craved the shot glass-full of civilisation that they served up. It was always just enough to fuel us for the next stint. It's not something we ever spoke about, but I had a feeling that Faye felt the same. Whenever we lay on plaza benches, in the shade of a nearby tree, drinking in the scene going on around us, neither one of us was in a rush to leave.

In the small town of Coripata, Faye and I were enjoying ice cream from a shop-cum-shack on the corner and eagerly engaged in our newfound sport of plaza people-watching. There was a low rumble of tyres as a tatty-looking white minibus pulled into the square. It was full to the brim with passengers and laden with luggage on the roof rack. We watched as bodies began emerging, nay flowing, from the doors at the front of the bus. Once the number of people got past 20, I wondered how in the world they had all managed to fit in.

In that moment, I also wondered how insurance worked in Bolivia, and whether there even was such a thing. Did the passenger capacity for the bus simply state 'as many as you can cram in there'? I didn't envy the passengers. The road into town had been narrow and winding, and the surface terrible. There had been just enough space for our two bikes on some corners, so what it would have been like to be dangling off the edge in a heavily laden minibus was beyond me. I concluded that the driver must now be done for the day and would be clocking off but, just then, he began to chant.

'Chulumani, Chulumani, Chulumani…' he said, almost singing the words, as if offering worship in a church. Chulumani was a town 25 miles from where we were sitting, and one we'd been struggling to work out how to pronounce, so the driver was doing us a great service by singing it so beautifully.

'Chulumani, Chulumani, Chulumani,' sang the man again.

'I think he wants to know if you want to go to Chulumani,' I said to Faye, grinning and licking the last of the ice cream from the stick with the tip of my tongue.

'I've always fancied a trip to Chulumani, you know… it's on my list of top ten Yungas must-see destinations,' she smiled back.

'Chulumani, Chulumani, Chulumani…' chanted the man.

'He seems really insistent, Faye. I think you should go,' I urged.

'It would be rude not to. But perhaps he's changed his mind?' Faye said, and there was a long pause.

'Chulumani. Chulumani. Chulumani,' called the man.

A day later, we made it to Chulumani, albeit under our own steam. We passed briefly through town and pushed on, deeper into the jungle. The days were sweltering, and the evenings were equally hot. At night, we set up camp wherever we could find a spot flat enough to pitch up, and our voices were drowned out by the noise of cicadas singing in the bushes.

It was a few days after passing through Chulumani that I leapt up from the shade on one of our mid-afternoon shade breaks.

'Faye! Faye! Check this out,' I said.

'What is it?' Faye asked. In my excitement, I'd stood up faster than I should have done, and almost toppled over. I took a few wobbly steps towards Faye, regained my balance and stretched out my arm, pointing to the temperature gauge on my watch.

'Look. At. That.'

'What?! Does that say… forty-one degrees?! Whoa!' She gawped.

'It blooming does. No wonder I'm dying out here. I thought my face was going to explode on that last climb… all over my handlebars… just like… bleurgh.' I made a dramatic outwards movement from my cheeks with both arms to mimic what I thought they might look like had they actually exploded from the heat.

'Well, I'm glad your face is still intact, mate. I wouldn't have wanted to clean up that mess,' said Faye. 'It is pretty extreme though,' she continued.

'It is pretty extreme… AND I've just decided that we are also pretty awesome,' I said.

'Yes, we are… Only if we have cookies though,' replied Faye.

'You're right. We're only awesome if we have cookies. Without cookies, I am just a shell of a woman, and much less awesome. On that note… how many cookies do you have left?'

Faye rummaged around in her handlebar bag. 'Err… oh no. Only four.'

Cookies were not what we had expected to use to fuel our journey through the jungle, but we were fast learning that Bolivia was not a country of convenience. I'd done adventures before where I would need to stock up on food and then ration it for a week or so, but I had never been anywhere where the choice of something decent to put into my stomach was so limited.

This was more of an issue for Faye, whose tummy-tantrums continued to come and go every few days, so she had to be more careful with what she ate. Most of what was for sale in the small shops in the Yungas needed to be cooked on a proper stove in order to be eaten, or it was in a can and, therefore, too heavy for us to carry. Instead, we had to opt for readily digestible things in light packets that would survive in the heat. That reduced us to a daytime diet of wafers, cheese puffs, cheesy biscuits and mini cookie sandwiches with a splurge of icing in the middle.

The wafers, cheese puffs and cheesy biscuits were okay, but the cookies came in a variety of flavours, from strawberry crème through to chocolate, so we decided that they were the best of a bad bunch. Plus, they came in perfect little packets so that we could easily ration them for rest stops.

However, as we entered the second week in the Yungas and our cookie consumption reached critical levels, I felt disgusted. Every time we had to eat, I didn't want to, but I knew that I needed to in order to have the energy to make the climbs. We began to joke that we would likely leave Bolivia with type 2 diabetes.

***

Soon the novelty of life in the jungle wore thin. Each day, I hoped that things would get easier. But each day we struggled in one way or another, whether it was with the steepness, the heat, the lack of decent food, the sunburn and even the rain. Things that had once seemed like an exciting new challenge became a daily chore. And the more tired I felt, the more irritated I became – not only with the conditions, but also with my own ability to cope with them.

One day, I'd made the mistake of working out that a 25-mile cycle had taken us seven hours. Seven hours! It was hard not to feel crushed when progress was that slow. We could have walked the miles faster. For a moment, I wondered whether I'd gone soft, but then I remembered the 41-degree-temperature reading on my watch. That was proof that I wasn't imagining it all. Riding in 41-degree heat was ridiculous at the best of times. Riding on an off-road track up a mountain in the jungle with humidity and goodness knows how many metres of ascent already in our legs, that was a whole other ball game.

On day 10 in the Yungas, the inevitable happened. The

heat, the slow progress, the bugs, the bad food, the punctures suffered on account of the rough downhills – all these things had ground us down. In our naivety, we'd expected that a 200-mile section should take a week, nine days at most, but there we were, on day 10, and still with a further two days of riding to make it back to the main highway. That realisation was enough for us to throw some toys out of the adventure pram, something that, thankfully, we both decided to do on the same day. Rage is always better when shared, after all.

Faye's rage started early that morning. As we loaded our bags back on to the bikes, some horseflies began swarming around her. Now, Faye hates flies. Not only flies, she hates any kind of bug, in fact. And especially bugs that bite her. One of the benefits of being at altitude during the first part of the trip was that bugs don't tend to hang out above 2,500 metres. But in the Yungas, at a lower altitude, the bugs were everywhere. While I found them a source of mild irritation, the constant stream of horseflies landing on, and nibbling at her legs had driven Faye to the edge. For every bug that bit her, a new swear word would leave her mouth, quickly followed by a profuse apology. Faye is so polite and mild-mannered 95% of the time that to hear a torrent of swear words pouring from her mouth was very funny. Naturally, I did what a good friend should do – I tried not to laugh, and failed.

Once we got moving that morning, the bugs couldn't hack the pace and so Faye's level of humour went up, and (much to my disappointment) the level of swearing went down. I'd woken up that morning feeling tired too, but Faye's morning bug-rage had cheered me up no end and was doing wonders to keep my own frustrations in check. I had been further distracted by an afternoon ride on the most spectacular zig-zag road yet. Leading to the town of Inquisivi, it was a rubble track that was easily visible from the mountain opposite, a dusty orange line cutting back and forth across the forest-covered mountain. From a distance, I could see that the bends on the road were sharp, and if I turned my head sideways, they looked like heartbeats on a hospital monitor.

During a short break in the Inquisivi Plaza, we listened to a rousing morning chorus, which was escaping through the doors and windows of an elaborate white stone church. As the final hymn ended, I reasoned that, if I could just keep a handle on my own slow boil of exhaustion for one more day, we would be back on the main road. Just as we began to pedal out of the town, the wind picked up, the skies darkened and a crackle of thunder sounded in the hills.

'Sounds like rain's coming!' shouted Faye, who was up ahead on the track.

'Yep! I'm just going to put a rain jacket on,' I shouted back.

I pulled on my brakes to bring the bike to a stop and went to unclip my foot from the left pedal, only the pedal cleat wasn't having any of it. My shoe got stuck and I fell sideways, on the bike, until I hit the road and slammed my wrist on the ground, grazing my hand and snapping the water-bottle cage on the front of the bike frame. Whether it was the shot of pain from my hand, my irritation at the fact that this was the third time my pedal had misbehaved that this week, or the fact that I was in a post-lunch-break carb slump, I will never know. But it was like someone had flipped a switch. My blood started to boil and a rage began to rise.

'Faye,' I said, standing up abruptly and dusting myself off. 'I'm just going to shout at the mountain, okay?'

'Errr… okay,' said Faye, looking confused. And so, with permission, I took a deep breath and hollered at the top of my lungs. I hurled expletives into the air and finished with a blood-curdling Braveheart-esque war cry. I shouted because of the slow progress. I shouted because I just wanted to ride my bike along and not up or down. I shouted because I was tired and sick of eating crap food. I shouted so hard that the back of my throat was red raw by the time I was done.

When I'd finished, I looked over at Faye who was clutching her stomach and laughing. I had learned that when Faye finds something *really* funny, she laughs so uncontrollably that her stomach hurts. My expression was still one of angst and irritation, but now it began to soften.

'What are you laughing at?' I asked.

'It's just… I can't…' She burst into fits of giggles again and now I started laughing too.

'What is it?! What's so funny?'

'It's that… I can't believe you just politely asked me whether you could scream at the mountain!' She burst into laughter again.

'Well… I just didn't want you thinking I was angry at you,' I said through my own laughter, now realising how absurd my request must have seemed.

'You are so funny, McNuff!' she panted, coming to the end of her giggles and trying to catch her breath.

'Delighted to be of service,' I said, feeling much better now that the angst was out of me and glad that I had amused Faye in the process too.

'Come on, you weirdo – let's get going again before the rain hits.'

The following morning, after we'd spent a night camped on the outskirts of Quime, our wheels met tarmac for the first time in two weeks.

'Oh my god. That feels INCREDIBLE,' said Faye.

'Oh… oh… oh… Yesss!' I shouted in sweet relief.

Many people want to win the lottery; they dream of diamonds and pearls and fancy cars and lavish dinners. All we had dreamt of for the past two weeks was a beautifully tarmacked road. Using up the last of the cookie stash as fuel, we cycled upwards from the jungle floor and headed for Abra Tres Cruces, the gateway back to the real world.

With every few hundred metres that we ascended, the landscape around us changed. The greenery became less dense and the trees were replaced by ankle-high scrub until, close to the top of the pass, there was no vegetation at all, just a large, barren, volcanic plateau, all browns and yellows with not a dot of green in sight. How strange it was to not see green. It was like walking out of a darkened room into direct sunlight.

At the top of Abra Tres Cruces, Faye pulled alongside me to take in the view at 4,700 metres. I breathed a huge sigh of relief. The Yungas was done. We had gorged on mangos, survived Death Road, eaten ten times our bodyweight in cookies and ascended over 23,300 metres in the space of 12 days. It was a Bolivian baptism of fire. Surely, everything would get easier from now on.

6

Peaches for Tea

Distance cycled: 532 miles

Metres ascended: 27,477

I was just a girl, standing in front of a long straight road, asking for a tailwind. And, oh, how the wind delivered. Thirty miles of gently winding, tailwind-assisted descent led us out of the Yungas and back to the main highway south. I must have turned my pedals three times in the 90 minutes that it took us to get all the way down. It was the same for Faye. We were 100% grinning and spinning, with no breaks, no stopping, just freewheeling and reaching speeds of up to 20 miles per hour. In comparison to the recent average of 2.5 miles per hour through the Yungas, it felt like warp speed. I took a selfie of us that day as we descended. In the photo, beyond my smiling face, you can see Faye in the background. She's sitting on the saddle with both her legs stretched out to the side, nowhere near the pedals. She looks fresh out of a 1920s comedy post-card; all that's missing is a set of white bloomers.

I was relieved to be out of the jungle at last but, during that descent, I had something else on my mind. I really want-ed to speak to Jamie. It'd been a few days since I'd managed to have enough phone signal to call him and, even then, it was a stuttered conversation over a crackly line with missed words and long delays. I was especially anxious to speak to him that day because I knew that he'd just been to an important appointment at the American Embassy in London. It was an appointment that would affect how the following year would pan out for the both of us.

It had been two years since Jamie had run 5,000 miles across Canada. Since then he'd set up a charity called the Superhero Foundation in our home city of Gloucester and now he was ready for a new adventure of his own. So he had decided to head off on a 6,000-mile run across the USA, dressed as a superhero (of course).

The American adventure would take him away from the UK for a year. Somehow, we had to work out how we would manage our relationship, in between his adventures and my own. Our individual need for adventure certainly added a layer of complexity to our relationship, but adventure is who we are, it's what we do and, most importantly, it's what had brought us together in the first place. Whenever I struggle with being apart from him, I am always quick to remind myself that, although we are boyfriend and girlfriend, we are not two parts of the same being. We have chosen to spend our lives together – and what a privilege it is to share this mad journey with someone else – but we are each a whole, with individual wants and needs.

As my own plans for the Andes journey fell into place, it

seemed to make sense that we should try to time our adventures so that there would be an overlap between the six months of my Andes trip and Jamie's year-long US run. Then I'd be home alone, in England, for a shorter period of time. Jamie agreed and the plan was set. The only spanner in the works was that Jamie isn't the most forward-thinking person in the world. One of the beautiful things about him is that he lives in the day to day. In the seconds, the minutes and the micro moments of life. He is also an eternal optimist. Everything will be okay in Jamieland (I would love to live in Jamieland, if only for a day). The reality is that everything *is* actually always okay. In fact, it's always more than okay, but sometimes Jamie ends up taking a long and winding route to get there, and that means I'm often detoured onto that long and winding route too.

As I prepared to leave for the Andes, I had casually asked Jamie if he'd applied for his US visa. Of course he hadn't. I was understandably nervous. He hadn't yet secured a visa for a run that was supposed to be starting a month after I left.

'It'll be fine!' he said. 'Of course they'll grant me a visa to do the run!'

'But what if it's not fine, J?' I asked.

'It will be,' he smiled, confident as ever.

Jamie's appointment at the American Embassy in London had been scheduled for the day we emerged from the Yungas, so I was keen to find some phone signal, maybe even some Wi-Fi, and give home a call.

All hopes were dashed when we discovered that the 'town' at the junction on the main highway was not a town at all – just a collection of shacks. There was no phone signal and certainly no Wi-Fi. Disappointed and unable to speak to Jamie, I dropped him a message via my GPS tracker.

'Made it back to the highway. Glad to be out of the Yungas. How did appointment at the embassy go? All good?'

Minutes later, a reply came in. 'Glad you're out of the jungle. I'll tell you about the appointment when we speak. :)'

I knew something was up. Jamie very rarely put emojis on messages. And if things had gone well, he would have said so. I felt frustrated. All I wanted to do was speak to him and find out what was going on, but I couldn't. Sometimes being disconnected from the world on adventures is a blessing but, at other times, it's a pain in the arse. I pushed the thoughts from my mind. It was getting late, after all, and a chat with Jamie could wait until the next day. Instead, I turned my attention to finding a camp site for the night.

The following day, we zoomed off along a well-paved road, enjoying yet another stonking tailwind. We were taking turns to ride at the front and averaging a meaty 17 mph. That kind of speed for us on the flat was unheard of. By midday, we'd made it to the town of Caracollo and headed into the plaza in search of food and phone signal.

Faye wasn't yet sure whether she liked traditional Bolivian cuisine and I didn't blame her. We'd tried to eat like locals a few times in tiny towns in the Yungas and it hadn't always gone well. There seemed to be several courses to each meal ordered, and we never quite knew what was coming next, or whether there was anything coming at all. We found it hard to judge whether we should force down what we'd been dished up (despite not knowing what it was) or take a chance that the next part of the meal might be something more recognisable. It was a classic game of stick or twist.

The meal we had the most experience with was *almuerzo* (lunch). We would walk in the door of a small restaurant and utter that one word. The restaurant owner would nod and then disappear. Usually *almuerzo* was a three-course meal which started with some kind of soup (often with meat, vegetables and the odd bone floating in it). The soup was then followed by more meat, with a side helping of rice and undercooked chips or plain fluffy potatoes (gotta love the double-carb action). To finish, there was always some kind of sweet dessert.

I actually enjoyed the fact that I never knew what was going to end up on my plate. Whenever it was an option, I would take 'real food' over dry crackers, cookies or cheese puffs any day, even if it did make me retch every now and then when I hit a piece of gristle or something unidentifiable and slimy.

It had been a few days since we'd found a decent *almuerzo* establishment and a few too many days on our high-sugar, low-vegetable diet (which I'm sure is the new Atkins diet). So I decided it was time to find some 'real food'. Once I had a full belly, I would call Jamie for an update on the visa situation. I spotted a traditionally dressed Bolivian woman on the corner of the main plaza; she was sitting next to a small white wooden box on wheels. Her dark skin was weather-worn and her long black hair was streaked with silver and flowed out from beneath a black bowler hat, which was set at a jaunty angle on her head. Her brightly coloured skirt was draped over the plaza steps and she worked rhythmically as she lifted various lids on the top of her cart and served up steaming bowls of food to those in the queue. I took my place in line behind the locals and, after a few minutes, I made the front.

The woman picked up a white tin bowl, then glanced up at me and stopped. She looked around. I looked around too, realising how odd I must have appeared. A 5ft 10 in., fair-skinned, blonde girl, clad in Lycra, still wearing her cycling helmet (safety first, kids) in a line of locals waiting for lunch. I'd read online that Bolivian businesswomen were hard-working and didn't trust easily beyond their family, so I wondered if this one trusted me. The woman looked at me and nodded, before opening up a lid on one side of the cart and letting a large burst of steam escape. Thrusting the bowl into the cart, she scooped a pile of white rice into it. She then pointed to a larger bowl, on a small stool, that appeared to contain some kind of chilli sauce.

'*¿Sí?*' she asked. Ooh, I have options, I thought. How exciting that this meal came with optional saucy add-ons.

'*Sí, por favor,*' I replied, and she plopped a large dollop of the sauce by the side of the rice. Then, she opened up another side of the cart and another burst of steam escaped.

Whatever was in that second side of the cart smelled really funky, like a mixture of Chinese takeaway and Christmas dinner. She pointed into the cart and I peered over the lid to see a vat of brown, translucent liquid with oil globules on the surface and what looked like chopped-up vegetables floating in it.

'*Sí*,' I said, thinking that it looked edible, warm and nutritious, and how nice it would be to have something warm and nutritious in my belly to water down the cookie mountain that must have formed in there.

The woman poured a generous helping of the Chinese-Christmas soup over the rice, before moving the bowl to another casserole-style pot which was sitting on the plaza step next to her. This was the final round. I could feel it. The *pièce de résistance*. She lifted the lid for the big reveal and, without even asking whether I wanted any, she shook her head and waggled her finger.

'*No.*' She said firmly.

'*¿No?*' I said, peering into the pot at what looked like a pile of oddly shaped pieces of meat, most of it still attached to bones. There was a pause.

'*¿Sí?*' she asked with a look of *well, if you really want to*.

'*¡Sí!*' I replied. I had made a resolution that I would eat like the locals, and if this is what they were eating today, then I would eat it too. The woman shrugged her shoulders and gave me an *if you're sure* look before dumping a piece of meaty bone onto the pile of chilli-infused, soupy rice.

I took the bowl from the woman's leathery hands, replaced it with the princely sum of five bolivianos (20p) and thanked her, doing my best to explain in broken Spanish that I would bring the bowl back later. Walking away, I looked down into my hands and knew I'd made a mistake. On the meat, I could see a layer of pearly white fat, so thick that it seemed to have its own pulse and personality. It glistened in the early afternoon sun, its sliminess rivalled only by the skin surrounding it, which looked like a lighter-coloured, wetter version of the skin on a rice pudding. I tried to work out what animal I might be looking at, or which part of it, at least. It looked like some kind of leg but I couldn't be sure.

I ate as much of the lunch as I could, and three times made an attempt to attack the strange meaty bony thing. I was embarrassed at not being able to eat it, after insisting that it should be included in the bowl. An animal had lost its life for this meal. The least I could do was eat it, I thought. But each time I tried, I retched as soon as I brought it anywhere near my mouth. I just couldn't do it. I gave up. I set the bowl down by my side and called Jamie instead. He picked up right away.

'Helllooo. How's it goin'?' came the Gloucester drawl that I had learned to love so much.

'Hello, my boy. Good, thank you – well, I'm trying to eat some disgusting bone thing for lunch… but I've given up on it… I think I'm going back to being a vegetarian. Other than that, we're good. The road is super-fast today. We're smashing it!'

'You always smash it,' he said.

'Err, well, except the jungle has been smashing me for the past few weeks, but we'll say that's a one-off... anyway. How did the appointment at the embassy go?'

In true Jamie style, he took a deep breath and began a long story. I knew I had to wait for the conclusion (he was a wonderful storyteller, after all), but five minutes later I got the news I'd been dreading.

'So, they said they can't grant me the visa for the run just off the bat like that. If I want to be in the USA for a whole year, I'll need to go through an appeal process.'

'An appeal? Right...' I said, trailing off. 'And how long will that take?'

'The woman said it could take up to six months. I'm sorry.'

In six months' time, I would just about be coming home from the Andes. This news meant that if Jamie got his visa and then left the UK, we would be apart for 18 months. I was gutted. It was a blow to our life plan. I told him I understood and that it was beyond his control, and that I just needed some time to get my head around the fact that things wouldn't be working out as we'd planned. I assured him that I'd be fine, I just needed a little time. I said goodbye, hung up and sat on the corner of the pavement with tears running down my cheeks. I knew I would get used to the idea, but the notion of us being apart for 18 months was just too much to think about right then. Faye saw that I was off the phone and came over.

'Oh, McNuff, what's up?'

'Jamie's visa got refused. He has to appeal, and it could take up to six months.'

'Oh, Anna,' she said.

'It's okay… I mean, it's not okay. But it will be okay.'

'You'll work it out. Something will work out,' she said, pulling me into a hug.

'Thanks, Faye-bomb,' I said, letting a tear drop onto the shoulder of her dirty orange cycling top.

In that moment, something shifted in the balance between us, and I relaxed. A hug can have that effect on someone. I realised that I had been holding back from Faye. I'd felt the weight of a responsibility that she enjoy herself and that, if we had a terrible time, it would all be my fault. This was my idea in the first place, after all. But that had led me to hold back. Until that moment, I hadn't let Faye know that I was still nervous about Jamie and me being apart. I hadn't shared the feelings I'd had during that first week in La Paz about whether I was making a huge mistake going on another adventure, in general. I had only shared half of what I was thinking or feeling with her. But that afternoon, with salty tear-stained cheeks, sitting on a dusty curb in a small Bolivian town, I realised that I needn't keep anything from Faye. In fact, I shouldn't. I didn't need to be the one responsible for making sure this adventure was a success. If it was going to be a success, I had to be looked after by someone too, and that someone for the next five and half months was going to be Faye. We had nobody to rely on except one another.

'You didn't fancy eating the mystery bone in your soup this time then?' Faye grinned, letting me out of the hug and pointing to the tin bowl on the ground next to me. I sat up and wiped the tears from my cheeks.

'Nah, I think it's llama bone, you know.'

'Oh, no! Not the llamas.'

'It's so slimy… look – it jiggles… Like bum fat. Maybe it's a bum bone?' I said, lifting up the bowl closer to Faye's face and wobbling the meat in it. She pushed my arm away.

'Ewwwww! Come on… let's get going. It's still a tailwind out there… who knows how long that'll last?'

We rode that tailwind all afternoon and I found comfort in being in motion again, switching places with Faye every five miles and taking turns at the front. The complex set of emotions swirling around my head were forced into submission by the simplicity of the repetitive motion of cycling. Life was no more complicated than turning the pedals – just two women headed for the horizon, sandwiched between a setting sun and a rising moon.

***

When we reached the city of Oruro, we decided to stop and take a few days off. After all the small towns of the past few weeks, being in a city of 264,000 people was a real novelty. There were actual shops and restaurants and vegetables and everything. We even allowed ourselves the luxury of a hostel room with an 'en-suite'. Although when you have to stand on the toilet in order to have a shower (this is no exaggeration), I'm not sure it counts as an en-suite. More an 'en-cupboard', and an eternally wet one at that. Still, it was reassuring to know that if I wanted to have a wee and a shower at once, I needn't choose between the two.

While in Oruro, we took the opportunity to buy new inner tubes because I had gone through three in the past week. We stocked up on food for the road, got extension stamps for our Bolivian visas (so that we could stay beyond the standard 30 days) and cleaned our bikes. We both spent a full afternoon on the pavement outside our hostel making Bernard and Gustavo spick and span. I had never spent that long cleaning a bike in my life. If ever I was in any doubt, Bernard and I had bonded.

I liked Oruro. Sitting at 3,700 metres and originally a gold-mining town, it was an eclectic mix of bustling markets, dark alleyways and fruit stalls, all leading to a plush city centre with grand white colonial buildings and the most opulent plaza we'd come across yet. I also liked that Oruro is a rule breaker. High up on a hill on the outskirts of this land-locked city is a lighthouse, the Faro de Conchupata. Oh, yes. Oruro doesn't care that it is not within a whiff of the ocean; its pristine white lighthouse, crowned with a golden ball, stands tall and proud for all to see. Built as a tribute to the president of the time, Manuel Isidoro Belzu, it was at this lighthouse that the

Bolivian flag as we know it today was raised for the first time, in 1851. The colours of the flag – red, yellow and green – were inspired by a mesmerising rainbow that the president had seen as he rode his horse from La Paz to Oruro. Faye and I hadn't arrived in Oruro on horseback as President Manuel had, way back when, but we did have our own beloved aluminium horses called Gustavo and Bernard and, after a couple of days rest, we were ready to saddle up and ride out. It had been nice to get an injection of city life and a taster of local history, but the open road was calling again.

During the days that followed our departure from the city, we often found ourselves alone. Out there, it was just us, the llamas, and cloud-spattered skies for miles upon miles as we pedalled across a flat and featureless landscape, bound for the edge of the infamous Bolivian salt flats. Every now and then a truck would whizz by, the driver tooting his horn, waving and offering a respectful thumbs up. We didn't speak much, Faye and I, wheeling along one behind the other, absorbed in our own thoughts. Sometimes I would stare at my handlebars and let my mind drift to all the things I would one day be doing in life. Sometimes I would look down the road and wonder if we'd made any progress at all. But the llamas were there, in small packs every few miles, chomping on tufts of grass, batting their long luscious eyelashes and letting us know that we were, indeed, moving forward through their vast and seemingly never-ending homeland.

On the second morning beyond the city, having exhausted any useful train of thought, I decided to be 'constructive on the road'. I liked the idea of using this 'dead time' to further my Spanish, so I listened to podcast lessons for the first three hours of the day. It could only help us on the journey ahead, and I had high hopes that I might one day progress beyond asking for cheese, Wi-Fi or answering questions about who we were and where we were headed.

When my mind grew weary and our tummies rumbled, we stopped for a roadside lunch of dry crackers and water, slumping into a large drainage run-off at the side of the road. The concrete slabs were set at a perfect angle to support our backs, and they were warm too. They were the ideal place to recline over lunch and look up at the clouds, which rolled off towards the horizon in tranquil procession.

At the town of Huachacalla, we turned off the main highway to stock up on water at a tiny store at the back end of town. We'd been filling up from fountains in small plazas wherever we could, but often we needed to rely on a shop to buy water in bottles or cartons. We'd then decant the water into our own bottles and hand the vessel back to the shopkeeper. I hadn't seen any sign of recycling in Bolivian towns, but I hoped that if we gave the bottles back, they might at least find another use for them. The stop in Huachacalla was supposed to be just for water because we still had enough food to last us for the following four days. After leaving town we would be heading up and over a small climb, squeezing between two volcanos and tootling down to our camping spot for the night. We were both in the shop, with a carton of water in each hand, when Faye yelped 'Anna. They have peaches. Tinned peaches.'

'Where?'

'Up there, right at the top,'

And there, on the top shelf, coated in what looked like three years' worth of dust, was a gigantic can of syrupy peachy goodness, and it spoke to me.

'I'm getting it,' I said, reaching for the top shelf.

'But… it looks heavy,' said Faye.

'It won't be heavy once it's in our bellies. Do you want peaches for tea tonight?'

'Errr… yes, of course, but…'

'Well, so do I. I'm doing it. I'll carry it. It'll be like resistance training up the hill,' I grinned.

Any extra struggle was worth it for that delicious dusty can of peaches. That night, after the traditional pack of instant noodles with cheese melted into them, we gleefully rinsed our oversized camping cups, and went in for dessert. As the sun sank lower in the sky and the mountains transformed into a silhouette against a backdrop of orange glow, there we sat, chomping on peaches. We chomped and slurped and licked our sticky peachy fingers until the moon began to rise and the stars lit up the sky.

7

The Demons of Coipasa

Distance cycled: 742 miles
Metres ascended: 31,292

The Salar de Uyuni is the largest salt flat in the world. It is also the most well-known. Flick through the South American section of any travel blog and you will likely see a photo of the Uyuni flats. The featureless, crystal-white landscape is so vast and so flat that it's easy to bend the rules of reality and play with perspectives. Out on the flats, through the lens of a camera, a toy dinosaur can be the size of Godzilla. Your friend can fit neatly in the palm of your hand and you can drink from a bottle of wine that's twice your height. And if you fancy something to accompany the oversized wine, you can cook a whole group of tourists in a saucepan for dinner.

The Uyuni flats are a playground for creative minds, and it was certainly that kind of PR that made us decide that it just had to be part of our route. But when working out how to get there, we'd discovered that Uyuni wasn't the only flat at the salt party – there were other, lesser-known ones, such as the Coipasa flats, that didn't get written about or slapped all over Instagram. From what we'd read on-line, these flats were more rugged, less pristine and more of a challenge to ride across. Plus, on account of their spongy, ever-changing surface, you certainly couldn't drive a busload of tourists across them. All this sounded right up our salty alley.

After our night of peachy decadence, we had ridden away from the camp spot, through the small town of Sabaya, and taken a sharp left. We left the smooth tarmac behind once again and turned onto a track heading south. I'd enjoyed the past few days of easy riding but my mind needed fresh input. It craved adventure once again and we hoped that the Coipasa flats would deliver.

Pedalling away from the main highway, I watched the ground change beneath my wheels – from light-brown sand, to sand spattered with white, to completely white salt. Having never seen anything like it before, my brain (as brains tend to do) began an attempt to attach the landscape I was seeing in front of me to something already familiar. And so my brain kept telling me that I was surrounded by snow. Then I'd shake my head and remember that it wasn't snow, it was salt. How cool is that? And yet, it still reminded me of snow – dusted like icing sugar through a giant sieve over the darker earth. As the ground beneath our wheels turned whiter, it even began to behave like snow, clumping together in mounds and ruts, which Faye took great joy in pedalling through, whooping and cheering as she went. In some patches, the salt was wet and sloppy – puddles of slush that threw splodges of watery salt onto our wheels, frames and legs.

In all the excitement of riding through the salty snow, I realised that I hadn't thought about the direction we were heading in. When I 'came to' from my dreamlike state, the trail had disappeared completely.

'Hang on a sec, Faye. I need to check the map,' I said, pulling on my brakes and bringing Bernard to a halt. In front of us was a fairytale landscape. A yawning expanse of crystallised salt stretched to the base of a green-grey mountain range in the distance. Above the distant mountains was a triple-blue sky, which changed from light blue on the horizon line to royal blue, then navy. There was nothing else in sight. Just the salt, the mountains and the sky.

Faye pulled her bike to a halt alongside mine. I looked down at my phone and then looked up.

'Where are we headed?' she asked.

'Between those two mountains,' I said, pointing to the sky between two faint peaks. With no road out there, it was the Wild West for directions. 'There's an island with a volcano on it, to our right. We want to stick loosely to the edge of that for as long as we can. But other than that… we just keep heading for those mountains.'

'Awesome. How long for?' Faye asked.

'About two days,' I grinned, staring ahead.

'Wow,' said Faye, now turning to look ahead too.

The first day of cycling on the Coipasa flats was electric. We were charged with adrenaline, in the love with the vast unknowing of what lay ahead. The mixture of sand and salt beneath our wheels was the gateway to another universe. The sun shone brightly for most of the day but there was a haze in the air, as grains of sand were gathered up by the breeze and tossed around. We pedalled on, enjoying the easy miles and the novelty of a new landscape. It was early afternoon when we spotted the first flock of Andean flamingos.

'Flaaaaammmmin' flamingos!' I yelled in an Australian accent. I'm not entirely sure why I chose an Aussie accent, it just seemed appropriate for the occasion. And who knew what nationality these flamingos were anyway.

'Wooaaahhh!' said Faye. 'Flaaaamiiin' flammiingooos,' she echoed.

I had never expected to see flamingos on the salt flats of Bolivia. In fact, I had never really thought about where the flamingos of the world live; I just knew there weren't any in the UK. And now there they were. Clear as day. A giant flock, some 500 metres away, just going about their daily flamingo business.

We then got a bit carried away and, in a bid to get up close to the flaaaamin' flamingos, we pedalled our way straight into a flaaaamin' lake. The flamingos fled and left us up to our ankles in mud that smelled like a cross between poo and rotting fish. Worse than the smell, though, we were now flamingo-less. I wondered whether the birds were mocking us from where they'd landed, half a mile away. 'Silly humans,' they would say. 'Look at them, ankle-deep in our flamin' poop.'

After failing to make friends with the local flamingos, we continued to pedal across the featureless expanse of white and towards the mountains in the distance. It was surreal to think that we'd been in the jungle just a few days earlier, surrounded by noisy bugs and dense forest. The Coipasa flats were the exact opposite. It was a calm, quiet place, still warm enough to ride in shorts and a T-shirt, but with a light breeze to keep us cool. Beneath our wheels the surface changed every so often, from pure salt crust to softer grey-white sand but, if we looked ahead, there was nothing. No people, no buildings, no vegetation, just the mountains, which didn't seem to be getting any closer no matter how hard we pedalled. A mile or so to our right, we could see the green-grey outline of Coipasa Island, a chunk of solid land which I glanced at every now and then, just to confirm that we were actually moving forwards.

After riding for seven hours that day, we attempted to set up camp in the middle of the flats. We'd talked about how cool it would be to wake up 'out there' in the salty nothingness, midway through our journey towards the gap between the mountains. Unfortunately, not only was it impossible to hammer our pegs into the hard salt but, also, a gale-force wind had picked up. With nothing to break up the wind, it was whipping across the flats, hammering into our cheeks and almost blowing us off our bikes. We soon realised that the only place we'd be able to pitch a tent that night was on the nearby island. We'd moved beyond the edge of the land 45 minutes ago but we had no choice but to backtrack. With our tails between our legs, we accepted defeat and retreated six miles to the edge of the island. It took us a full hour to make the distance but it was the right decision. The ground on the island was softer and, as a bonus, the volcano in the middle of it provided shelter from the brutal wind. Once the sun disappeared from the flats, the temperature dropped quickly – we were still at 3,600 metres, after all. We wasted no time in piling on our down jackets, beanies and trousers, before cooking up a simple, hard-earned dinner on the stove.

The following morning, I woke up to the sound of Faye giggling outside the tents.

'McNuff! McNuff, get out here. Check this out.'

I rubbed sleep from my eyes and unzipped my sleeping bag. Opening the porch door, I stuck my head outside and squinted in the bright sunlight.

'What is it?' I asked.

'Look!'

Faye was standing in front of the tent, holding up my socks. One was blue and one was pink (my socks never match because life is too short to bother matching your socks). They had become sodden in yesterday's mixture of watery salt and flamingo poop, so I had draped them over my handlebars to dry. They had dried alright. In fact, they had excelled in drying and had gone one step further to turn themselves into impressive sock sculptures: stiff and frozen in the exact shape that they had been draped over the handlebars. Faye threw one of them into the air and I watched as it helicoptered back down to earth.

'Well, I'm not looking forward to putting those on,' I said.

'These are pretty bad too,' said Faye, holding up her exceptionally crusty pair of cycling shoes. I looked over at the bikes. They were coated in salt icicles too.

'Oh, Bernard. Oh, Gustavo. Look how dirty you are. And after all that time we spent cleaning you,' I said, a tinge of disappointment in my voice.

After choosing a fresh pair of unmatched socks, I had to work hard to shove my feet back into my own stiff cycling shoes. We then sped away from Coipasa Island and headed back across the dirty-white flats, enjoying the warmth of the morning sun and making great progress across the lightly rippled ocean of salt. By mid-morning, we'd hit some significant lumps and bumps. The salt had crystallized into hexagons and the edge of each hexagon was raised some 10 cm from the ground. The hexagons must have moved at some point, like the meeting of two tectonic plates and they had formed little ridges. At first, crashing through the ridges was fun. We laughed and cheered as we ploughed onward and I took great joy in seeing just how quickly I could break each one.

'I am a juggernaut! You cannot stop meeeee!' I yelled, shoving harder on the pedals as I bounced around on the saddle and struggled to hold on to the handlebars.

At first, the challenging surface was a source of excitement. It added some spice to our progress during what was otherwise plain sailing. We laughed and whooped for the first 30 minutes, careering through the deep, salty crusts, not knowing if the tyres would break through or if the crusts would stop them dead. Oh, what fun! Fun, that was, until the 'fun' went on for more than those first glorious 30 minutes and reality dawned on us. Our steady 10-mph progress was long gone. As the hexagonal crusts got bigger, our energy levels began to dip. The salt got thicker and our speed dropped to 3 mph. At one point, I was locked deep in battle with one of the crusts of doom, when I noticed Faye alongside me. Then I noticed that she was walking with her bike… and going at precisely the same speed as I was. I let out a loud sigh, dismounted Bernard to join her and we pushed our bikes for the next two hours, stopping every 45 minutes or so for a rest.

'It'll get better soon, I'm sure,' said Faye, plonking herself down onto the ground and trying to pour some optimism into our dwindling salt-infused well of adventure juice. Sitting down next to her, I began tugging at the edges of the salt crust. I pulled a chunk of it free and found it to be hugely satisfying, like picking a giant scab. Peering into the surface below the crust, I noted that it looked decidedly sloppy and dark brown, just like the flamingo-poo lake. It smelled the same too – a mixture of earth and brine.

'Maybe it'll get better, maybe it won't,' I said, tossing a piece of crust into the air and watching it break into clumps as it hit the ground. 'But I suppose we should see this pain as an opportunity… an opportunity to learn, to grow… to become better people,' I smiled, my voice now laced with sarcasm.

Faye was decidedly unimpressed and let out a loud sigh as she flopped backwards onto the ground. There she lay, in silence, staring up at the sky, likely wondering what on earth she had agreed to, and what on earth she was doing there.

An hour after leaving our rest stop and still pushing our bikes, we noticed that the crusts had finally begun to disappear. I looked ahead. The ground seemed smoother and the ridges were thinning out. Gradually our bike-pushing speed picked up and the walls of the crusty hexagons melted away. We got back on our bikes and were soon able to cycle at a whopping 7 mph. The surface was softer than the previous day but it was rideable, at least. There were now just 35 miles to the town of Llica, on the other side of the flats. At our current rate, we would be there by late afternoon.

'Wahoo! Now we're moving!' Faye hollered, streaking ahead of me across new firmer ground.

'Faye, hold up! I just want to check the directions,' I called after her. Once I'd caught up, I got my phone out to check the map.

'Huh, that's odd,' I said, zooming in on the red line which showed the route we should be taking.

'What's up? Are we headed for the wrong mountains?' Faye grinned, her sense of humour now back at top-notch levels on account of the smooth, non-crusty ground.

'No, the route says we should head left, over there, then hit that land, and go right, to end up over there. In front of us. That doesn't make any sense.' I furrowed my brow and looked at the map again. The route, which we'd downloaded from another cycle tourist's blog for this particular section, was saying that we should cycle along two sides of a triangle, as opposed to taking the most direct route, which would be to carry straight on ahead.

'What do you reckon?' I said to Faye.

'I'm not sure,' she replied, squinting into the distance.

'I mean, it looks okay straight ahead. But we could end up hitting that crusty stuff again,' I said.

'Yeah, I wonder what's so much better about going around the edge, rather than through the middle?'

'Maybe it's a seasonal thing? It says in the notes that the ground changes depending on the time of year. So maybe it was a bad time of year and this bit was waterlogged or something when the guys who wrote the blog came through?'

'We could just go for it?' said Faye.

'I was thinking the same thing. Shall we?'

'Yeah! Let's do it,' she replied.

And so, riding high atop a horse called Optimism, into the kingdom of Positivity, we set off on a direct route across the flats. For the first hour, we repeatedly congratulated ourselves for such a bold and daring decision. The ground was a tad spongy but, if we kept our cadence up, we could stay on top of it like a pair of hovercrafts and make good progress. Oh, how fabulous we were. Oh, what great decisions we had made. Oh, how we were the most amazing adventuresses on the planet. Oh… how were we now sinking in deep sand on our bikes!

'Waa… Faye… I'm sinking,' I shouted, trying to keep moving forwards but eventually coming to a halt. I sank until the bottom third of my back wheel was covered in salt, sand and mud. Faye, having chosen a bike with larger wheels and wider tyres, was better equipped to stay 'afloat' on the sea of sponge and was able to keep going a while longer. But soon enough, Faye began to sink too.

'Eww, it stinks!' she said, her feet breaking through the salty sand and into the layer of stagnant sludge beneath it.

At that point, we knew we had many miles of pushing our bikes ahead of us. But we stayed positive and told ourselves that things would get better. Just as quickly as the ground had changed from rideable to not, it would change back again. We pushed on with the belief that this spongy ground couldn't possibly go on all the way to Llica, which was 30 miles away.

So, we pushed on. We pushed, and we pushed, and we pushed some more. We pushed for 5 miles, then 10 miles, then 12 miles. Miles and miles through soul-destroying, energy-sapping salt sand. After 15 miles, the chatter between the two of us died. We trudged on silently, side by side, in the 30-degree heat, at 3,600 metres high, stopping only to guzzle water every now and then. Even during the stops, we didn't speak. We were both locked in a silent battle with the demons of Coipasa.

As the hours passed, Faye and I began to separate. There

was no need to push together all the time, because there was no danger of losing sight of one another in the featureless landscape. After three hours of pushing, during a particularly deep sandy section, I reached breaking point. A voice screamed in my head. *That's it! I am done. I'm so bloody done! I'm not going on. I can't. I'm stopping. I am going to lie down on this god damn sponge until I sink into it and wind up somewhere on the other side of the world, far from here!*

Then a second voice followed, *Anna. Really? And where exactly will stopping get you? Nowhere. That's where.* The second voice was right. The overwhelming urge to throw down my bike, to stamp and scream at Mother Nature would get me precisely… nowhere. In fact, it would get me further from where I wanted to be, which was that shore over there, between the two mountains. So instead of stopping to throw a tantrum as planned, I just whimpered, took a deep breath, re-gritted my teeth and forged on.

After five hours of trudging over the spongy ground, we reached the edge of the flats. We shoved our bikes up a small sandy slope, through more ankle-high scrub, and over to where the road was marked on the map. It was 5 p.m. and we had just 12 miles left to ride to Llica. We would smash those final miles to town! That thought was shattered when we discovered that the road, our saviour, our glimmer of hope, was actually deep sand. Not even spongy sand this time. Deep, red, dunes-of-the-Arabian-desert, sand.

I let out another sigh and we resumed pushing. Faye had

been silent for a long time now, but as we shoved our bikes headlong into a sixth hour out of the saddle, she appeared beside me.

'McNuff, I need to let you know that I am approximately twenty minutes away from really losing my shit,' she said very calmly, but through gritted teeth.

A smile started in the corners of my mouth. It progressed to a grin, then a giggle, and then I was full-blown belly-busting laughing so hard that I could no longer push my bike. I stopped and collapsed over the handlebars.

'This is ridiculous!' I wailed.

'It is!' Faye wailed back.

'Oh Faye-bomb. What the hell are we doing?'

'I dunno, mate, but it is not cycling,' she replied.

We both let out a long sigh. I hung my head between my arms over the handlebars, then looked up.

'How about we just camp?' I said.

'What, here?' she asked.

'Yep. There,' I said, pointing to a patch of scrubland to the right, back towards the lake.

'Best idea you've had all day,' said Faye.

That night, we sat out in front of our tents and cooked up a dinner of noodles and cold cut-up sausages. I felt so proud of us. We had both just pushed ourselves to the brink of exhaustion. We could've got ratty with one another and lashed out, but we didn't. Either of us could have refused to carry on, but we didn't. Faye could have blamed me for suggesting a terrible route option, but she hadn't.

The wind had picked up, just as it had done the previous night. As we readied ourselves for bed at 7 p.m., the sky above the flats began to glow. There was something about its ethereal orange that compelled me to call out to Faye, telling her that she just had to come out of her tent and see this.

We both stood, in our socks and jammies, bellies full of dinner, with tired legs and smiling faces, bracing against a near gale-force wind. We marvelled at the colours which were seeping, the way ink does into a pot of water, from behind the mountains to our right and into the sky. Purples, reds, oranges, all shifting position and hue ever so slightly by the second, as the clouds and sky colluded to create one of nature's greatest paintings.

The day had been brutal; there was no doubt about it. But watching the colours unfold in the sky above us reminded me that the world was always turning beneath our feet. And as tough and unbearable as a day might seem, one thing is certain: sooner or later, the sunset will arrive. And if you can just cling on long enough to make it to that sunset, it might contain enough beauty to restore your weary bones and fragile mind. It might just soothe you, and steel you, for the challenges to come.

8

Faffletics

Distance cycled: 862 miles
Metres ascended: 31,558

Faffing is one of the greatest words in the English language. It is a popular British pastime, often employed as a tactic by children who are late for school and want to do anything and everything except what they should be doing in order to leave the house. Many adults also like to faff, much to the frustration of non-faffing, organised and punctual people around the globe. If, like me, you are not always organised and only sometimes punctual, fear not – for *you* are a professional fafflete. We faffletes like to compete in the Olympic sport of fafletics, doing all we can to maintain our position on the winners' podium. Like me, Faye is a professional fafflete. And so, on our journey through the Andes, we had been passing the imaginary 'baton du faff' between one another on a daily basis. Whoever was clutching the baton on any given day, rest assured, they would be faffing.

We had made it through Llica and were now packing up after a night spent just shy of the Uyuni flats. I had everything sorted and was ready to roll. Bernard sat waiting patiently, bags loaded. Faye had been a slow-moving creature that morning and was… faffing. We knew well enough just to let one another get on with the day's faffletics, so I busied myself by picking some salt from Bernard's trusty frame. Until I heard a shout. Faye had been stung by a scorpion! I winced as I watched her go through several stages of post-sting emotion: fear, agony, anger, frustration. I felt so helpless to see my friend in that much pain – it looked excruciating. And we got really freaked out when her big toe started to go hard. After I'd done my best to ease her suffering with new-found knowledge about the various species of scorpion in Bolivia (courtesy of Google), Faye moved into the final phase of post-bite feelings: relief.

The relief coincided with the pain easing, and Faye managed to regain some composure as she manoeuvred her hard toe back into her cycling shoe. She felt silly for having been walking around camp barefoot in a place where there were scorpions, and I felt equally silly for not having known that there are scorpions in Bolivia. I wondered what other harmful beasties there might be out there, which I had been blissfully ignorant of.

Ten minutes later, after Faye had promised to let me know if any other parts of her body went exceptionally hard (like her scorpion-stung toe), we set off again across the Uyuni salt flats.

What with the Coipasa salt-flat disaster and a scorpion sting having been thrown into the adventure mix, we felt that we deserved a good day's ride. We prayed to the gods of the

Salar de Uyuni to be kind to us, to grant us safe and speedy passage across the flats, and to hold fire on any more dramas. Our prayers were answered. For 47 miles, we pedalled across beautiful crystal whiteness, following a jeep track that had just enough crunchy character to be exciting, and just enough wear to make for easy progress.

Before visiting the flats – and having only seen videos and pictures online of other cycle tourists visiting them – I had wondered how anyone knew where to go, in the white noth-ingness. Now that I was there myself, I could see that there were sections of salt where the crusts of the hexagons had been worn down over time, meaning that faint, makeshift roads were visible.

It's difficult to describe what being on the Uyuni flats felt like, but it seemed as if we had wandered up and onto a per-fectly flat, snowy plateau. In front of us was a white carpet that sparkled in the sun. The faint, smooth road began at our feet and whooshed towards the horizon like a set of train tracks: dead straight, in perfect perspective until it disappeared en-tirely. The only defining features of the landscape were the blue sky and the white salt, the view split 50/50 between the two. Being the middle of the Bolivian summer, it was warm, around 22°C, which meant that we could ride in shorts and T-shirts, even though we were at 3,900 metres above sea level. Life on the flats was beautiful. Serene, stunning, calm. There was nowhere else on earth I would have rather been and, as we cycled, nothing changed. It was as if we were on a convey-or belt, pedalling in one spot as the earth rotated beneath our wheels. To make it even more dream-like, there wasn't a sound out there. Silence belonged on the Uyuni flats.

We spent much of the day riding side by side, listening to podcasts or music, chatting and laughing. We were carrying most of our water in canvas hydration bladders, slung over the back panniers on the bikes. When we ran out of water in the bottles on our bike frames, we would stop to refill with water from the bladders. During these breaks we would discuss any geography questions bubbling in our minds, such as 'How were salt flats formed?', 'Why are there hexagons everywhere?' and 'Did this used to be the sea?'

With some aid from Google, we discovered that the salt flats of Bolivia were once prehistoric lakes. When these lakes dried up, some 30,000 to 40,000 years ago, they left behind two smaller lakes (Lake Poopó and Lake Uru Uru) and, where the water had evaporated entirely, two massive deserts of salt. These became the Coipasa and Uyuni flats. Below the crusts of salt is a layer of brine, followed by a layer of mud. We had glimpsed the brine every now and then, when we found a hole in the salt crusts on the road, and we had gotten to know the layer of mud very well on the previous day's crossing of Coipasa.

When not discussing the local geography, we tested how salty the salt was by bending down and actually licking it. Well, I say we. It was just me who thought that this was a good idea. It was a test that shrivelled my tongue, made me gag, and only needed to be done once. We also played hopscotch with the hexagons, and we even invented a new game (my favourite game of the whole trip, in fact) which was to see whether one could fill up an entire hexagon with wee when one needed a pee. I managed it once, but it was sort of a pentagon, rather than a hexagon, so I'm not sure that it counted. Faye only ever managed a triangle, which lent further support to my claim that she was often dehydrated.

That afternoon we followed a track to the middle of the flats, which was to take us to the tranquil Isla Incahuasi, a small rocky outcrop less than half a mile wide. It was rumoured to be covered in 700-year-old cacti, some of which stand up to 10 metres tall. I later read online that the island is the remains of a volcano and was, historically, a resting place for the Incas, who crossed the lake with their llamas, looking to trade with Chile, some 100 miles away.

We had enjoyed a day of solitude so much that the thought of encountering anyone who might burst our bubble of serenity wasn't appealing. But we didn't need to worry about that, as I had read about the island on a blog, which described Incahuasi as having one inhabitant, or rather, two – a man and his dog. I relayed this information to Faye as we neared the island. You can, therefore, imagine how perplexed we were to see a hive of activity on the shores of Incahuasi.

'Is that… are those… buses?' Faye said.

'It looks like it… and there's people too,' I replied.

'Oh, no. People,' said Faye, and I laughed. We were getting like a proper couple, Faye and I. We loved our time together, alone as a duo, with no one else in sight. 'I thought you said that there was just a man and a dog on the island?' she continued.

'Err… yeah. I've just realised that the blog that said that was written in 2010. So, I guess the place has gotten popular since then?'

'I wonder if the dog still lives there though?' said Faye. She really does love dogs, after all.

Having not eaten much that day except the boring dry food that we'd stocked up on in Llica, my stomach made a deep gurgle as we pulled off the flat and onto the blackish-brown sand of the island. 'On the plus side, if there are tourists, they might have a shop. And if they have a shop, I'm going to buy chocolate and then hug the owner. Or I might hug the owner first, and then buy the chocolate. We'll see how it goes,' I said.

And then I saw it. A wooden sign that said 'Restaurant'. This island didn't just have a shop, it had a freaking restaurant! Set among a collection of small stone buildings, each one with a straw roof, the restaurant was the largest building of all. It was definitely more shabby-chic than shabby-shack, boasting wood-framed windows, stone tables out the front and a full bar inside. I wondered how on earth they managed to keep a restaurant stocked out there, some 50 miles from the nearest town. At least they didn't have to worry about a steady supply of salt.

Cue two very smelly cyclists (now six days without a shower) abandoning their bikes and bowling straight into the small

Incahuasi island eatery for a late lunch. There, we filled our pie holes with chicken, chips, carrots and green beans. Oh, sweet crunchy, buttery, peppery green beans. Faye had a hot chocolate and I had a beer, before we moved over to the small shop, which was in a separate stone building opposite, and stocked up on nuts, chocolate and (boring but sensible) crackers for the following day's ride.

Bellies bulging, we paid our island camping fee of 10 bolivianos (£1.10), and retreated to a tent spot in a small cove, just at the edge of the flats. It was 6 p.m. by then and, from our secluded pitch away from the crowds, we watched the last vehicles leave the island just as the sun went down. It wasn't long before we were back to having the flats to ourselves, which felt greedy but wonderful.

Later on, during a dinnertime treat of mashed potatoes *avec saucisses et fromage*, I started wondering about the surrounding landscape. 'Faye, what's the plural for cactus?' I said, spooning steaming mashed potato into my mouth.

'Err, I dunno. Is it cacti?' she replied.

'Maybe it's cactuses?' I offered.

'It could well be. Why, are you thinking of writing a blog about them?'

'Not yet, but don't you think that that cactus right there looks like a giant penis?' I said, pointing to an especially grand, phallic cactus, with two smaller cactus nubs next to the main shaft of the plant.

'Ha! I was thinking exactly the same thing!' she replied.

'They do say that great minds think alike,' I smiled.

'In fact, that one over there looks like a penis too. A very hairy spiky one,' said Faye, pointing to a different cactus.

There was a long pause. 'So, Faye of Cornwall, are we both in agreement that all of these cactuses look like giant penises?'

'Yes, we are. Peniseseses are everywhere tonight,' she said.

The following morning, we packed up early and began pedalling away from the island of giant penises, before the first crowds had a chance to descend. We had asked the shop owner the night before which track the buses took from the island to the town of Uyuni and had deliberately chosen an alternative route in a bid to have the road to ourselves. Having grown in confidence at our ability to cover the miles quickly, I decided that it was time to set Faye a 'personal development challenge'.

The previous week, I had loosely dropped into conversation that I believed we should get naked on the salt flats or, to be more specific, go for a naked cycle. Faye, who hates to be naked, even to get into the shower, had point blank refused, but I was still hopeful. Perhaps the flats would weave their magic on Faye's mind and, once we were out there, she would reconsider.

We'd been pedalling for an hour and had covered a decent 15 miles across the salt. During that time, we hadn't encountered anyone else. But we had been looking into the distance, watching what looked like toy cars and buses move along roads adjacent to ours. They must have been at least five miles away, but we could still make out their hazy silhouettes against a backdrop of blue and white. I pulled on the brakes and brought Bernard to a stop. Faye followed suit with Gustavo and appeared alongside me. She pulled her headphones out of her ears and blinked at me with a confused look on her face.

'You alright, mate?' she asked, as Faye often does.

'Yes, great thanks. It's time,' I said.

'Time for what?'

'Time to get naked,' I smiled.

'Oh, no!' said Faye, remembering the conversation we'd had the week before. 'I thought you'd forgotten about that.'

'An elephant never forgets, Faye.'

'McNuff, did you just call yourself an elephant?!'

'I did. And do you know what?'

'What?'

'Elephants don't wear clothes. They walk around naked all the time. It's good for them.'

'But we're not elephants,' said Faye.

'No, but we are animals. And animals are supposed to be naked.' There was a long pause during which I could tell that Faye was contemplating her options. I took the chance to add further weight to my argument. I wasn't convinced that my elephant angle had been entirely successful. 'Come on, Faye. Where else in the world can you take off all of your clothes and cycle naked?!'

Faye bit her lip. 'But what if someone comes by?' she asked.

'Then we'll see them coming. Look, over there. You can see those buses and they must be miles away. If we saw a bus coming in this direction, we'd probably have time to boil up a cup of tea, eat a whole packet of biscuits, and then put our clothes back on before they even made it here.'

Faye laughed and then fell silent. In that silence, I had a pang of guilt. I felt guilty about forcing her into doing something she really didn't want to do.

'Okay, you don't have to, of course. It's up to you. I just think... we'll never be here again. But it's totally your call,' I said.

'Okay,' said Faye.

'Okay?!' I shouted.

'Okay, okay, okay! I'll do it,' she said, laughing.

'Yay! Right then, bikes down and clothes off. We are getting naaaaaked!'

And that's just what we did. We laid our bikes down at the side of the road and peeled off our clothes. Given that we were just in shorts and T-shirts, it didn't take long until there we were, two grown women, naked as newborn babies in the middle of the Bolivian salt flats, 3,900 metres above sea level. We picked up our bikes from the ground and hopped back on them. One turn of the pedals, two turns… and then full birthday-suit speed. Oh, how glorious it felt. The sun was shining down on every square inch of my skin. The breeze moved uninterrupted over every area of my body and there was no clothing cutting into me, no restrictions to my movements. The warm leather saddle offered heat and comfort to my bum. I felt liberated and free as a bird!

At first, I could see that Faye was trying to cycle one-armed while covering up her boobs with the other arm. We were both pedalling in a figure of eight, passing one another in the middle, because, well, this was an experience that should be shared rather than enjoyed alone. On the first pass on our cycling circuit, I called out to Faye.

'Faye, I've seen it all before! And I've got those too, you know!' I shouted, pointing at my own boobs, and Faye laughed. By the second pass, she'd stopped trying to cover anything up, and seemed to be enjoying the sense of liberation as much as I was.

'This is awesome!' she giggled, her bright red hair flowing out behind her.

By the third pass, we were lining up for naked fly-by high-fives and, on the fifth pass, I tried to get close enough so that I could slap Faye's bum, and I succeeded.

'Oh! Cheeky, cheeky!' I yelled, Carry-On style, as my hand made contact with her naked arse.

We wheeled around on the flats for a good 10 minutes, whooping and cheering, before realising that our bodies were completely exposed to the sun and we didn't have sun cream on. Captain Sensible tooted his horn and we decided to call it a (naked) day. I picked up my camera from the salty ground, where I'd set it down before our naked free-for-all, and pressed a button for it to stop recording. I was now the proud owner of 10 minutes of footage which showed Faye and me freewheeling under the Bolivian sunshine, butt-naked. This footage, I promised, would not be shared publicly. In fact, I think I might have promised Faye that I would delete it. I can't remember now. You can, of course, see the footage if you go to this link on YouTube… No, I'm kidding. I wouldn't do that to her. Not yet, anyway. I'm saving it for her wedding day.

We decided, probably wisely, to pedal the final 45 miles into the town of Uyuni fully clothed. We passed more throngs of tourists, a salt-extraction plant and even a hotel built from salt, just before we reached the main tarmac road. It felt surreal to be back on a man-made surface again. The road into town was mostly straight, so the miles ticked by quickly. I watched as the land around me slowly shifted back to colour once again, from white to greyish-brown and then to orange. I kept looking back towards the flats as we cycled away, wondering if I'd imagined the serenity of it all. I didn't fancy repeating the spongy ride across Coipasa, but the second section, I hadn't wanted to end. When I think about riding across the flats now, all I can remember is the feeling of it – the warmth of the sun on my forearms, the smell of the salt and the soft crunch beneath our wheels.

Flanked by the flats to the west and mountains to the east and south, Uyuni is home to 30,000 people. It's laid out in a grid of dusty streets with local, open markets at one end and tourist-centric restaurants, hotels and tour offices at the other. It was the largest town we'd been in for a long while, and once again, it felt strange to be surrounded by so many people. We pulled up in the middle of town, beside a neatly painted, bright yellow clocktower, to consider our options for accommodation. Sleeping indoors was a monumental event so we always took the time to discuss where our bolivianos would be best spent. After a week without a shower, we decided to splash out and treat ourselves to a couple of nights in a hostel (one that wasn't built from salt). We chose a hostel with a courtyard and a hosepipe so that we could give Gustavo and Bernard showers too – the salt would corrode their parts in no time at all, if we didn't take care of it, and we still had some 4,000 miles to go.

That evening, we went through the pictures of us out on the flats, including the ones of us in our birthday suits. Faye was still smiling, in slight disbelief at the whole event. She then did something that really surprised me. Faye Shepherd, who hates getting naked even to get in the shower and describes herself as a 'semi-cuddly 6 ft 1in. redhead who has spent most of her life trying to blend in' posted a picture of herself cycling naked on her social media. It was far enough zoomed out so that you couldn't see anything apart from the fact that she wasn't wearing any clothes. Her caption read: 'This isn't a post about me being naked on a bike. Although, there I am. Naked on a bike! It's about stepping outside of a comfort zone and doing something that, for me, was really, truly scary.'

I decided to follow suit and post my image too. I thought for a moment about whether it would offend anyone. But then I realised, there was absolutely nothing sexual about those images. Nudity doesn't have to be a sexual thing. After all, it's our semi-pornographic music videos and provocative adverts that make us believe there should always be something sexual about naked flesh. Our bodies are our bodies. They are what we live in every day. They are the most wonderful things, which propel us across countries, allow us to comfort others in times of distress, to laugh, to talk, to bear children. They have floppy bits and wobbly bits and bits that make me wonder quite what evolution was thinking when it created them (noses, for example?!). But whatever their shape, whatever their size, human bodies are the most amazing, complex machines on the planet, and they should be celebrated at every opportunity.

By posting that picture online that evening, Faye showed that she was a woman who was proud enough of who she was on the inside to celebrate what she looked like on the outside, too. It was a perfect end to a perfect day.

9

Sally Attacks!

Distance cycled: 966 miles
Metres ascended: 32,797

When planning our route through Bolivia, Faye and I had agreed that we were after a mixture of superb scenery and a spattering of remoteness. After all, we weren't going to drag our bikes 6,000 miles from the UK to take a route through South America that could be seen from the window of a tour bus. Oh no, if there was even the faintest chance of us having a unique experience on our Andean adventure, we were going to take it.

The Lagunas area of south-west Bolivia is a popular tourist destination, so named because of the many sulphuric, smoking, salt-encrusted lakes dotted in volcanic surrounds. But if we headed slightly east, away from the Bolivian-Chilean border, we could explore some of the lesser-known Lagunas via a remote eight-day route that passed through the tiny towns of San Vincente (population approx. 50), San Pablo de Lípez (population approx. 220) and the evocatively named 'Pueblo Fantasma!' – a ghost town with a population of zero (that is, unless you count the ghosts that live there.) All in all, beyond

Uyuni, it was set to be 200 miles of dusty, remote riding, during which we would meander around at an average of 4,700 metres above sea level. We had also chosen the route because it would allow us to take a short side trip, to attempt to climb a 6,000-metre volcano, called Volcán Uturuncu.

We took a couple of days' rest in Uyuni, most of which was spent pottering around town, both together and apart. Faye's stomach was still causing her grief and I really felt for her. It was a pain to have to manage an 'altitude tummy' all the time, but she seemed to be taking it in her stride. She found a new stash of Imodium at the local pharmacy and kept her food intake to the bare minimum. I, on the other hand, took the opportunity to eat as much pizza as humanly possible, something that I'd learned was only on offer in the more touristy towns and so needed to be taken full advantage of. Especially because they have a strange tendency to put broccoli on pizza in Bolivia. And I really do love broccoli.

In between pizza inhalations, I spent time writing postcards to friends in the UK, because, well, it's nice to get actual mail. I had also sent a present home to Jamie. I'd decided that one of the ways to keep the love alive when on opposite sides of the world was to pepper his doorstep with random gifts from South America. It's a little-known fact that Jamie has unusually large thumbs, so you can imagine my delight when I came across a pair of embroidered, woollen llama gloves, complete with disproportionately large thumbs. The thumbs on these gloves were as long as the middle finger section. Not only that, but each thumb splayed out widely from the palm of the glove like a giant navy banana. For the large-thumbed man in my life, it was the perfect gift. So I bought a pair and sent them home with a note which read, 'Thumbs up for Bolivia! Missing you xxx'. By the time the third morning in Uyuni rolled around, I had sent all my cards and gifts, we were well fed, rested and ready to go exploring again.

I pulled Bernard to a halt at a junction 20 miles south of town, and Faye soon appeared beside me. This was it; we had arrived at the point of no return.

'That's our road,' I said, pointing to a grey rubble track off to the right, leading away from the tarmac highway and snaking its way across the dusty landscape.

'You sure you still want to do this, Faye-bomb?' I asked.

'That road?' she said, squinting into the distance.

'Yep,' I replied.

'Let's do it, McNuff,' she said, and we were off.

At first, the scenery looked very much like it had done leading into and out of the salt flats. But as the day wore on, the landscape began to change. Gone were the dusty grey roads with short, sharp inclines and in rolled longer climbs surrounded by a sea of sand. Terracotta reds, burnt oranges, cedar... I was used to seeing different greens, but I'd never seen quite so many reds and oranges as I did that day. I tried to count how many different shades I could see, but it was like looking at a sky full of stars. Each time I focused on an area of land, more colours appeared – creeping, seeping, oozing from the earth.

The colours were all the more impressive because they were accompanied by mountains and, at any one time, I could see ten volcanic peaks, some of them closer to the road, others far off in the distance, at the end of their own winding tracks. During one afternoon lunch break, I took a deep breath and stared at the mountains, thinking about what it was that always drew me to them. I decided that when I look at a mountain, something inside me shifts. I am pulled towards it. With each painstaking turn of the pedals, deals are being made and broken, unspoken, between the mountains and me. I find a deep comfort in being near mountains – their sharp peaks, rolling ridges and snow-spattered faces. There's something nurturing about them. Above all, mountains have the power to make me feel like everything is going to be okay. And that's exactly how I felt that day – happy, secure and positive about the road ahead, my connection to Faye growing as strong as our connection to the Andes themselves.

As the days rolled on, the road continued to be corrugated, sandy and undulating. It rose and fell just a few hundred metres at a time, keeping us roughly at an even 4,000 metres above sea level but making us work for every inch of forward motion. The going was slow and the terrain was rough, but we didn't mind too much because everything about it reeked of adventure. By day, we sang, we chatted, and we laughed. Or we cycled apart, listening to music and podcasts, lost in our own worlds. We pedalled and pedalled along desolate flats, between peaks, around sand-banked bends, across rocky riverbeds, moving further from civilization with every turn of the wheels. At night, we dined on instant noodles and cold, cut-up frankfurters, catching drops of precious soupy broth before it dribbled down our chins. We wild-camped wherever we pleased. There was no one out there to ask for permission, after all, and we weren't in search of it. In the Andes, Mother Nature was in charge and she was welcoming us with open arms.

One morning, I stopped and watched Faye ride away toward yet another volcanic peak. We were pedalling along a peach-coloured road that was lighter than the surrounding sand. Off to the side of the road, dotted over red earth, were small green-yellow plants – little tufts of them, as if there was an army of trolls submerged in the sand with only their hair poking above the ground. I watched Faye ride on, across the folds of the earth. And it really did seem that way, as if the earth were folding and flexing, weaving and shifting in shape and form as we passed through it.

I could see shadows cast on the ground, created by the white-grey clouds hovering above. The clouds were so perfectly formed that I imagined someone hidden behind the mountain in front of us, manually pumping puffs of white into the sky. I remember noticing how Faye's auburn ponytail neatly matched the colour of the earth and how the blue of her jumper matched the sky. It was like she belonged there. Like the landscape had changed in order to blend in with her as she pedalled onwards.

In Bolivia, I often heard locals talk about their respect for Pachamama, the Andean goddess of the earth. Bolivia is one of the few countries in the world that recognises Mother Earth, and her accompanying life systems, as having legal rights. Just as we have rights as human beings, so does Pachamama have rights in Bolivia. On the road that day, it was easy to see why the law of Pachamama meant so much to Bolivians. There was certainly something motherly about the road to Uturuncu. It nudged us, it tested us, it didn't let us get away with anything, but it looked after us all the same. In its arms, I felt safe. I felt free. And best of all – without a soul around – we had its undivided attention.

Although people were few and far between on the road, wildlife was everywhere. One morning, I was standing outside my tent, brushing my teeth, when I noticed something moving on the horizon. Was that? Yes… that was a llama. And it was strolling casually towards us.

'Err, Faye.'

'Yes?'

'There's a llama out here. Well, it's not here yet, but I'm pretty sure it's coming over here,' I said.

'Really? Cool,' Faye replied, poking her head out of the tent porch so that she could see the llama too. 'What do you think it wants?'

'I don't know. Maybe it's come for breakfast. There was that tiger who came to tea once, wasn't there? So perhaps this will be the llama who came for breakfast,' I grinned.

We soon learned that a morning visit from a llama wasn't unusual. We passed dozens every day, each one halting a three-course shrub dining experience to crane its neck ever so slightly upwards and stare at the two women passing on bikes. We would often stop to stare at the llamas, as they stared at us. Chomp, chomp, chomp went their gigantic camel-like lips; large, round eyes watching from behind long, unblinking eyelashes. Each face was so expressive. Often, they appeared confused, sometimes intrigued, but whatever their facial expression, their lips kept on chomping.

The llamas weren't our only friends out there. We began to see rheas (small ostrich-like birds), desert donkeys (much like ordinary donkeys but surrounded by sand) and a bird with the most beautiful royal-blue feathers on the underside of its wings. There was also an animal that looked as if it was descended from a llama that had had an illicit affair with a deer many moons ago. I now understand these to be vicunas but, without knowing their official name at the time, we simply called them deellamas. The deellamas seemed afraid of us and mostly ran away, at speed.

When we grew tired of being entertained by the wildlife (which was rare), we would play spot the dust devils. These were miniature tornados that swept across the landscape, forming in a flash and dancing across the horizon before dispersing in a gust of wind. We didn't actually find our first dust devil; it found us. And that was a shock. When it first happened, I heard an unusual roar, like the sound of a car engine and then WHOOSH! I was suddenly engulfed by a cloud of swirling red dust, the particles violently biting and clawing at my skin. It then left me and headed for its next victim. 'DUST DEVIL!' I yelled at Faye, but it was too late. Although she was five metres ahead of me, she was swiftly swallowed up, disappearing completely in a tornado of dirt.

In contrast to the availability of phone signals on the salt flats, we had nothing of the sort during the first four days of our Lagunas loop. So I was delighted when I crested a pass to see a 3G tower in the distance. I promptly got my phone out and, sitting on a rock at 4,700 metres, dialled Jamie's number. He picked up right away and said that he was just about to set off for a run with his dad (the legend that is Donald McDonald) in Gloucester. After that, they would be going for a skate on the ice rink, which had just arrived in Gloucester ahead of Christmas. We didn't chat for long before he had to go, but I said I'd call him the next time I found a phone signal. I hung up and thought for a moment about the world we lived in. A world where I could sit on a mountainside in Bolivia and speak to someone looking out on an ice rink in Gloucester. The injection of normality and the thought of people whizzing round a Christmassy rink at home made me smile for the rest of the day.

In those first few days of the ride to Uturuncu, everything went swimmingly. There were a few side effects from the altitude, Faye's tummy trouble being one but, otherwise, everything was manageable. That was until day five, when we encountered the arch nemesis of all rubble-road travellers: corrugation. Corrugation is quite possibly the worst type of road surface you can inflict on a touring cyclist. It forms as a result of heavy trucks or cars moving over loose, sandy ground. Something about the way the wheels move pushes the sand into horizontal ridges, which form small peaks like waves on an ocean. If you're in a car, you judder gently over the waves, compacting them as you move forward. On a touring bike, though, it's like riding over an endless cattle grid. The wheels dip into each small trough, and it's impossible to maintain any kind of speed as your hands grapple with the handlebars and you bounce around on the saddle.

It was all that bouncing around on the saddle that resulted in Faye and me being joined by a third team member in the Lagunas. She was a saddle sore and, because I like to name everything, I named her Sally. Sally had decided to make a home for herself right at the point where my left leg met my bum. Sally the Saddle Sore was welt-like and she became angrier and angrier as the week wore on. So much so that she had now begun to fill with pus. And not just one layer of pus, but two. Sally was a complicated character, with many layers indeed.

In a bid to appease Sally, I had started trying to ride the bike with my butt hanging off one side of the saddle. But every now and then, I would come across a particularly vicious patch of corrugation. Then I'd be thrown into the air and bounced back onto the seat, landing directly on top of Sally. A wave of searing pain would follow as Sally burst under the pressure and ejected pus into my cycling shorts. Soon, I developed a system for getting ahead of the game. Each night I would heat up a safety pin on the stove. I would then sit in my tent and burst through my skin to the two layers of pus and squeeze the poison out. Mostly this worked, although sometimes I would wake up to find that Sally had reassembled herself overnight. Just like the other two members of our cycling team, Sally was one determined lady.

Although Sally was a literal pain in the arse, I was okay with pain, I could handle pain. But I did start to get concerned when, on the seventh day into the loop, I noticed a swollen lump in my groin. I knew (from recalling a secondary school biology poster) that I had lymph nodes somewhere down there, and that the swelling was likely a result of my body fighting the infection that Sally was holding onto so tightly. I knew that I really needed to get hold of some antibiotics, and fast. Luckily, in Bolivia, antibiotics are available over the counter, so it was just a case of hanging on a few more days until we were out of the loop and I could find a *farmacia*.

As the week wore on, it wasn't just my nether regions that were taking a pounding on the rough roads. There was something else I was battling with, a force far greater than Sally and that was… my ego. Faye had confessed at the start of the journey that one of the things she was most worried about on this adventure was that I would be faster than she was. As it turned out, that couldn't have been further from the truth. Not only we were pretty much evenly matched in terms of speed but, on a number of days, Faye left me for dust. And I mean literal, llama-poop-infused, volcanic dust. I had asked Faye to come with me to South America because I suspected that she would be physically strong (because I knew her to be mentally so), but there were days in the Lagunas when Bernard and I were gasping to keep up with her.

Of course, it wasn't always the case (my ego just wrote that). On some days, Faye would struggle and I would be faster. But there were, without a doubt, days when Faye was the faster rider. At first, those days challenged me. Unbeknownst to Faye, I began to question who I believed I was as a person. I prided myself on being physically fit and capable, after all. I was the Great-Britain rower, I was the more experienced adventurer… I was… I was… I was… Ego. Ego. Ego.

Fortunately, just before we'd left for the trip, I'd read a book by Ryan Holiday called *Ego Is the Enemy*. He believes so strongly in that statement that he's had it tattooed on his forearm. Holiday talks about ego not in the typical Freudian sense, but as 'an unhealthy belief in your own importance. Arrogance. Self-centred ambition.' In short, the book makes the case that it's this kind of self-centred ambition that can get in the way of a lot of things – and that, actually, many of the emotional reactions we have to certain situations are a result of our ego flaring up.

One afternoon, Faye was up ahead and I was riding further back, not out of choice but because I couldn't quite keep up. For some reason I'd decided not to listen to any music that afternoon because I wanted to be alone with my thoughts.

After a few days of feeling uncomfortable about being left behind and even, at one point, silently cursing Faye for going so fast, it hit me like a lightning bolt. These were just thoughts, they weren't me. I loved Faye. She was my friend. I shouldn't be angry that she was doing so well and going so quickly. It was my ego. It was bruised, hurt and angry. Once it stepped out of the shadows and into the light of my consciousness, I could see it for what it was. And by god that ego looked ugly. I felt sorry for it. It had no love for itself. It was validated purely by the exploits of others. Worst of all, it suffered terribly from the dreaded *comparisonitis*. According to my ego and the laws of *comparisonitis*, because Faye was doing so well, it must mean that I was doing badly. Because there could not possibly be enough space in the world for more than one person to do well.

In that moment, I also realised that I had confused a sense of leadership with a need to be 'the best'. Yes, we were a small team, but even small teams have leaders and I saw myself in that role. I did the majority of the planning (mostly because Faye is a fly-by-the-seat-of-your-pants kinda gal). I made a lot of the decisions about the route and food stops. We worked well as a team because Faye was willing to let me take on that role. But, as team leader, I also carried the misconception that I had to be the fastest. I had to be THE BEST. Because surely, if I was dragging behind, that was embarrassing? Was it? I wondered. The answer was no. It wasn't embarrassing at all. Once I had had this personal revelation (which I didn't share with Faye, because I felt it was too shameful), I was relieved.

And soon after that revelation, I felt our relationship begin to shift. I no longer needed to be in control of everything. I no longer needed to be the best. I just needed to do my best and let Faye do hers. To let us ebb and flow naturally, as humans tend to do.

It was no coincidence that, around this time, we worked out that it was easier if Faye navigated, something that I had been doing since leaving La Paz. Faye had a mount for her phone on the handlebars of her bike, which meant that she could always see the map. In contrast, to look at the map, I had to stop and get my phone out of one of the small bags attached to the handlebar. It made much more sense for Faye to take charge of the directions. So, our new routine was that I would still set the route, but I would then pass it on to Faye and she would tell us when to turn left, right or carry straight on. At first, that felt weird. The navigation was yet another thing I was letting go of. An element of control I was losing to this person who was supposedly less experienced than me. It felt weird for a day or two and, on a few occasions, I had to resist getting my phone out to double-check that we were on track. But I never did. And soon it felt quite lovely to let go and trust Faye with the navigation entirely. It was like a weight had been lifted, like a burden had been shared and we were closer as a team.

***

One chilly morning in the Lagunas, I unzipped my sleeping bag and waited for the call from Faye's tent. Faye was always awake before I was, and I knew she waited for sounds that I was stirring.

'Morning!' came the call from my neighbour. 'Morning!' I yelled back, before absent-mindedly beginning a rendition of Bill Withers' 'Lovely Day' – a rendition that Faye (naturally) joined in with at the chorus. Packing away my tent, I decided that my day would surely be better than the previous one, which had featured the internal issue of ego conflict and the external issue of Sally the Saddle Sore. That day then, Bill Withers and I decided, had to be a lovely day. It was simply the law of averages.

Post-morning sing-song, after engaging in some light faf-fletics, Faye and I wheeled out of camp at 9 a.m. We were more eager to get going than usual, because there was a special offer at the mountain-pass superstore that morning. It was a BOGOF (buy one, get one free) and, instead of cycling up just one pass, we had decided to have a bash at two. Greedy, I know.

Pass number one came and went with minimal drama and wasn't too much trouble. We slugged and groaned up and over 4,700 metres and stopped for a brief high-five, to celebrate reaching the top, before gliding (or rather bumping and bouncing) back down to 4,200 metres for a spot of roadside luncheon next to a dry riverbed. With weary legs but hopeful minds, we left our lunch stop and began the climb back up to the lap of the gods for pass number two.

The road surface was terrible and, when things got really steep, I wrestled with the bike as if it had become a hydra. Side winds buffeted me in my already fragile climbing position, and the loose stones beneath me did their best to play mountain buckaroo. At one point, I felt the 11 litres of water I was carrying slosh violently to the back of my bike. Bernard's front end reared up and I had to throw my entire body weight forward just to stay upright.

Struggling on, I decided that it was time to change tack. I got up out of the saddle and pounded on the pedals just as the back wheel spun out on a section of deep sand. 'Waaaaaa!' I screamed, tumbling sideways, falling off the bike and landing in a crumpled heap with it on top of me in the sand.

Faye was still ploughing ahead and, admirably, managing to stay upright, so I hauled the bike up, clipped back in on the pedals and set off after her. I began to make steady progress up the incline at last and, with every rotation of my legs, I repeated the mantra 'Pasta' (left leg), 'sausages' (right leg). My motivation now reduced to the dinner lying in wait in my panniers.

Faye and I had agreed to split the 4,800-metre climb into 100-metre blocks of ascent. I looked often, far too often, at the altimeter on my wrist, willing the metres away. In between staring at my watch and thinking about sausages, I glanced at my hands on the bars. They were cracked and bleeding. I ran my thumb against the place where I had slammed a rock accidentally into my forefinger a few days earlier, while trying

to peg in my tent. It was still an open wound and I was reminded how nothing healed at altitude. There was no moisture to
allow it. I noticed that the skin around my nails had started to
crack and bleed, too, so I made a mental note to dig out the
antiseptic cream once I got into my tent that night.

By the time we made it to our final rest stop, just shy of
the top of the pass, Faye had turned her customary shade of
monochrome. White had hijacked every feature of her face,
so that they all seemed as one. Nose: white, cheeks: white, lips:
white (slightly tinged blue). Despite Faye managing to stay on
her bike better than I could, I knew that she was more done
than a Sunday slab of roast beef, and I was too.

After finally making it to 4,800 metres, we had a modest
celebration. There was a brief hug and we spent a few moments taking in the view, revelling in the sweet relief of having
done the last climb of the day. We could see for miles. Looking
out over the vast volcanic surrounds, I caught a glimpse of sulphuric smoke rising from a white *laguna* way off in the distance.
I then turned to Faye and let her know that I had a searing
headache. It had started that afternoon and I just couldn't kick
it – a sure sign that the altitude was really getting to me. So
we cut our mountaintop celebrations short and descended to
4,500 metres as fast as possible to set up camp.

It was beginning to get dark as we pitched up, but there
was just enough time to whip up the long-awaited pasta and
sausages before bidding one another goodnight and burrow-
ing deep into our sleeping bags. There were no savage winds

that night and I had managed to keep my thoughts in check. We had survived the day without any mechanical issues and even managed to enjoy a small victory salute at the top of each pass. As I closed my eyes, I made a note to thank Bill Withers for what had been a tough but lovely day.

10

A Bloomin' Big Volcano

Distance cycled: 1,169 miles

Metres ascended: 37,970

At 6,008 metres high, Volcán Uturuncu is one of the highest volcanic peaks in South America. It is also the home of one of the highest roads in the world. Once upon a time, the area around the volcano was used for mining and a rough rubble road had been built for the trucks to move up and down the mountain. Although the road was apparently now blocked off by a barrier, we'd heard that we could just about sneak a couple of bikes around the edge and ride along the road until it ends at 5,600 metres. From there, we'd need to continue our skyward journey to the 6,008-metre summit on foot.

Having spent three weeks getting acclimatised to the higher altitudes of south-western Bolivia, we were now ready to start the assault on the main event. If we could make it, 6,008 metres would be the highest that both of us had ever been on earth, although Faye had been close to that height when she'd climbed Kilimanjaro in 2014. We hadn't spoken much about Uturuncu over the past week. We'd been consumed with the task of making it over all the lumps and bumps to get closer to it but, as the turn off to the mountain neared, we mentioned it more often. It was during those chats that I realised our reasons for taking the detour were very different.

I was excited about the challenge of going up a bloomin' big volcano but, seeing how everything in South America was higher than I'd ever been before, it was all a bonus to me. I was still enjoying the novelty of any place where there was a limited amount of oxygen in the air, and I was less concerned with how high Uturuncu's summit actually was. As someone with more experience at altitude, Faye was more attached to each one of those six thousand and eight metres of elevation. She'd found Kili a huge challenge back in 2014 and now wanted to use the Uturuncu ascent as a test of whether she could go higher, and without porter support, like she'd had on Kili. It was a reminder that adventures are such a personal thing. We all use different measuring sticks throughout our lives to prove our worth and ability, and Uturuncu had become one of Faye's.

We arrived in the small town of Quetena Chico at 1 p.m. It was a dusty Wild West kind of a place and I knew from what I'd read online that, like many other towns in Bolivia, Quetena Chico was once a mining town. Knowing that the chances of a shop being marked on the map were slim to none, we launched into the usual routine of stopping the first person we came across in the town and asking them where there was a *tienda*. We were directed to one building which had *cerrado* (closed) plastered across the front. So, we asked again and were directed to another building on the main drag through town. That too had *cerrado* on a sign across its door. We accosted a group of passing kids and, in broken Spanish, I fumbled through words, asking whether it was closed for the day. We managed to gather from the reply that the shop would be open at some time that afternoon. When I asked exactly what time in the afternoon that might be (because I'm British and I like to know that there is some order to things) the boy simply shrugged his shoulders and repeated, 'This afternoon.'

We needed to stock up on supplies before attempting to climb Uturuncu, so we rested our bikes against a nearby wall, sat in the shade on the pavement outside the shop, and waited. It was a warm afternoon. The temperature was hovering around 20°C and there was very little breeze, so it was a relief to be out of the sun for a while. I must have fallen asleep in the cool of the shop's shadow because a few hours later I was awoken by a rattle of keys from the other side of the white, wooden shop door. It creaked open and a woman appeared in the doorway. She glanced down at us, understandably bemused at two smiling British women lying on the pavement outside her shop. I checked my watch. It was 3.17 p.m., a fact that confirmed that there was no specific opening time – unless the shop opened up at 3.17 p.m. each day, which I very much doubted. Although, given the order of all other things in Bolivia, I couldn't rule it out as a possibility.

Once inside, we stocked up on as much food as we could carry. Having not found a decent-sized shop since leaving Uyuni, we bought far more than we needed. We then sat outside the shop and unthinkingly ate a disgusting amount of it, which was a terrible idea. Our stomachs weren't used to eating that much food, not during the past week at least.

By 4 p.m., we were back on the bikes and pedalling along the old miners' track out of town. Taking directions from a blog I'd found online, we followed a faint sandy trail to behind a white house, pedalled past a llama munching merrily in the front garden, ducked under a washing line, passed three black spotted pigs wallowing in a pool of mud, and headed towards the base of the volcano. It was only a 10-mile ride to where we planned to set up our base camp at 4,400 metres for the night, so (ever the optimist) I reckoned that we'd be there in an hour, tops.

Of course, two hours later, we were still bouncing around on a surface that resembled broken crockery, and to further slow the base-camp mission, Faye's stomach had not reacted well to having an unusual amount of food thrown into it. Between you and me, it was the fourth time in an hour that we'd had to stop so that Faye could compost the landscape (I can now only assume there are blossoming orchards in her wake). Having been at over 4,000 metres for a week, my adventure buddy was suffering from altitude tummy in a bad way. But that day, things tipped up a notch. Her stomach had given up trying to hold anything in.

After one stop for water, Faye remained curled up in a ball next to her bike, moaning. 'I can't do it,' came the faint wail from her lips. 'I just can't!'

'Where is it?' I asked. 'Where's the Imodium? Can I get it

for you?'

'Ow. It's at the BOTTOM of my bag,' she groaned. 'It'll take you ages to find it.'

'I don't care, Faye-bomb. I'm going in. If anything else comes out of you, I'm worried you'll disappear entirely.'

'Owww!' said Faye, wincing at yet another stomach cramp. 'Okay… let's find it.'

Clearly, Faye was not well. Considering this was the day before we were intending to summit Volcán Uturuncu, it was quite possibly the worst day for her to be so ill.

Successfully bunged up by Imodium, Faye managed to muscle on, cycling in short bursts and letting me know when she needed a break to do some composting. Eventually, we made it to our base camp at 4,400 metres. Dusk was beginning to fall and, after laying Bernard on the ground, I walked over to Faye for the customary end-of-day high-five. Palm poised, smile affixed, I was three steps out from high-five initiation when she burst into tears. My heart sank. Faye was distraught – exhausted and frustrated that, due to tummy issues, a dream of hers to summit Uturuncu was about to go up in smoke.

I dropped the high-five hand, put my arm around my now unusually subdued red-haired friend and took a deep breath. I had to say it. I didn't want to say it, but I really needed to put it out there.

'I'm not sure that we'll be going up that mountain tomorrow, Faye,' I said softly.

'I know,' she sighed. The truth was I felt a responsibility for Faye's safety out there and, of course, my own.

'I'm not saying we definitely won't, it's just that we've got to be safe. Right now, you're not in any fit state to go up there. And I'm not sure I'm okay going up there with one of us feeling so rough,' I said.

I had no idea what to expect at 6,000 metres after all. I was worried about how I would cope, given that it would be 1,200 metres higher than I'd ever been. I had to be realistic that I couldn't promise I would be in any fit state to look after Faye, much as I always wanted to. That said, this was her decision too.

'I suppose we can see how I am in the morning?' Faye asked.

'Yeah. Let's do that. If you can manage to keep some dinner inside you overnight, then we might still be okay.' Faye nodded. I hugged her again.

'Okay?' I asked.

'Okay,' she said, wiping her tears away.

I crawled into my tent that night and prepared myself for the reality that we would likely just head back down the mountain again in the morning. By 7 a.m. the following day, I could hear Faye shuffling around in her tent next door.

'Faye?'

'Morning, mate!' she chirped.

'How you doing over there?' I asked.

'Good. Really good!' she said.

I got dressed, unzipped my tent and walked over to the outside of hers.

'Faye Shepard of Cornwall. I would like a full overnight stomach-acrobatics report, please. STAT.'

Faye unzipped her tent door and grinned. 'Nothing to report, McNuff of Londonshire.'

'Nothing?'

'Nothing. No activity in the south of my body, whatsoever,' Faye affirmed with a grin on her face – a face that was flushed with twice as much colour as it had been the night before.

'Wow. I'm impressed,' I replied.

On the basis that Faye's stomach had 'behaved' overnight, and that she had managed to keep breakfast inside her too, we decided that we would give Uturuncu a crack. The plan was to go steady, to attempt a summit, and allow enough time to turn back and make it 'home' to base camp before dark. We decided to leave the majority of our belongings stashed behind rocks at base camp and ride up to the volcano with just the bare survival essentials. I say 'survival essentials'… We still had an awful lot of crap with us. I mean, I for one couldn't bring myself to stash the knitted Christmas snowman and Santa my mum made for me when I was eight (which I carry for Christmases away from home). Senti-mental, I know.

'Ready?' I asked Faye.

'Ready,' she said.

'And we turn around at four p.m., wherever we are?' I affirmed.

'Four p.m. Yes. Agreed,' said Faye.

By 7.30 a.m., we were pedalling away from the tents and upwards on one of the highest roads in the world. Leaving camp, we were buzzing, although we were both quieter than usual – our collective nerves colliding with apprehension and hammering headlong into excitement. I was nervous that Faye wasn't well enough to be doing this. Maybe I wasn't even able to do this? What would happen if I started to suffer from altitude sickness on the way up? What happened if neither one of us could look after the other? There were so many unknowns, and it was the unknowing that scared me. We cycled on, in our own worlds, focused on the task of splitting the climb into 100 metres of ascent at a time. After ticking off the first 100 metres of climbing, we made it to 4,500 metres. We didn't say much on that first break, instead just pausing briefly to take a swig of water before setting off again for the next 100 metres of ascent. We were both so absorbed in our own thoughts and concerns that I had failed to notice – the tension created by such a cocktail of nervous energy was ripe for an explosion. At 4,600 metres, the pre-explosion touch paper was lit.

'I'm not sure we're going to make it,' said Faye, and I couldn't believe my ears.

'Faye! Did you actually just say that?' I shouted in disbelief, unable to control the level or tone of my words as they left my mouth.

'What?! It's taken us almost thirty minutes to do that first hundred metres of climbing. I'm just saying that if we carry on the same speed, we won't make it to the top,' she replied.

'You can't say that after an hour in!' I snapped back, and Faye fell silent.

It's natural that when we are fearful, our thoughts are fragile. My thoughts were so very fragile at that moment. I was apprehensive about making the top and doing all I could to maintain a blissful bubble in my mind that it was possible. I was fighting so hard against my own self-doubt that, when Faye added hers into the mix, I crumbled under the weight of our collective doubts. Well, I didn't crumble. I snapped.

The moment the words had left my mouth, I regretted the way they'd come out. They were laced with irritation and borne of frustration. It's so deep-rooted in me to always maintain a positive outlook that I was angered by anything in my environment that didn't support that. We didn't say anything more at that 4,600-metre rest stop, but set off again, bound for the next break.

After leaving the next stop at 4,700 metres, the disagreement seemed to be behind us, but I was evidently still carrying some anger when Faye said, 'Do you think we should have brought a tent with us?'

Why was she talking about a sodding tent? Is she still thinking we're not going to make the top?! Why is she thinking we won't make it?! My mind raged.

'Why are you worried about a tent, when we're going to make it?' I said. Faye fell silent.

At the 4,800-metre stop, Faye didn't say a word and I knew something was up. I ventured a few meaningless questions and her replies were all one-word answers. Oh, crap. She was annoyed. I hated falling out with friends. I hadn't fought with any of my friends in years, probably 10 years in fact, so falling out with Faye felt hideous. What was even more hideous was the thought of carrying on to the summit being annoyed with one another. I took a deep breath and took a few steps towards her.

'Faye, are you annoyed?'

'Yes, I am.'

'Right,' I said, pulling my gloves off, dropping them on the ground next to her, and sitting down. 'Shall we talk about it? Let's not go all the way up there with an atmosphere,' I said, gesturing to the top of the mountain.

And so, at 4,800 metres high, we sat on the side of a volcano and we discussed things, like adults. As usual, it was a case of words said, intentions misinterpreted and assumptions made, on both sides. I explained that I was irritated by her sharing a negative thought in the first hour of the ascent. I drew on a rowing example to try to get across why it had had such an effect on me.

'It'd be like starting a two-thousand-metre race, then one member of your crew saying after five hundred metres that they don't think we're going to make the finish line. It affects the rest of the crew.'

'I get that. But you made your point once. You didn't need to tell me again,' said Faye. Her words were clipped and she sounded really pissed off. It was the angriest I'd ever seen her.

'But then after that you said we should have brought a tent in case we didn't make it,' I said, now rising to a level of anger too.

'I didn't say that,' Faye said, still angry. 'I was just thinking out loud about whether we might have needed a tent in case of an emergency,' she continued. 'I didn't say we wouldn't make it.'

I realised, actually, she hadn't said that we wouldn't make it on that occasion. I felt like an idiot. I was so irritated by the first comment that I had assumed anything she said after that would be negative. She could have said that she'd like to look for a pot of gold at the end of a rainbow and I'd have likely taken it the wrong way.

'Oh, I'm sorry then. I misunderstood,' I said, and there was a long pause.

'I'm sorry too. I shouldn't have said that thing at the start. I was just nervous.'

'Me too, mate, me too. And you're entitled to your own thoughts. I shouldn't have snapped,' I said.

There was another long pause.

'Are we okay?' I asked.

'Yeah,' said Faye, and I moved in for a hug.

What I was beginning to understand was that Faye and I were an ecosystem. If one of us was right and the other one was wrong, then one of us would be hurt. And if one of us was hurt then the environment we lived in was damaged. And if we caused damage to our environment, the very air we breathed, day in, day out, became toxic. With that in mind, we were learning to approach arguments not from a point of view of who was right and who was wrong but, rather, of what we had and hadn't understood, and then looking for where there was a difference between what had been said by one of us, and what had been heard by the other. The argument we'd just had was a textbook example of that.

Post-hug, we were friends again. The air between us was cleared, but the air on the mountain was getting thinner all the time. For the next few hours, we pedalled and pushed our way to over 5,000 metres. Faye was looking strong. I, on the other hand, was faltering. At 5,100 metres, we stopped for a rest. It was now 12.30 p.m. As we'd made a promise to turn around wherever we were by 4 p.m., we had just over three hours left to make the 6,008-metre top. It was still possible, but we couldn't afford to go any slower.

I got off the bike and flopped onto my back, staring at the sky. My chest was tight, my heart was pounding and I shut my eyes through waves of nausea. I felt horrendous. The energy

I was using to pedal and negotiate the uneven rubble surface was far more than I had to expend. I knew we were going to have to leave the bikes at some point and set out on foot and, for me, this was that point.

'You alright, McNuff?' Faye asked.

'Just give me five minutes,' I replied, eyes firmly shut, and still panting. Once I'd recovered a little, we agreed that it was time to switch to walking. We locked the bikes up behind a rock, took only our *essential* essentials in a backpack (knitted snowman and Santa stayed behind to guard the bikes) and set off up the volcano on foot.

It was then that something odd happened. I started to feel sha-mazing! My chest loosened, my heart rate dropped, and I found that walking was a breeze, compared to cycling or pushing the bike. I felt 'normal' again. I looked to my right, expecting to see Faye skipping along next to me, only someone had replaced Faye with a ghost. She was white, breathless and struggling. 'Anna, do you still feel horrible?' she gasped between steps.

'Um, no. I feel fine. How are you doing though?' I asked, even though I knew the answer.

'Terrible. Just terrible,' she replied, shaking her head. Clearly, something about the way our bodies operated was very different. I couldn't believe Faye had had the energy to cycle just a few minutes earlier, and now she couldn't believe I had the energy to walk.

Keeping a watchful eye on Faye's state, we slowed our pace, resting after every measly 50 to 75 metres of ascent. I looked sideways at Faye often and thought about that fine line we were treading. I had to trust that she would be honest with how she was feeling. I needed to respect her judgement, but at the same time I had to be aware that she might not be best placed to judge her own state. I opted for trust, first and foremost. Because, after all, I could be delirious too.

By 2.30 p.m., the wind on the volcano had really picked up. We slumped behind a large boulder at 5,557 metres and paused to consider our final route to the summit. From where we were sitting, it looked tangibly close and, according to the map, we had three options to get there. We chose the shortest, steepest path, which was just half a mile long, and set off again.

Our pace slowed even more and the slope got very steep. Every three steps, I paused to rest with both hands on my knees. I checked in on Faye and looked upwards, scouting for foot placement on the next three steps. By 3.30 p.m., we'd made it to 5,650 metres. The rocks under hand and foot were becoming increasingly loose and we were reduced to scrambling. I started to hear a quiet voice in my head. It was Captain Sensible. 'And just what do you think you're doing, young lady?' he asked.

'Uh… trying to climb a volcano, Cap, can't you see?'

'Well that doesn't sound like a very safe thing to be doing, not now it's getting late in the day.'

'Shh, Captain, pipe down… we're almost there…' I

pressed.

Thirty minutes later, Faye and I had made it to 5,791 metres and were sitting next to one another, our own voices (and Captain Sensible's) barely audible above the rising wind. 'Wow', I mouthed, looking out over a spectacular lunar landscape. I hadn't grasped how high we were until that moment. Even the grandest of mountains in front of us looked dwarfed. And there were dozens of them. Some a dark shade of red, some more pink, some marbled with white and others just ghostly outlines in the distance. I felt humbled. Like they were watching us watching them from our Uturuncu throne.

Perched precariously side by side on scree and stone, we discussed the final section. I could not for the life of me see how to make it to the top. Everything seemed to steepen and the rock looked looser than ever. I still thought making the summit was possible, but I was now struggling with the why of it all. I thought about my folks, and then I thought about Jamie. For me, the risk we were taking to push for the summit had now gone beyond being worth it. Faye interrupted my thoughts.

'What are you thinking, Anna?' she asked.

I looked at her white-washed face and lips, which were tinged blue, and I was entirely honest in my reply. 'I'm thinking that if we zoomed out from here and looked at us at this point, I'd say things were getting silly.' Faye nodded, solemnly. 'And, for what it's worth, I also think you look like shit,' I added, grinning.

There was a long pause.

'Well. That's it then. Let's go down,' said Faye.

It had to come from Faye, that decision. Yes, my comment was a leading one, but the decision to turn around and let go of the dream, that had to come from her. It was now approaching 4.30 p.m. and we'd got as far as we could. Decision made, we sat for a few more minutes in silence, drinking in the beauty and surrealness of it all.

'I just think I needed to know I could do it. And I do now,' sighed Faye.

Then down we went. Back to the bikes, forcibly gripping the handlebars for the return journey over the broken-crockery surface. We didn't say much. We just juddered and jerked back down, absorbed in our thoughts, mind cogs processing the madness of it all, Faye's Uturuncu dream now cut free and carried off on the clouds.

It was gone 7 p.m. by the time we made it back to base camp. After collecting our stash of extra kit from behind the rocks, we pitched the tents and inhaled a small dinner – as much as our throbbing heads and nauseous tummies would allow.

'Well, Faye-bomb,' I said, putting the last of a packet of dessert lemon wafers in my mouth, 'I think it's time for bed. I am beat.'

'Absolutely. Me too,' she replied.

I left Faye sitting on the ground outside the porch of her

tent and returned to my own. 'Goodnight!' I shouted, before unzipping my front porch, and clambering inside.

'Anna?' Faye yelled a few moments later.

'Yep? What's up?' I asked.

There was a short pause.

'Sorry for being a total muppet today,' shouted Faye.

'Well, in that case, I'm sorry for being a muppet too,' I called back.

'Night, night then, muppet! Sleep well,' she said.

11

Friendship = Cheese Puffs

Distance cycled: 1,221 miles
Metres ascended: 39,012

One evening in southern Bolivia, I reached up and ran a hand absent-mindedly through my hair. It got stuck, just behind my right ear. Where the arms of my sunglasses usually sat, I found a wad of knotted hair. I tugged at it a few times and, on account of not having a mirror, took a picture of it with my phone to further investigate the issue. Wow. That little nubbin was tighter than Bob Marley's dreadlocks. I thought back to the last time I'd had a shower, which was 10 days ago in Uyuni. It was official: the grime on my body had reached a critical level.

'Faye!' I yelled from inside my tent.

'Yes, mate?'

'Have you got any scissors over there?'

'Err… yeah I have. I've got some in the medical kit. Do you want them?'

'Yes, please. I'm coming over.'

I got out of my tent and walked over to collect a small pair of nail scissors from Faye, who was poking them out from a crack under the bottom of her porch.

'I would open the door, but I'm stark naked and you don't want to see that… so here they are,' she said.

'Faye, I've seen all your bits now, you know!'

She laughed and I took the scissors. 'What do you need them for?' she asked.

'Oh, I need to cut my hair.'

'Oh! Getting a mini hairdressing McSalon on the go over there, are you?'

'Not really, but I've got a knot the size of Bolivia and it needs to come out. Although if you had a razor with you, I'd gladly shave the whole lot off right now.'

'You'd suit the *Prison Break* look, you know,' said Faye.

'I was thinking I'd look more like Demi Moore… all sexy and aloof,' I replied.

Scissors in hand, I returned to my tent and set about hacking out a knot that turned out to be 3 cm in diameter. I pulled out my phone and took a video for posterity.

'So, it's ten days without a wash – without a shower anyway – and I have just had to cut a knot out of my hair.' I picked up the clump of hair and brandished it at the camera, before ruffling the rest of my head. 'I think I could pretty much be in a L'Oréal advert right now. Because god knows, I'm worth it!'

As I started to get undressed for my nightly wash, I realised that not only had I not had a shower in those 10 days, I hadn't looked in a mirror either. I didn't really know what I looked like but I figured I must be pretty feral by now. I took a selfie of my face and torso and was shocked by what I saw. I barely recognised myself. Usually a C cup, my boobs had shrunk to the size of peanuts. Not even monkey nuts – they were dry roasted peanuts. My collarbones were stripped of any fat and sticking out at jaunty angles, and I could see the outline of individual ribs around the sternum on my chest. I ran my hand over the lower portion of my front ribs and noticed that there didn't seem to be much fat left over them either. Venturing a hand around to the back of my body, I reached for my back fat. That never dwindled. I was like a camel in that respect. Like many wonderful women, I store any blubber I need back *there* for a rainy day. To my horror, someone had been illegally withdrawing funds from the bank of back fat and I was well into the overdraft. I had been verging on skinny from the moment we left La Paz, but the tough work in the Yungas and now the 10 days of dancing around between 4,000 and 5,800 metres had stripped me of any remaining reserves.

My body was falling apart. In fact, everything was falling apart. I'd somehow managed to tear my rear bike tyre, which I'd had to replace with my spare one, and even my shoelaces had given up the ghost that morning and snapped. We could no longer keep up the 60-mile days that we'd been averaging in the lead up to and across the salt flats. In fact, on some days on our current loop, covering 30 miles over the corrugation and sand was a huge achievement. The past few weeks had been the kind of stuff that adventure dreams are made of, but that night I would have paid a handsome sum to be transported to a town and be done with the Uturuncu section. I was ready for a rest and a shower and I knew that Faye felt the same.

***

When I woke up on the morning before our penultimate high pass of the loop, I felt absolutely dreadful. It had been two days since we'd climbed Uturuncu and an underlying fatigue was festering in my bones. I had zero energy, a tight chest and a stuffy nose. In fact, I felt like I'd spent the night with a WWE wrestler sitting on my chest (with his fingers pinching my nostrils). To add a little extra somethin' somethin' to my personal pity party, we had also begun to run low on food. Many of the shops in the tiny towns we'd passed through had been shut, or the shop ended up being a glass cabinet in a local grandma's bedroom.

Leaving Uyuni, we'd expected to make it through the Uturuncu section in eight days, ten days maximum. Ten days had now passed and it would be at least a further four before we crossed the border into Chile and reached the town of San Pedro de Atacama. As our energy levels dwindled and our food supplies followed suit, the thought of making it to San Pedro and getting a decent meal was often all that kept me going.

I knew that I had a couple of choices for how to deal with feeling under the weather. I could have chosen to pretend that I felt marvellous, which I did try. But in the end, I settled on beginning the day mildly pissed off – which I tried and excelled at. By the top of Hedionda Pass, which was marked 'very steep!' in our notes, Faye was going great guns. She was trucking along in a steady rhythm and I watched her move further and further ahead up the climb. I, on the other hand, wasn't even able to turn the pedals fast enough to stay on the bike. The only thing for it was to get off and push but, even then, I was having to stop every 30 metres of ascent to suck in some air through what felt like a straw and relocate the lost city of My Lungs.

'Come on, McNuff. Just a bit longer,' I muttered under my breath at each rest stop, as I collapsed over the handlebars and then looked towards the crest of the pass. I genuinely thought I was going to keep it together. I thought I'd managed to swallow the lumps in my throat enough times to hold in all my emotions. Exhaustion and frustration flowed through me like a river, but I had built a dam in my mind. A giant wall that now held back an overspilling lake of fatigue. The dam wall began to crack.

Cresting the pass, I saw Faye sitting at the side of the road taking a rest and was relieved that I could stop too. I opened my mouth to speak.

'Oo eee. That was a tough one. That really nearly got me you know… I almost cri…' And that was all it took. The dam burst, the flood of frustration surged forward and I melted into tears. I knew that I just had to let it all out. 'Tears are just chemicals. Get 'em out and move on,' as my hard-as-nails friend Naomi says. I sat at the side of the road and had a good old-fashioned sob. My shoulders shook and big blobs of salty tears rolled down my cheeks before dropping onto the dusty road. I was just so frustrated, mostly at how slow I was going, and so very, very tired.

'You alright, mate?' Faye asked.

'Yeah… I suppose it was going to happen. You had your cry the other day, and now I'm having mine,' I sniffed.

'You go for it, McNuff. Get it all out,' Faye said.

'It's just… I woke up feeling dreadful… my nose is blocked, my lungs hurt and all I want to do is get out of this fricking loop and get some food!'

'I hear you… me too,' she said softly, and there was a pause.

I let out a big sigh.

'But I do have Cheesy Poofs,' Faye said, brandishing a packet of our favourite cheesy snack. A smile crept into the corners of my mouth. 'And I'm very good at sharing you know,' she continued.

'You are *very* good at sharing,' I said, reaching into the packet for a handful of cheesy, puffy goodness. So there we sat on the roadside, divvying up the 120 calories of the cheese puffs, hoping that they would keep us going until we made the next 30 miles and could get some food at Polques.

Away from the high passes and now riding along, rather

than upwards, we nudged closer to roads that were more frequently used by the tourist buses and jeeps that passed through the area. Gone were the deep reds of the start of the loop and the dark browns of Uturuncu. Around the Lagunas, the landscape was lighter, orange-brown with patches of white. The Lagunas themselves were nestled between surrounding volcanoes and each looked like someone had submerged a giant bowl of soup in the ground. Threads of steam, which rose from their white surface, were scooped up by the wind and whisked away. We trundled onwards, dodging a few dust devils and stopping to look at the Andean flamingos that gathered in the lakes. The bright scarlet on their feathers and their gangly legs never failed to make me smile.

With six miles to go till Polques, Faye and I cycled headlong into a wall of wind. We battled for a few hours in the strongest headwind known to humankind. It blasted our cheeks almost clean off our faces but we pushed on. I remember looking over at Faye, knowing we had been surviving on 800 calories a day for the past few days, and wondering how on earth she was still going. And then I wondered how I was still going. And then I concluded that – if it was ever in any doubt – human bodies are amazing. At that moment, I was in love with mine. My rib-revealing, peanut-boob, no-back-fat scrappy body was still managing to propel me across the windswept Lagunas on less than half the daily calories it needed. Dear body, thank you.

At last we made the main road to Polques and the transition to a more well-travelled route was immediate. The road surface was hard packed (although still dirt) and jeep after jeep began to zoom past, coating us in thick dust each time. We pedalled on, eager to make it to the town and buy some food at the shop, which our notes told us was there. Pulling into the lay-by off the road at Polques, both of us immediately clocked that something was wrong. Our hearts sank and our bellies rumbled. There was no shop.

Despite dozens of tourists and three minibuses waiting, there was nothing but a large thermal pool and a seemingly empty, long, cream-coloured building. It was a further three days to San Pedro de Atacama and we literally had nothing left to eat. Well, except my left arm – but I was ruling that one out.

We had a brief chat to a group of tourists at the front of the building. They told us that they were staying in the cream-coloured building that night as part of a package tour. We were lightly swaying on our feet as we chatted, our faces ashen and gaunt, trying to smile at the group through cracked lips. Having not seen anyone in several days, it felt strange to be surrounded by so many people. I had almost forgotten how to interact with anyone who wasn't Faye. Having a conversation with the tourists was like painting by numbers. My mind began offering a running commentary.

That woman has smiled at you, Anna. You should smile back. She has now asked you a question – initiate response mechanism. Oh, this man is paying you a compliment – activate modesty sequence and insist you are not brave really, just stupid…

After 10 minutes of chit-chat, my stomach gave a deep gurgle and drew my attention back to the fact that I was ravenous. I asked the group who was 'in charge' and headed into the building to find the tour guide, who was apparently in the kitchen. Stepping out of the bright sunlight and into the dark of the hallway, I took a moment to let my eyes adjust. When everything was back in focus, I spotted a blue wooden door to my right. Shoving open the door, I found three Bolivian men sitting on low stools in the kitchen, chatting and chopping onions. A rush of onion-air flooded my nostrils. I assumed that these were the tour guides, and so I began my mission.

'*¡Hola! ¿Hablan inglés?*' I asked, hoping that one of them might be able to understand an explanation of our nosh-less plight. One by one the men said that they didn't speak English. I could have, of course, attempted to continue in broken Spanish, but I was exhausted. And it was too late. There were no two ways about it – I was going off on one in English, and what I lacked in language skills, I would make up for in physical drama.

For the next few minutes, I talked to the men in English. Well, I say *to* them; really, I talked *at* them. Arms flailing wildly, rubbing my belly, pointing at Sally the Saddle Sore, showing them the cracks on my thumbs, retracing our route from Uyuni in thin air. At one point, I even mimed climbing a volcano and gasping for breath. It was my finest Charades hour, during which the men looked understandably perplexed. By the time I had finished the dramatic enactment of 'ten days in the volcanic wilds', I had managed to negotiate a deal. We would hand over all the money we had left in our wallets (around £20) in return for dinner and a bed for the night in the cream-coloured building. We had effectively hijacked a package tour and scored ourselves an all-inclusive deal for the evening. Marvellous.

I was delighted that this solved the immediate problem of having run out of food and being exhausted, but as we began to take advantage of the complimentary coffee laid on for the paying guests, I started to wonder how we were going to make it to San Pedro de Atacama, a few days away, with no other food. And then, there she was: Patricia. A doctor from Cheltenham in the UK. Brown hair, blue eyes, English white-rose skin and a comforting smile.

'Eat some crackers,' she said, motioning to the complimentary snacks laid out next to the coffee. The rest of the tour group now began to rally around too. Egged on by travellers from England, Russia, Italy and Germany, we began cramming crackers into our mouths and into our pockets, stocking up on supplies for the following few days. We wolfed down five crackers each and pocketed the same amount, but Patricia still wasn't happy with our hoard. She was a doctor, after all; she had our wellbeing at heart.

'Come with me,' she said, getting up and moving away from the dining room and into one of the bedrooms off the adjoining long hallway.

As it turned out, Patricia (who had become our angel-in-residence) was on month three of a four-month journey through South America. She plonked her bag onto one of the beds.

'Girls, do you have any more food to get you to San Pedro?' she asked, a concerned look on her face.

'Not really,' I replied, now feeling embarrassed, although knowing full well we'd done our best in trying to get hold of food en route.

'Okay. Well, I'm not long off from going home. I've got some spare stuff in here,' said Patricia, patting her Mary Poppins-esque black bag.

'Right. Let's see what we've got. Peruvian granola? It's a bit weird, but do you want it?'

'Yes,' said Faye.

'Hot chocolate sachet?' she asked.

'Yes,' I said.

'Earl grey?'

'Yes.'

'Cereal bars?'

'Yes.'

'I don't suppose you want these mandarins?!'

'YES!' I shouted, wondering what on earth she was going to produce next from that bag. A lamp? A spoonful of sugar? And then it happened. Patricia paused momentarily, before moving her hand slowly and seductively deeper into the bag. She was almost up to her armpit when she finally extracted her arm and said, 'How about this?'

In Patricia's palm was a 250-g bar of Galaxy chocolate. And I am talking BRITISH carried-from-home chocolate.

'YES!!!!' we screamed in unison at the top of our lungs.

***

Fully stocked up on good vibes and good food, we pedalled on for the next few days. We were regularly coated in dust by passing tour buses but enjoyed knowing that we were now close to crossing into Chile and arriving in San Pedro de Atacama. On our final night on the Uturuncu loop, we camped just 2 miles shy of the Bolivian-Chilean border. It wasn't the cleverest thing we could have done, and we were mildly terrified by a surprise visit from the border police at midnight. Still, they were friendly as they checked our passports and, having convinced themselves that we were not intending to enter Chile illegally, they let us be.

The following day, we had a reunion with our midnight callers at the immigration shack, as they stamped us out of Bolivia at the border. We slogged the final few miles up to the Hito Cajón pass and were welcomed into Chile with the greatest gift anyone could have bestowed upon us: a paved road. Oh, how our lady bits rejoiced! After two weeks of sluggish progress, the tarmac felt terrifyingly fast. Especially as it was all downhill from 4,700 metres to the town of San Pedro de Atacama at a balmy 2,400 metres above sea level.

Clad in leggings, down jackets and full-face buffs, we glided downwards for 90 minutes. I sang most of the way, following Faye as she zoomed ahead, flicking my legs into motion every now and then, just to remind them what cycling felt like, but otherwise I freewheeled. We stopped at intervals to take off layers of clothing as the air temperature rose steadily, giving the impression that we were slipping, ever so gently, into the warmest of baths.

By mid-afternoon we had arrived in the mecca of San Pedro de Atacama (population: 2,500), just on the edge of the Atacama Desert. Thanks to the slow-descent striptease, we were now in shorts and T-shirts in 21°C, a far cry from the −10°C we'd slept in the night before. Without a second thought, we wheeled straight into the main plaza, which was full of restaurants and cafes. When I say full, I mean that there were at least five eateries, which was five times as many as we had encountered in the past two weeks. We propped our bikes next to the largest one and sat down at one of the outside tables, in the shade of a large umbrella with a beer brand on its cream-coloured canvas. I ordered a giant tankard of lager, some water and a pizza with pepperoni, fresh tomato, rocket and avocado. Avocado… on a pizza?! Wonders will never cease. Faye ordered a pizza with chicken, goat's cheese and red onion and a Sprite. Once our food had arrived, I looked over at Faye and grinned. And when I took the first bite of that fresh and juicy pizza, heaven was a place on earth.

Gorging on high-calorie food and drink, I began trying to process everything that had happened since we'd left Uyuni.

The past two weeks had taken us to hell and back but through some of the most beautiful landscapes imaginable. We had laughed, we had cried and often it was one of us laughing that had saved the other from crying. In the space carved out by a silence that can only be comfortable between two people who know one another deeply, I felt the net around our friendship tighten. Not because we had behaved admirably. Not because we had maintained a stiff upper lip and always said and done the right thing, but because we had stumbled a few times into doing quite the opposite. We had been thoughtless, impulsive, careless even, with our actions toward one other. We had been very human.

I let out a long sigh before folding the final slice of pizza in half and cramming it into my mouth. Then, remembering that we had a phone signal at last, I loaded up Jamie's number and hit dial. He answered.

'Helloooo me Annnerr. It's so nice to hear your voice. How are you?' he said in his West Country drawl.

'Ah, it's so nice to hear your voice too,' I replied, immediately feeling my whole body relax.

'What's been going on over there?' he asked.

'Oh, you know,' I said. 'Not much…'

San Pedro de Atacama
to Santiago

San Pedro
De Atacama

Paso De Jama

Jujuy

ARGENTINA / CHILE BORDER

Salta

Cafayate

Santa Maria

J+K

Chilecito

Aconcagua

Talampaya
National Park

Mendoza

Santiago

12

Do Not Feed the Animals

Distance cycled: 1,284 miles
Metres ascended: 39,678

I had a friend called Joy once. At the start of the final section through Bolivia, she had packed her bags, written me a Dear John letter and left my life. I confess, I thought she was gone for good – kept at bay by a wall of exhaustion and buried under layers of volcanic dust. So imagine my surprise when, a week after Faye and I left San Pedro de Atacama, Joy showed up again, refreshed and ready to roll. Everyone's Joy is different, of course. My Joy loves crunchy vegetables (broccoli, especially). She loves soft squishy beds. She likes strong coffee and she goes weak at the knees when faced with a slice of oozy lemon pie. All of which I'd been eating during our rest days in San Pedro de Atacama.

Faye and I had originally intended to spend only two days in town. We were behind schedule, so we really needed to crack on and make headway south, towards Santiago and the mid-point of our journey through the Andes. Arriving in Santiago on time was important because we'd planned to take two weeks off the bikes and hang out with our loved ones.

Jamie was flying in from the UK, and (thanks to a surprise early Christmas gift from Faye's dad) Faye's mum, Libby, was flying in too. Both Jamie and Libby had booked their flights, so arriving later than we'd planned would mean missing out on quality boyfriend or mum time. And that just wasn't an option. Time is the most precious commodity on the planet, after all.

It was late November in San Pedro de Atacama; we were still 1,500 miles from Santiago and now had just five weeks to make those miles. Some swift pizza-infused calculations led to the scientific conclusion that we needed to get a wriggle on and leave town as soon as possible. The only problem with that conclusion was… we were exhausted. And so, two days in San Pedro slipped easily to three and then into four. Staying in a hostel for that long was hammering our trip budget but neither of us could face the thought of heading back into the mountains just yet. And besides, I was keen to make sure that Sally the Saddle Sore had made an exit from my life. Or at least shrunk in size before I left civilisation. So we stayed a little longer. I spent much of each rest day sitting in one of the many cafes in town eating slices of lemon meringue pie and drinking coffee. I'd really started to get addicted to lemon meringue pie but I decided that there are far worse vices to have.

In between resting, eating and drinking, I'd also made a bold decision to cut off 80% of my hair. The salon session in the tent halfway through the Uturuncu loop had planted a seed in my mind. I'd always wondered what life would be like with shorter hair. When I was a kid, I remember watching the adventures of Elizabeth and Jessica in the 90s TV show

Sweet Valley High. The girls were twins and one of them had short, pixie-cut blonde hair. I remember thinking 'Wow, that girl must be so confident to have her hair cut short like that'. I associated shorter locks with confidence and I had picked up some more of that since leaving La Paz.

Having curly locks down to my shoulders was proving troublesome so, one afternoon, after finishing my daily slice of lemon pie, I marched into the nearest hair salon. There I found a very excitable Chilean man in a pale blue Hawaiian shirt. He was all arm gestures and smiles and, with my limited Spanish and the help of some Google images, I showed him what I wanted. A few snips and a bit of buzz-cutting later, and I had a hairstyle that made me look like one of the X-Men. Short and dark around the sides, with longer blonde curls in a quiff on the top. I bloomin' loved it.

By day five in San Pedro, Sally the Saddle Sore had finally calmed down, the lymph nodes in my crotch had shrunk to normal size and, safe in the knowledge that dealing with matted hair was behind me, it was time to hit the road again. Even though it was a long two-day climb back up to the Hito Cajón pass at 4,700 metres, we didn't mind one bit. With good food and good sleep, we had fully recharged our minds and bodies, and even the bikes had had a tune-up at the local bike shop. The hardship of the Uturuncu loop faded into memory and the lure of the road grew stronger again.

The appeal of riding out of town was enhanced by the fact that we would be going into Argentina for the first time, via Paso de Jama, one of the mountain passes that I had read about in countless adventure books. I'd seen pictures of its snake-like tarmac road wiggling down the mountainside, looking like a line of syrup drizzled over breakfast pancakes. It was a long, sweeping pass, set in a volcanic landscape, straddling the most-northerly border crossing between Chile and Argentina. It certainly seemed popular among motorcyclists and cycle tourists alike. I had a number of friends who had been up and over the pass and I couldn't wait to experience all its wiggly loveliness for myself.

Back on the road, we made steady progress towards Argentina. The landscape on the 4,000-metre-high plateau that led to the border was stark and stunning. A single light-grey road streaked off along the flat plain into the horizon, the double yellow lines down the centre shifting to one side or the other whenever the road turned a corner. There was so much space out there. The colours were less vibrant than they had been in recent weeks, but being surrounded by softer shades of volcanic orange, peach and smudges of white was like riding through a watercolour painting. By far the boldest colours were the grey road and the blue sky, and it was a pleasure to be sandwiched between the two.

Our easy ride towards the Argentinian border was not only aided by the baby-bottom-smooth tarmac but it was also broken up by occasional tour-bus traffic. Much as Faye and I both enjoyed remote riding, seeing and meeting other people was a welcome change. There was something comforting about the company of strangers after the hardships of the recent few weeks.

One afternoon, a small white tourist bus passed us and slowed down alongside. The driver honked his horn and the group waved from inside the bus. Honking and waving from tourist buses happened a few times a day but there was something different about this particular one. It seemed to be moving more slowly than others had. I watched as it came to a complete stop just ahead of us in the middle of the road. The front passenger's window slid down and out of the window floated... a baguette. A large, freshly baked, crusty baguette.

'Here! Take!' said the driver, leaning across the passenger to hand us the bread. I cycled up to the window so that I was eye to eye with the baguette. I wrapped my grubby little fingers around it and pulled it towards me. Wafts from the freshly cooked loaf charged up my nostrils as memories of summers spent in France flooded my brain. I went in for another sniff before grinning at Faye and then holding the loaf aloft, as if it were Excalibur and I a Knight of the Round Table. The group in the van cheered. And lo, what next? Something for our goblets? A carton of orange juice followed the baguette through the open window and floated into my hands. Sweet, sticky orange juice.

Two hours later, having gobbled up the bread and downed 90% of the orange juice, we were resting our weary bods by the roadside when a small silver van pulled up. Again, from an open window on the passenger side came a whole French baguette. *What is going on?!* I thought. The baguette was followed by two tins of fish, some oranges, a banana, a block of chocolate and an apple. This particular group had completed their tour of the nearby Lagunas and, just like the group in the white van, they had decided that they would like to stop and feed the cyclists. We weren't complaining, we didn't even mind that each time they passed food out the window they all got their cameras out and began taking pictures while we ate. It was like feeding animals at the zoo. We were the star tourist attraction out there and we were very happy about it.

I have several photos from that day. In one, Faye is gratefully receiving a tin of tuna via the bus window, while the tourists squish themselves against the glass and take photos of her with their phones. And in another photo, I am posing next to my bike, standing on a long grey road in a *Saturday Night Fever* John Travolta-style disco pose, with one arm in the air, thrusting a fresh baguette up towards a cloud-spattered sky.

In the days spent pedalling between feasts delivered by tourist buses, we learned that we weren't the only animals out there on the plateau. Each day we saw hundreds of what was fast becoming my favourite Andean wildlife: flamingos. We'd been seeing flamingos since the salt flats in Bolivia, but back then I was too exhausted to appreciate them. And besides, we were mostly caught up accidentally wading into their poop on the Coipasa flats. But on the smooth tarmac roads and under the blue skies of Chile, I became more and more enamoured of the flamingos. Every time I saw them on the horizon, gathered in a lake or taking flight as we neared, I just had to stop and stare. Flamingos are surely the most Disney-esque of flying things. The perfect mix of graceful and gawky. That long ungainly neck, the droopy black beak and lanky legs interrupted by the knobbliest of knees. But then, when they fly, when the sky is awash with pink and scarlet, oh my, they are majestic.

Naturally, as one does when one is on an expedition, I spent a night in my tent googling 'do flamingos have knees?', which led to the discovery that flamingos' knee joints are actually hidden under the main body of their feathers. The joints visible on their legs below the feathers are, in fact, their ankle joint. I'll pause for a moment to allow you to be blown away. I know. After relaying details of this anatomical anomaly to Faye (who had also been unaware of it) I decided that, once home, I would launch a widespread media campaign to improve flamingo #AnkleAwareness. There are so many fascinating things to learn about flamingos that I didn't stop there. I went on to find out why their feathers are so pink. It's because the algae and crustaceans they eat contain red pigments. A flamingo's digestive system extracts the pigments from the food and dissolves it in fat cells. The fat cells are then deposited, over time, in any new feathers that grow, and so the birds appear a whole range of colours, from orange to pink. Magic. Flamingos really are what they eat. My final question of the evening was 'how do flamingos sleep?' I won't tell you the answer and will leave you on a cliffhanger there. As always, this journey had opened my eyes and forced me to ask questions that I never would have done at home. It was school on the move at its finest.

Out there, on the high plateau between Chile and Argentina, the days just got better and better. I was sleeping soundly, waking naturally with the sunrise and, from the moment we rolled out of camp each day, everything seemed darn near perfect. All the hard work of weeks spent slogging through Bolivia had upped my fitness level and, with a higher proportion of smooth tarmac roads, we were able to get up to riding 70 to 80 miles a day.

With smoother roads came less of a need to concentrate on actually trying to stay on the bike. I could take some additional sensory input, so music began to play a large part in the return of my long-lost friend Joy. With a headphone in just one ear (so I could hear any approaching traffic), I would begin spinning my legs, warming them up in the morning to the ballads of Journey, singing at the top of my lungs about being a small-town girl, living in a lonely world.

I enjoyed looking down at the road as I cycled, seeing how, at speed, the multicoloured patches of tarmac blurred into a single shade of grey, and I was deeply satisfied to note that I was in the highest gear on the bike again. It was so nice for big-gear cog to get an airing. Considering I had worn the small 'granny' cog I used for climbing to a pulp, the big one was due a bit of action.

Every now and then, a bump would appear on the horizon. Having negotiated the major passes of this section, it would only ever be a small climb, maybe 300 metres of ascent, but I could feel my legs start to twitch. They were poised, like (oversized, over-fed) greyhounds in a starting gate. They could see the hill, they could smell it, and they were ready for it. I'd change the song in my headphones again, this time to a dance track, just as I hit the start of an incline.

I could feel my hamstrings start to pull, the pressure on my sit bones increasing as gravity tried to claw me backwards, but as I was being repeatedly told by the max-volume dance track entitled 'Gravity', it couldn't hold me down.

Faye had also decided to bring some music into her pedalling, and we continued listening to an assortment of 80s and 90s hits long into the evening, with grins on our faces. In between bouts of euphoric on-bike dancing, we used any spare energy to play games of 'would you rather?' As it turns out, I would rather sweat mashed potato than have garlic butter for saliva and, if Faye were a man, she would rather have one large testicle the size of a football, as opposed to twenty small frogspawn-esque testicles.

As dusk began to fall, a strange feeling came over me. It had been so long since I'd last felt it that I barely even recognised it. It started as a mere tingle in my toes and clawed its way, just a few millimetres at a time, up my legs, swirling around my stomach like a tornado before reaching my chest, from where it exploded in a hundred different directions. 'YEAH! I am alive!' I hollered at the top of my lungs, feeling euphoria take hold. I was liberated and high as a kite. Down the other side of the small hill, my legs throbbed. It was a dull ache that brought me no end of satisfaction. I had transcended. I was completely content. I was no longer on my bike – I was in my head, in my future, in my past, I was anywhere and anyone I wanted to be.

In the miles of euphoria towards the Argentinian border, everything about life seemed crystal clear. With the struggle of past days gone, for a while, at least, I could let my mind roam. Each day I spun the roulette wheel, I dropped in a thought ball or two and waited to see where it stopped. Often it landed on thinking about how I wanted to spend my days when I was back home. I wanted to write books and I wanted to give talks, both of which effectively boiled down to storytelling. Anything else was just detail. I wasn't entirely sure how I would manage to make those two things my full-time living just yet but that's what I wanted to do. I breathed a sigh of relief, amazed at how a life that seemed so complicated 90% of the time could be distilled into the aim of doing just a few simple things. That, when given the time and space to actually think rather than do, the thinking about what to do ceases to feel so overwhelming.

A week after leaving San Pedro de Atacama, we had crossed the border into Argentina, whooshed down Paso de Jama, and were now pedalling south, headed for the cities of San Salvador de Jujuy and Salta. One afternoon, we followed a faint grey road, snaking and switchbacking between orange-red hills peppered with green scrub. At the top, we stopped for a lunch break. Faye was sitting on the edge of the road, looking down on the pass we'd just ridden up. Her royal-blue T-shirt looked out of place against a backdrop of burnt-orange hills and pastel skies but I noted that, after two months in the sun, her tanned skin fitted in perfectly.

Munching on crackers and cheese, I watched how shadows cast by the clouds moved across the undulations of the valley below – their dark, shifting outlines like giant manta rays gliding over an ocean floor.

The peace and calm from that lunchtime break on the pass soon faded, as we joined the main highway heading south and spent the following few days fighting for space and fresh air amid plumes of truck dust. Thankfully, beyond San Salvador de Jujuy, we found that we could stay off the main roads and follow neatly signposted, sweeping 'garden routes', passing between small patches of woodland, past green farmland, or meandering through suburbia. As we approached Salta, I realised that we hadn't discussed spending a night in the city. I had assumed that we wouldn't but now I was concerned that I'd made the decision without consulting Faye. When we pulled up at a junction outside the city, I thought I better check in with her on the subject.

'Um, Faye. Did you want to stay here tonight?' I asked, fiddling with my handlebars and doing my best to keep my tone neutral so as not to sway her decision.

'In the city?' she asked.

'Yeah,' I replied.

'Err, I hadn't really thought about it.'

'Okay, well, I suppose it could be nice. Having a bed and a shower and all that,' I said.

'Nah. I prefer the tents,' said Faye, and I heaved a sigh of relief.

'Phew! Me too.'

'Great. We could get some lunch though? That might be nice?' she said, and I agreed. I was always up for lunch, after all.

I was relieved that Faye felt the same way I did about camping that night. Staying in San Pedro de Atacama a few weeks earlier, with its population of around 2,500, had felt busy enough; the idea of staying in Salta where there were more than 600,000 people, would have been too much to take. Entering cities always felt like moving from a 10-day silent retreat to a seat next to a giant speaker at a rock concert. It physically hurt my senses to be in cities for too long. So much noise, so many people, so much of... everything.

We found a small cafe on a street corner with outdoor tables and Faye ordered a glass of fresh orange juice, something I had begun to learn was her go-to midday treat. Faye and I were at opposite ends of the spectrum when it came to deciding what to eat. Faye's tummy was always sensitive, and even more so when we were at altitude – she had to be careful what she put into it to make sure the contents stayed put. She often marvelled at my willingness to eat (or, at least, try to eat) anything. I think this was an overhang from having been a fussy eater as a child and my mum going on a one-woman mission to stamp out such picky behaviour. Conversely, I was learning what Faye did and didn't eat. Nothing too spicy (we'd learned that in Oruro when spicy pasta had turned her guts inside out). No caffeine – she'd really never gotten into the tea and coffee thing – and she wasn't keen on alcohol either. She liked mangos, but not mango juice. She would never eat an apple because she hated powdery apples and couldn't take the chance that an apple might be powdery. Cheese was a firm favourite, as was pizza (we really connected on those two) but, by far, her fave treat was a '*submarino*', which is the mother of all hot chocolates. It's brought out as a glass of hot milk with a small chocolate bar on the side. While the milk is still hot, you unwrap the chocolate bar and drop it into the milk, stirring it until dissolved. Heaven.

Since crossing into Argentina, my new favourite thing had become *medialunas*, which are miniature, extra-sweet croissants. They usually come in a basket of three or four and are served with coffee. I love coffee. I love to dunk things in my coffee (my dad had raised me as a dunker). And so I loved nothing more than dunking a *medialuna* or three in my coffee. Sitting outside a cafe on a street corner in Salta, with Faye sipping her freshly squeezed orange juice and me mid-dunk with a *medialuna*, knowing we would soon be heading back out of the city, life was rosy.

With full bellies and veins coursing with juice and coffee, we wound our way through the backstreets of Salta and out into the surrounding countryside. Now down at 1,500 metres above sea level, the heat and humidity had begun to rise. By 4 p.m. that day, our bodies were drenched in sweat and our skin coated in a fine layer of city smog. My legs throbbed from the new addition of small, sharp rolling hills and we were both more than ready to pitch our tents for the night. Finding a place to wild camp had become increasingly difficult over the past few days. With more cities came more suburbs, more people and more restrictions on land. Long gone were the mornings when llamas would come for breakfast at our tent spot in the middle of nowhere. Now we had to begin looking for a camp spot at least an hour or so before we intended to stop.

There were a few criteria we needed to fulfil for our camp spots. The land should be flat and dry. We needed to be able to get the pegs in the ground, so it couldn't be too hard or on gravel. The pitch should be hidden from the road so that we wouldn't be seen or disturbed by any passers-by and we also needed to be able to get two fully loaded touring bikes from the road to the camp spot. The latter was often the greatest challenge because there are so many fences along the roads in northern Argentina. It was times like that when I longed for the simplicity of a running adventure and being able to just hop off the road or a trail and duck into the forest with no worries about puncturing tyres or dragging bags over rough ground.

After a few failed attempts at finding a camp spot and with it now approaching 5 p.m., we glided over a small bridge and spotted a potential pitch, off the road to the right. It was at the bottom of a small gully which led into a forest. It was flat(ish), hidden from the road (although directly next to it) and, as a bonus, it was sheltered. The only downside was that it was fenced off, but after deciding we were doing no harm, we shimmied our bikes and selves under the wire fence and pitched up, just out of sight from the road and next to a long concrete tunnel that passed underneath it.

I felt mildly uncomfortable to be on a fenced-off piece of land. Pitching in places like that always made me nervous in case someone came by. But after some discussion, we agreed that the worst thing that could happen would be for a farmer to ask us to 'gerrr off my laaaannnddd' (or the Spanish equivalent) – an event for which I prepped my best blank stare and an apologetic look, just in case. We set up our homes for the night, cooked up dinner and were just settling in for bed as dusk fell. All was going well. Well, that was until it became abundantly clear why the fencing was around the land.

I heard the scuff of hoofs and a few grunts, so I unzipped the top part of my tent porch to see what was occurring outside. Plodding down the slope to our left were three large black and white dairy cows. The first one stopped just shy of our tents, likely confused to find us on their grazing patch. The second cow walked into the bum of the first one and then stopped, before the third cow followed suit and came to a halt as well. Oh good, I thought. Now that they had seen us, they would surely turn around and go back up the hill. But after a few moments, the cows resumed their onward march, on a direct trajectory for the front of my tent. Now, I will confess that I find cows scary. They are massive when you get up close and they can run super-fast too. I know this from experience, when Jamie and I accidentally ran between some mumma cows and their calves and were chased across a field by a herd of them in Gloucestershire.

But I also knew that Faye had a degree in animal science and a master's in agriculture, so I decided to get an educated take on the likelihood of death by hoof trampling that night.

'Err, Faye,' I called out.

'Yes, mate?'

'In your professional opinion, is that first cow getting a bit close to my tent?' We were both now poking our heads out of the top of our porches like birdwatchers.

'Nah, we'll be alright,' said Faye, ducking back inside her tent as the first cow's udder passed within touching distance of my porch. The cows hung around for a while and, once it became apparent that they weren't going anywhere (and I realised that they would do us no harm), I found that there was something oddly satisfying about cow-watching. So I indulged for the next hour as the cow gang milled around our camp, nuzzling, munching, pooping and, every now and then, stopping to stare at me. I even named them: Daisy (big mumma cow), Peaches (the calf) and Sandra (the bullock).

As dusk gave way to darkness, the cows continued to provide amusement, their long straight backs and black noses lit by the soft light of the moon. Eventually they moved on, heading off for an evening of bovine adventure on another part of the land. And as they did, I noted that there was a new entertainment show kicking off in the forest behind them. A Firefly Spectacular!

At first, there were only a few fireflies, just a flash of yellow light every now and then. But, before long, the forest was teeming with them. It was as if someone had adorned the trees with a hundred fairy lights, which pulsed erratically and ever so briefly, but with all the intensity of a mini explosion. It was a humid night, and a warm breeze tickled my nose as I called to Faye to unzip her tent and enjoy the show. Eyes wide, and smiling, I marvelled at how something so tiny could create something so infinitely magical. Their numbers grew, with more and more fireflies appearing until even the blackest recesses of the forest began to sparkle with life. Eventually my eyelids grew heavy. I could barely keep them open and so I ducked back inside my tent and drifted off to sleep, surrounded by the enchanted forest.

13

An Unlikely Rescue Mission

Distance cycled: 1,679 miles
Metres ascended: 48,078

It's 100 miles from the city of Salta to the famous vineyard town of Cafayate. If you take the most direct route that is. But something about taking the direct route didn't feel right. The past week on smooth tarmac roads had been dreamy. Yes, there had been long hours in the saddle and tired legs but in the context of the trip as a whole, life had been a breeze. So, when we started planning our continued route south, the direct route to Cafayate began to feel like so many of my secondary school reports, which all too often read: 'I suspect she is cruising. Could do better.'

I do love a good cruise through life from time to time. When not on adventures, I am extremely happy to stay in my pyjamas for the entire day, especially if it's a Sunday, drinking coffee and making pancakes, watching *Sunday Brunch* on the telly and chatting to Jamie. But the masochist inside me also craves pain and suffering and... adventure. And that's the thing about adventure: it rarely just plops into your lap as you go about your daily business. More often than not, you must seek it out. After establishing that Faye was also keen for a return to some off-road pain and suffering – I mean 'adventure' – it made logical sense that we take the illogical route from Salta to Cafayate. Instead of staying on paved roads down at an oxygen-rich 1,000 metres, we would opt to tack on some extra miles and head off onto some rubble roads via a 3,500-metre mountain pass.

Leaving our camp beside the enchanted forest, we set out on what was to be a day of going upwards. I liked going upwards. Faye liked going upwards. So, we climbed steadily and in good spirits. I was still loving my self-imposed audio Spanish lessons via the 'Coffee Break Spanish' podcast and, that day, I learnt how to say 'my hotel room is smelly'. Faye and I had fallen into an educational routine with the language learning. I would study Spanish via podcast and then teach the relevant bits to Faye during our roadside snack breaks. It was good for me because repeating things to Faye solidified the learning in my mind, and it was good for Faye because I could sift out all of the phrases that we would likely never use, such as: 'I would like a room with an en suite and a view of the ocean, please' and 'my car has broken down'. While cycling, instead of listening to Spanish podcasts, Faye chose to indulge in back editions of Radio 4's *Desert Island Discs*. She would then tell me which *Desert Island Discs* episodes were the best and I would listen to those in the afternoon. The routine worked beautifully and everyone was a winner.

As our pedals turned slowly through the Pukamayu Valley, so did the colour wheel on the surrounding landscape, shifting from pastel pastures, to vibrant greens, to greyish blues and then, all of a sudden, we were in another world. The road hadn't yet turned to rubble and so it was still a pale grey. I watched as it curved around a bend to the right, cutting between two steep cliffs of blood-red rock. Layers of burnt orange and flickers of peach ran in horizontal lines along fragile-looking cliffs, from which small, sharp pieces had broken off, presumably through force of water or wind, and were scattered across the road. Green shrubs lined the roadside and were climbing the cliffs, scaling them slowly and thinning out to just a few plant fingers halfway up. Down the valley, I could see more mountains, their red rumpled spines creeping towards a sky that was heavy with thunderous grey-white clouds. We pedalled on through the afternoon, winding in and out of steep canyons and past tall cacti and small crystal-clear streams as they tumbled into the muddy Chicoana River.

While perched on a rocky outcrop and eating lunch in the slim shade of a cactus, we spotted a purpose-built lookout a few hundred metres up the road. Deciding that it was probably more sensible to rest up there instead, we pedalled up to it. At the lookout, we met a friendly Dutch couple who were travelling by car around South America with their four-year-old daughter, Quinn. I looked around at the mountainous vista, at the kind of sight I hadn't seen until I was at least 12, when my parents took me and my two brothers to the Grand Canyon (lucky us). And there she was, little Quinn, seeing it all aged four.

'She has twelve stamps in her passport,' her dad, Michiel,

said. We later learnt that Quinn's first adventure had been to Everest base camp when her mum, Gwen, had hiked there seven and a half months pregnant. When Gwen then told us about another trip she'd made to Antarctica, complete with tales of penguins and 'a dozen different shades of white', I began to see that she, too, suffered from a wanderlust I know only too well. Gwen went on to tell us why she felt it was so important to continue travelling, even after they had had Quinn. Every day, Quinn the explorer makes a video for her class back home in Holland. Apparently, it's easy enough to get permission to take your kid out of school in Holland – how wonderfully liberal.

'Yesterday's video snippet was about a dead donkey,' Gwen said.

'It's good to show the reality of the world as well as the beauty,' Michiel added.

'Otherwise kids think that everything lives and dies on the shelves of the supermarket,' Gwen added.

After chatting for a while longer (about donkeys both alive and dead), Gwen casually dropped into conversation that she was a psychologist. 'I did my thesis on the mindset of a long-distance cycle tourist, actually.'

'Oh, really?' Faye and I cooed in unison.

'Give me the headline,' I said. 'I mean, if you had to sum up your findings in one sentence, what would it be?'

Gwen paused and I could tell that she was choosing her

words carefully. 'I concluded that you are… a special breed,' she laughed.

So, there you have it, from the mouth of a *bona fide* doc. We cycle tourists are a special breed.

After leaving Gwen, Michiel and Quinn the mini explorer, we spent the rest of the afternoon riding up the mountain in simple silence. Above 2,500 metres, the landscape changed again, shifting from red back to fields of green, cleared for farmland. We were hoping to make the top of the pass and camp somewhere in Parque Nacional Los Cardones that night. I was feeling fantastic, enjoying the winding road, the landscape, the people… everything. But it soon became clear that Faye was feeling quite the opposite.

Sometimes it was frustrating when one of us felt great and the other less so, because there was an element of compromise in deciding whether to push on or to stop. But I also had come to understand that we are all strong and weak at different times – through our lives, within a week and even over the course of a single day. Our energy naturally waxes and wanes. There is a natural ebb and flow to life, too, that's often beyond our control (if you meet someone for the first time during one of their lows, you'd be forgiven for thinking them miserable). It's only in spending a significant amount of time with someone else, in being close to them as they move through their own energy cycles, that you begin to see the full measure of who they are. By this point, Faye and I had been through countless highs and lows together. We had a decent feel for one another as a whole – and how lovely it was to have another person be strong for you when you are feeling weak.

That day, Faye was having a low. Her tummy was acting up again and she was exhausted. I could see it in her ashen face, somewhere beyond the smile she was desperately trying to summon up. So, rather than push on, we decided to spend the night camping just shy of the top of the mountain pass. I'd love to tell you that we found an idyllic spot overlooking the picturesque valley below but, in reality, we camped just off the road, behind a crumbling white building with black peeling paintwork across the front, which said 'Bar'. I slept not far from an area that had clearly been used as a toilet and Faye kicked a few rusty old cans and broken bottles out of the way to pitch up her tent.

A few days later, after we had made it up and over the mountain pass, through Parque Nacional Los Cardones and into the Calchquí Valley. Faye's energy levels had begun to return to normal and, now that we were onto the rocky surfaces we'd come in search of, my energy upped from good to next-level fantastic!

'Here. We. Go!' I shouted, taking a hand off my handlebar and raising it above my head as my legs made the final few revolutions on their way to the top of another short, steep incline. One more half nudge of the pedals and my heavily loaded bike and I reached a tipping point: 'Waaaaa-hoooooooo!' I felt a rush of air across my face as I zoomed down the other side.

The rubble-licious terrain threw us around the valley like a pair of rag dolls. Arms flailing, hands gripping, teeth clenched. Up, down, up, down we went – around sharp bends and pinned to steep rocky walls under our own momentum. There was just enough respite between the 'ups' to trick my legs into believing that they could take on another climb. And so I started each ascent with a grin, and finished it with a grimace.

During the morning we'd bumped into two cycle tourists from Canada. They'd warned us 'aboot' the corrugated and sandy roads in the valley but it didn't faze us. Like the Dark Knight (aka Batman) we had been well trained by roads further north (although sadly not by Liam Neeson). We were pedalling ninjas – there was no surface that could possibly outdo the broken crockery of Bolivia. So, even when deep sand bucked me from my steed on more than one occasion during our rocky descents, I picked myself back up and pushed on.

As the mercury tipped over 34 degrees and afternoon haze turned to evening sun, I found a third wind of energy (I concluded that there had been no second wind, so I had skipped to the third).

'Do you want to go in front or behind?' Faye asked in one of our usual pre-departure chats about who would lead and who would follow for the next hour.

'I'll go behind if that's alright. I like that you go faster on the downhills and flats, then I can chase you up the hill!' I said.

'Ha! I know, I can feel you hunting me down like a dawg,' she replied.

'Ace. You be the rabbit. I'll be the greyhound. Let's GO!'

Off we went, up the two final steep climbs, through two beautiful dusty canyons. We were surrounded by rock spires that reminded me of Utah in the USA, although the rock here was sandier in colour. Each formation was fabulous in its own right and no two sets of rock were the same. Whenever we got up high enough to look back down the valley, it was like looking out over an egg carton. Every spire peaked next to a mini trough. We took it in turns to cycle ahead and take pictures of one another. When it was Faye's turn to be the photographer, she dashed to the top of the hill and got in position.

'McNuff, stop smiling! You look like you're having too much fun!' she shouted as I approached, and I did my best to look more serious, as all good adventurers should.

By early evening my legs were leaden and, with each uphill effort, I felt as if my quad muscles might just detach themselves from my knees. Call me sick, but I was still absolutely LOVING it. The sun beating down on my back, surrounded by spires of straw-coloured rock, I felt like I could ride forever, long into the evening and well into the night.

'This is awesome!' I shouted at Faye, who was just about done in.

'Oh great,' she sighed. 'Fifty miles into the day and you've just warmed up.'

That evening, the Argentinian heat reached a sticky crescendo at 35°C before the skies gave way at last. Just after we pitched our tents, thunder rumbled and lightning flashed, so we sat ooo-ing and ahh-ing from the porches of our respective homes. Faye wasn't enjoying the storm as much as I was – she was always more wary of being frazzled by lightning, but I adored the wildness of it all: the violence of the storm and the power of Mother Nature dancing right in front of my eyes.

Once the storm had died down, I unzipped every possible flap of material in the tent in a bid to cool off. I welcomed any available breeze through my shelter and lay on top of my sleeping mat, starfishing in pants and bra, doing all I could to bring my body temperature below boiling point from a day of exertion in the valley of rollercoaster and rubble. I fell asleep to the patter of rain on the ripstop roof, legs throbbing, grinning all the way into the land of nod.

***

We didn't stay long in Cafayate because we were keen to keep munching up the miles towards Santiago, and it was while packing up camp a few days after leaving town that Faye had a sudden realisation.

'Err, Anna,' she said.

'Yep.'

'I've lost my tracker.'

'What do you mean… lost it?'

'I mean, it's not here. It's definitely not in my handlebar

bag where I normally keep it.'

'Nah, it's got to be somewhere,' I said dismissively, and went back to packing up my tent.

I was very used to hearing that Faye had misplaced something. In fact, Faye, as her Twitter profile at the time confirmed, is 'a pro at losing stuff'. So far on the journey, we had waved goodbye to Faye's driving licence, two credit cards, a debit card, a sleeping-bag liner, a pair of sunglasses, two water bottles, a bag of SD cards, a key, a plug, an adaptor and an iPhone cable. We had also momentarily thought we'd lost a buff, pants, socks and another key. I had learned that Faye's ability to lose things is an offshoot of a wonderful aspect of her character and that is her ability to live entirely in the moment. I often wished I could live in the moment as much as Faye does, although I'm not sure I could afford the loss in possessions.

'Are you sure you don't have it?' I asked.

'Yep, I've definitely lost it. Oh, no,' said Faye, interrupting her own sentence.

'What?'

'I know where it is,' she said.

'That's great! Where?'

'By the tree where I took a poo.'

'You took your tracker for a poo?! Did you think you'd get lost?!'

'No, I mean, I left it where we sat down, after I went into

the bushes for a poo.'

The barely memorable, indistinguishable tree where Faye took a poo was almost a two-hour ride back from where we were camped off the side of the road. After a few more minutes of searching, we established that the tracker really was lost. SPOT or GPS trackers are important and expensive things. Just like my own tracker, which I'd been using to keep my mum and Jamie updated when we were out of phone signal, Faye's SPOT tracker allowed her to send a message to her family each night to let them know that she was okay. On a more important note, it also had a big red SOS button, which would tell the emergency services to come rescue our asses if we got into some real trouble.

We were only 10 miles from the next city of Santa María, and so, for the first time since leaving La Paz together, we decided to part ways. I couldn't remember much of the discussion about Faye going back to get the tracker, but it was brief, and I do remember thinking that it was a blow to lose a day of progress towards Santiago. Still, I pedalled onward to wait in town with a coffee in my hand as Faye set off, back towards Cafayate to locate 'the poo tree' and the tracker.

As I rode away from our camping spot, I was struck by two things. The first was that it seemed weird to be riding alone. How strange it was not to be watching Faye's wheel in front of me or hearing the crunch of her bike on gravel behind me. It was liberating and sad all at once, like I was missing a part of myself, a shadow. It felt as if I might wobble and fall over with the imbalance of it all.

The second thing that struck me was that I was annoyed, although I couldn't quite work out why. I wasn't annoyed that something had been forgotten – no one wants to forget things and I forget things all the time too. Perhaps I was annoyed that Faye had gone back to get the tracker? But no, that wasn't it. The tracker was an expensive bit of kit, and it would be a pain in the arse to get a new one. Why then, did I have an icky feeling in my stomach?

I spent the 10-mile ride to Santa María trying to work it out and, just before I rolled into town, I found the missing piece of the puzzle. I realised that, in the swift decision to turn around and return to the tree, I hadn't heard the magic words 'I'm sorry'. Perhaps it had been said, but if it had, I had missed hearing it. And that had led me to feel like Faye didn't care that forgetting the tracker had impacted my day as well as hers. I knew that wasn't true. But for some reason I felt like I hadn't been considered, and the only thing I could put that feeling down to was the absence of that one little word... sorry.

I shrugged off the feelings and decided to look for the positives in the day. As it turned out, that day my little brother Jonty was getting married. Somewhere in a church in London at 3 p.m. UK time, he would be saying 'I do' to the beautiful, witty Kate Anderson.

On account of this momentous event, I had taken the time to craft Jonty and his wife-to-be a love heart from donkey poo. Nothing says love like sun-dried crusty shite, after all. I'd taken a picture of the heart and was planning to send it to them later as a surprise on-the-day gift. I was very sad that I couldn't be in two places at once, but I was also so very grateful to have a younger brother and sister-in-law who understood and embraced my wandering ways.

I had no idea how long Faye would be – she didn't have a phone signal out there in the Argentinian boonies, so I stayed in a cafe and enjoyed a steady stream of photos that came in via messages from Jamie (who was at the church representing 'us'). In a stroke of genius, my dad had also arranged for a life-sized cardboard cut-out of me to be present at the wedding. My dad, being a dad, had naturally chosen one of the most unflattering pictures of me from the past 15 years to blow up to life-size. And so, as the next few hours passed, I received pictures and videos from friends next to the cardboard cut-out, taking selfies with 'me' and hoisting 'me' onto the dance floor for a boogie.

After the buzz from the wedding messages died down – I presumed that they were all now partied out and fast asleep back home – I moved on to sending some pre-Christmas emails to good friends, wishing them a very merry Christmas. It was the seventeenth of December and the festivities were in full swing. Emails done, I checked my watch. It had been five hours since we'd left the camp spot that morning. The man running the coffee shop was likely starting to suspect I was a caffeine addict and homeless (both of which were technically true), and I was beginning to worry about where my red-haired shadow had got to.

Fifteen minutes later, after a 62-mile round trip to 'track down the tracker', Faye appeared outside the window of the cafe. She looked exhausted. Strands of red hair were plastered to her sweat-soaked face and her shoulders were reddened by the sun. She stopped, grinned and pulled a small object from her bar bag.

'No way!' I mouthed, from beyond the window.

'Right, Anna. Time to bring it up,' said my brain. 'Do it now, just get it out the way, tell her how you feel about the sorry thing.' But of course, I didn't. Because another part of my brain said, 'The poor girl's exhausted. Be a friend and let her be.'

We pedalled for 30 minutes out of town before pulling off the road to camp. As we brought the bikes to a stop, I knew I wasn't going to be able to sleep. My brain and body were both buzzing, as I was used to pedalling all day, every day, and I still couldn't shake the feeling of being annoyed.

'Err, Faye.'

'Yep?'

'I'm just going to leave my bags here, then go for a little pedal up the road for a bit.'

'Umm… okay. Why?'

'Well, I won't sleep tonight with this much energy in my legs. I know it.'

Faye looked confused, so I quickly dumped my bags and

set off before she had a chance to ask any more questions. What I said to Faye wasn't a lie, I did have a lot of energy in my legs. But, truth be told, I knew that the thoughts whizzing around my brain were still toxic, and that letting them come out of my mouth at that stage might do some harm to our friendship. So, I rode off down the road, hammering on the pedals and pushing myself harder and harder. For some reason, I wanted to feel pain. After a day of sitting still, I wanted to move more than I had ever done before. I wanted to expel any anger from my veins and my mind and come back to that camp exhausted. I kept thinking that I'd turn around in 10 minutes but 10 minutes turned to 30 and, before I knew it, I was 45 minutes down the road from the camp. I let out a war cry. A roar into the wind, just to be sure I had expelled all my anger. Then I turned around and headed home, just as a small storm began to roll through the valley.

On the way back to camp, the red mist lifted, I was in a much calmer state and I decided that I really needed to let Faye know I was upset by the way things had gone down that morning. It was no biggy, I told myself. I would simply explain how I felt, get it off my chest and we'd move on. When I arrived at the camp, Faye was sitting on the floor outside her tent and had dinner on the go, carefully tending a pot of boiling water. She looked up.

'You alright, mate?' she asked, smiling.

'Yes, thanks. It's a bit breezy out there!' I said. I took a deep breath and opened my mouth to start the discussion. 'Faye…'

'Mm hmm,' she said, now chopping sausages on an up-turned soup-cup lid and popping them into the boiling water. I looked at her and felt a wave of guilt. It was late. She was tired. She was all tucked up in her beanie and down jacket. I didn't want to have the chat then, I didn't even quite know what I was going to say anyway. In that moment I decided that I had two choices. I could bring it up, or I could let it go. Could I let it go? Yes. I could. No harm was done. We'd just chalk that day up to experience. I was sure we wouldn't end up in the same situation again – it would all be water under the bridge.

'… what's for dinner?' I asked.

'O, something extra special tonight, McNuff,' Faye replied.

'Noodles and sausages?'

'You got it.' She grinned.

14

Rage and Calm

Distance cycled: 1,863 miles

Metres ascended: 53,294

'Anna, Anna, are you awake?!' Faye's voice broke the early morning silence.

'I am now!' I groaned, wiping sleep from my eyes.

'Attack! We're under attack. They are everywhere!' she shouted.

It had been a few days since the losing and finding of the tracker near Santa María. Things were back as they should be: we were back to riding together and enjoying the quiet dusty roads of central Argentina, wild camping in the bushes every night. The previous evening we'd pitched up in the shelter of some trees. Upon arrival, we had a brief chat about the abundance of ants of all shapes and sizes milling around camp but we'd decided that it would be okay because, surely, the ants would just go to sleep when we did.

As it turns out, they didn't. While we slept, the ants had raved on through the night. Gold-bummed ants, red ants, flying ants, little itty-bitty English-looking ants. They'd all been at it, and I'm talking glowsticks, string vests, headbands 'n' hot pants, happy hardcore-type raving. I'm pretty sure they'd invited all the ants from the neighbouring colonies over too, such was the mess they'd created.

Faye has a mild bug-phobia (read: strong hatred), so that, even in the boiling Argentinian temperatures we were experiencing, she would sleep cocooned in her inner tent mesh. She called the inside of the mesh the 'lockdown zone' and no creature with more than two legs was allowed in. I, on the other hand, can't stand to be caged. So, in hot climates, I'll remove my inner tent entirely and sleep under just the outer tarp, allowing a breeze to pass through the shelter. This means that I often wake a few times in the night to find bugs investigating various areas of my body but, in general, that doesn't bother me.

Unfortunately, during the midnight rave-a-thon, the ants had found a tiny hole in Faye's inner tent mesh and piled through into the lockdown zone. The cheek of it. She had awoken to an army of ants marching across the ceiling, dropping one by one onto her sleeping bag as the overhang on the tent wall became too much for their little ant-biceps to take. Far worse than the morning 'drop-ins' was the fact that the ants had taken command of Faye's banana. Her one remaining precious, delicious, breakfast banana. She held up what should be a yellow fruit so that I could see that it was entirely black – coated in a seething layer of six-legged mini-monsters. Yummy.

I was rather impressed with the ant performance in my own tent too. I had to applaud them for managing to scale the great rock that was my pannier (for an ant, I would put this akin to taking on an ascent of El Capitan in Yosemite National Park). In the pannier, I found ants in between layers of clothing, on electrical goods – one was even clinging hopefully to a rogue tampon. They seemed particularly fond of a packet of crackers in the outer pannier pocket; they had managed to eat through the bag I kept my tent in (ants in South America will eat through anything); and I even found one cheeky little bugger, the budding hygienist of the bunch, hiding in my toothbrush.

After two hours of packing up, shaking everything out and sadly witnessing the death of many an ant, I picked up my rubbish sack, only to find that there were hundreds more little creatures inside it. We often carried many days' worth of rubbish with us on the trip, until we reached somewhere to dispose of it – something that had made me acutely aware just how much waste we produced, even when living frugally. I inspected the rubbish bag more closely, feeling sorry for the brave souls inside. They'd gone in search of dinner and were going to get far more than they'd bargained for that day. Sad that some ants would never see their husbands, wives or children again, I sighed and said, 'Okay, kids – road-trip time!' Strapping the plastic bag to the back of my bike, Faye, the army of rubbish-bag ants and I took off for the nearby town of Bethlehem.

It was very cool to be pedalling through a town called

Bethlehem just a few days before Christmas. Of course, this wasn't the real Bethlehem but its name cheered me up all the same. We spent longer than intended in town. Partly to dispose fully of the ants and partly so that Faye could visit a pharmacy. The past week of riding on dusty roads had caused Faye's right eye to get all puffy 'n' red. To put it politely, she looked like one-eyed Willy the Pirate. She also said that, as of that morning, it was itching like crazy. As luck would have it, we found an open pharmacy in Bethlehem. This was rare in the middle of the afternoon, when shops in South America were usually closed for a siesta. Even luckier-er-er was that it just so happened that my audio Spanish lesson the day before had focused on pharmacy and doctor visits. Imagine that?! So, I packed Faye off with the Spanish words for 'My eye hurts. Do you have something for a painful eye?' and sat on the wall outside the pharmacy while she went inside.

Two minutes later, Faye emerged from the pharmacy. She was wetting herself with laughter.

'What's so funny? What happened?!' I asked and Faye could barely get the words out between her snorts. Apparently, the moment she'd crossed the pharmacy threshold her mind had gone blank. My imparted Spanish knowledge went out the window and all she could muster were words to the equivalent of 'Do you have an eye?' Sadly, there were no eyes to be purchased in the pharmacy that day and so Faye had to make do with her own as we trundled on. She did at least manage to score some eye drops.

Some 10 miles further on, we pulled to a halt at a minor T-junction. Just outside the town of Londres, at an inconspicuous corner of Argentina's famous Ruta Nacional 40, there's a turn-off to an old section of the road. Once upon a time, this 40-mile stretch of old road was the primary route for traffic between Londres and Tinogasta. These days, since a new, faster highway was built, the old Ruta 40 has fallen into disrepair. It was impassable on four wheels but still very much do-able on two. We'd learned about the road from our friends 'The Pikes on Bikes' and couldn't resist the sound of turning 90 degrees off the main highway and heading into the mountains.

As our wheels met rubble once again, there was a whiff of suspense in the air. I felt like Frodo approaching the mines of Moria, at the gateway to an ancient realm. Within 5 miles of leaving the main road, we had been transported from mundane straw-coloured plains to jagged skyscrapers of green and brown rock. A trail of sand and gravel snaked steadily through tall green shrubs, leading us gradually skyward as the mountains closed in behind us. Soon we were entirely alone. Not a car, not another person, just us and a few bike tracks in the dirt – a memory of those who had passed this way before. Suddenly, the gradient increased and the surface got rockier. We returned to the familiar bouncing around on our saddles, squirming to stay on our bikes, swearing, yelping and whooping when one of us managed to save herself from a potential tumble. I took great delight in witnessing Faye's second-ever fall from her bike (my fall count was well over 20 by that point). She was gunning it down a small dip in the road and ground to a halt on the sand at the bottom of it. She'd then fallen sideways onto the ground and started laughing at herself. By the time I caught up with her, I was in fits of giggles too, but I did my best to help her scramble out from under a tangle of pedals and chain.

As the heat of the day started to creep towards 40°C, we plunged deeper into the mountains. I gawped at a bug the size of a bird (I kid you not), followed by a snake the size of a small chapstick. *Aren't snakes supposed to be bigger than bugs?* I thought. The animal–insect world was topsy-turvy in Argentina, and at times I felt like Alice in Wonderland. At last we reached the summit of the climb and the thermometer on my watch read 43°C. The balls of my feet were on fire – a side effect of wearing thick black cycling shoes combined with a substantial amount of time spent standing up on the pedals to protect my lady carriage from all the rubble-bouncing. Beads of sweat tumbled down my nose and dripped onto my thighs. My arms and back were drenched too. The sweat was mixing with recently applied suntan lotion and red dust from the road, turning the surface of my skin into a congealed salmon-coloured mess. I daydreamed about a drink of icy cold water but had to swallow lumps of hot air instead.

After cresting the top of the pass, we found ourselves on a narrow ledge which tip-toed around the mountainside. I tip-toed on the pedals as well, too frightened to look to my right, where I knew there was a stomach-churning drop to the valley floor. I wasn't keen on messing around up there. We'd passed three graves by the roadside in the past hour, and I didn't fancy my name being added to those carved on the crosses. We stopped to look out across the flat plain below, which led to green mountains way off in the distance, some 50 miles away. Then on we went, over more rubble and sand, switchbacking down to earth on a dusty yellow road from our heavenly perch. At last the road flattened out and streaked off towards the horizon in a dead straight line between crop fields. We glided along gracefully for another hour on light sand, assisted by the gentle nudge of gravity, and arrived in the centre of Tinogasta. Hearts pounding, heads throbbing, dehydrated and caked in dust, we spotted an oasis on the main street: an ice-cream shop. I tumbled in and ordered a gigantic waffle cone with two scoops: one chocolate, one lemon pie. Lemon-pie ice cream? Argentina really knows how to make a girl's dreams come true.

With ice cream smeared over my face and a bottle of icy water in one hand, I flopped onto the grass in the town plaza and Faye followed suit. I slipped into a sugar coma and allowed the dreams of my afternoon snooze to transport me back to the mountains.

***

By Christmas Eve in Argentina, the Yuletide songs blasting from every shop were reaching a near-deafening crescendo. I had learned all the words to 'Feliz Navidad', and it went round and round in my brain from morning to night. Over breakfast at a cute B&B in the town of Chilecito, we hatched a plan for the supplies we would need to carry for the days ahead. It didn't take much of a discussion for us to agree that, if we weren't going to be at home, then we really wanted to be 'away' for Christmas. That is, not to spend the day in someone else's home, or go in for some attempt at replicating a normal Christmas dinner, only without the best part: our families. No siree, we decided that we wanted to be away from it all. Up a mountain, in the wilderness – somewhere worthy of a Christmas adventure.

I'd checked the map a few days earlier and noticed that there was the option of taking a road through Talampaya National Park – a place where it was rumoured that we could travel back in time to see dinosaur remains and petroglyphs left by indigenous people from thousands of years ago. Even better was that we'd also got a message from Campbell (the English cycle tourist we'd met in La Paz) who told us that there was a secluded wild swimming hole just beyond the park. That settled it. We would head for Talampaya National Park and spend Christmas Day cycling 80 miles, with a stop at the swimming hole on Christmas morning. Perfect.

At 3 p.m. on Christmas Eve, we were standing outside the supermarket in Chilecito, our bags laden with all sorts of fine goodies for a Christmas on the road. Orange juice, serrano ham, cheese, extra bananas, marshmallows. We were even going to attempt to make popcorn on the stove that night. What. A. Treat. By the time we'd finished cramming everything into pannier bags, the bikes were unusually heavy. To top it all off, we had loaded up with 17 litres of water each. With temperatures in the low 40s and three days of riding through nothingness towards and through the National Park, we wanted to make sure that we had enough to keep us hydrated, and to cook meals in the evenings too. We worked out that that meant carrying 3.5 litres of water for every day, each.

Faye had just received some bad news from home: one of her dogs, Jack, was poorly. So she was in a subdued mood as we rode out into the dusty countryside of La Rioja province. We munched up the first 10 miles easily, rolling over a few lumps and bumps on an otherwise flat road, which cut between modest green-brown mountains. It was a hot afternoon and there was a fizz of excitement in my belly. We'd had a few days' rest in Chilecito and it was nice to be on the move again but, also, I was excited about how the following 24 hours were set to unfold. I was caught up imagining precisely how wonderful it would be to spend the night camped under the stars, just shy of the national park, and how the following day we'd be at the watering hole, enjoying a refreshing dip before an afternoon of relaxed Christmas cycling. Everything would be worth it, being away from home and all that, everything would be perfe—

'Anna,' said Faye, interrupting my train of thought.

'Yep?' I called back to her.

'I've forgotten my tracker,' she said.

There was a long silence. I didn't know what to say in reply. Surely, I'd misheard her.

'You've forgotten your—'

'My tracker. I think I left it back at the hostel.'

'Are you sure?'

'Yes. I think so. It's not here in my bar bag. What should we do?' she asked.

Suddenly a wave of anger rose up in me. It came out of nowhere. Well, I knew exactly where it came from. It came from the thoughts I'd swallowed down 10 days earlier near the town of Santa María. Evidently, I was still upset and hadn't let it go. In fact, I had just stored that upset somewhere in a dark corner of my mind. It had been festering, waiting for a chance to hitch itself to a new event, and there it was. The tracker had been forgotten again and the upset had stepped out of the darkness, transformed into full-blown anger. I was shaking.

I was up the front so Faye couldn't see my face. I remained silent, took a deep breath and continued staring down the road ahead. I meant to speak, to say anything, something, but a tornado of thoughts was swirling in my mind and I wasn't sure which parts of it to let escape my mouth and which parts to contain. So, I didn't dare risk saying anything at all.

'Anna, should we go back and get it?' Faye asked again.

I took another deep breath. 'Okay,' I said, pulling off to the side of the road. 'Do you want to just double-check that it's not in your bag?'

Faye nodded and began to rummage in her handlebar bag for the tracker. While Faye searched, I became aware that there were now two distinct characters doing battle in my mind.

Let's call them Rage and Calm. Rage is raw and angry and wants to explode out of my mouth in a cascade of expletives. He wants to scream, 'This is F***ING RIDICULOUS!' Calm is concerned about Faye, making sure she doesn't feel upset, and most importantly, about me being a good friend. Calm needs to soothe Rage, because they've been friends for years and Calm has seen the destruction that Rage has caused in the past. The internal conflict between the two of them began.

Rage: You cannot possibly expect me to turn around and go and get that sodding tracker!

Calm: Come on, Rage, be understanding. It's just a mistake.

Rage: If this were me, I'd just leave the bloody thing. She should be saying, let's just leave it!

Calm: But she's asking for your opinion. She genuinely doesn't know what to do.

Rage: Well, I can't really say no, can I?!

Calm: Well, you can. But the tracker is expensive. She can't afford a replacement. And it's how she lets her mum know she's okay. You know that's important to her.

Rage: If it's so important then she shouldn't forget it! If we go back now, we'll end up spending Christmas Day in town.

Calm: Is that so bad? I mean, does it really matter?

Rage: It does matter! Because I WANT TO ENJOY MY CHRISTMAS DAY! And now that's been cocked up. And she doesn't even care.

Calm: Rage, this is Faye. Of course she cares.

Rage: Well, she hasn't said she cares!

Rage threw his toys out the pram and began to sulk. In the meantime, Faye had affirmed that she had indeed left the tracker behind. It was on the windowsill in the hostel, she said. I took another deep breath.

'Okay, let's go back. There was a gas station a few miles back there. Maybe I can sit there while you go back to get it or something?' I said, and Faye nodded.

We turned the bikes around and began the ride back down the road. By the time we got to the gas station, I was still shaking with anger. Rage was winning the battle in my mind and I knew I had to say something. Whatever it was, those thoughts I'd held in for the past 10 days, they had to come out. I really didn't want to do it. Faye was having a crap day as it was, what with Jack her dog being ill at home. This was the worst possible time to say anything that might make her upset. But I knew that if I didn't say something then, it would only keep poisoning the friendship well on the way down to Ushuaia. We stepped off the bikes, and I took a deep breath.

'Faye, can I say something?' I asked.

Faye looked at me and then at the ground. I could tell she knew it was coming.

'Go on,' she said.

I took another deep breath and thought hard about the way the words needed to come out.

'I really don't want to say it, but it's not about you forgetting the tracker. I get that. I forget things all the time. It's just… when it happens… I don't feel like we're being a team about it.'

Faye stayed silent. I felt horrible, but I knew I had to carry on. I daren't look at her face for fear of confirmation that I was upsetting her. I ploughed on.

'Whatever happens to you, happens to me too. And when we don't talk about the fact that it's impacting my day as well as yours, well, it makes me feel like maybe you don't care, which I know you do, it's just, that's the way I feel.'

Only now did I look at Faye, and I watched as her eyes started to well up. That made me feel even more terrible. I felt a lump in my throat start to form.

'Oh, I know,' said Faye, looking back at the ground and sounding downtrodden.

'I know you don't mean to. I'm really sorry, I just had to say it,' I said, and now my eyes were full of tears, the pent-up emotions from the past 10 days began to tumble down my cheeks. Faye started to cry too.

'I'm such an idiot,' she said between sobs.

'You're not an idiot,' I laughed.

'I am!' she sniffed.

'Well, you're my favourite idiot then.'

There was more back and forth before Faye took a deep breath and said, 'Oh, mate. I'm so sorry. Really, I am. This is turning out to be the crappiest day ever. First Jack being sick, and now I've upset you. I'm sorry.'

'I know! And I'm sorry, I know you're having a crap day. And I know you care. I just needed to say it.'

I took a few steps forward and opened my arms to give her a hug. And so, in a gas station forecourt on the outskirts of Chilecito, two British women hugged it out next to the diesel pump and all balance was restored to the world.

Post-hug-a-thon, we turned our attention to the logistics of retrieving the tracker. We had seen that there was a building just across the road from the petrol station with 'Taxi' scrawled on the side of it. It was strange for a taxi rank to be at a dusty corner 15 miles out of town, but we took it as a stroke of luck in what had been an otherwise unlucky day. Faye left her bike propped up outside the petrol station, and while she hopped in a taxi back to Chilecito, I went inside to fill my face with coffee and *medialunas*.

Dunking a *medialuna* into a decidedly average gas-station coffee, I thought about the feelings that I'd bottled up for the past 10 days. I realised that in holding in my thoughts, in sweeping them under the rug, I wasn't giving our friendship the respect it deserved. I'd tried to muscle on, believing that when the trip was done, I wouldn't need to deal with those thoughts anymore. In fact, we wouldn't need to deal with one another anymore. But I was a fool to think that I could just paper over the cracks in our relationship and carry on: we needed to heal them. And the only way to start the healing process was with honesty. At last, I had been honest – with myself and with Faye.

I decided to call Jamie, who was back home in the UK, gearing up for his own Christmas. I relayed the whole event to him in a torrent of words and feelings.

'I thought that it was Faye, that she wasn't considering me… but I just realised. I was the only one with the power to change how I felt. It was me! It was me all along,' I exclaimed. It felt so good to get it all out and put what had happened into perspective.

There was a long pause at the end of my spiel, during which I could hear Jamie chewing on something, and I knew he was thinking carefully before he replied. I also knew that he loved a good story, especially one full of emotion, so I knew he'd enjoy the one I'd just told.

'Oh, me Anner,' he said in his beautiful West Country drawl. 'This is what I love about adventures. It's Christmas Eve and you're out there, learning, growing as a person. And I'm sat here in my underpants eating Quality Streets'.

15

Roasted like Turkeys

Distance cycled: 2,158 miles
Metres ascended: 57,673

Following our gas station heart to heart, Faye returned from Chilecito with the tracker and we rode late into the night. We tore up the missed miles, both of us pushing hard on the pedals and sweating buckets through the humid evening air. As it happened, those few hours of late-night riding turned out to be some of the best we'd had in three months. The road was quiet as the moon started to rise in a pastel-coloured sky. We were delirious from our emotional exchange but took comfort in the fact that there were no walls between us now. There was nothing left unsaid, just the shared joy of being back on the move in the calm of a lilac dusk. By the time the sun disappeared completely and we pulled over to camp at 9 p.m., our friendship felt stronger than ever.

After a light dinner, I struggled to get to sleep. Partly on account of the emotionally charged day and partly because, in just a few hours, it was going to be Christmas. And I was *very* excited about that. As a 32-year-old in the middle of nowhere, I wasn't sure why I was quite so excited. I think it was the knowledge that everyone I loved at home would be well-fed and happy. That, or it was 'Christmas residue' – excess excitement leftover from years of exuberance as a child. In which case, I have a well of Christmas residue deep enough to last me into my seventies.

'Happy Christmas!' I yelled at Faye from my tent as fireworks went off in the distance at the stroke of midnight. I'd like to say I didn't wake Faye up, but I definitely did. It was Christmas for gawd's sake. There ain't no time to be sleeping when it's Christmas. I poked my head out of the tent at our roadside camp spot. Faye appeared, bleary eyed and we oohed and aahed together at a night sky now lit up with reds, greens, purples and gold. After that, I was definitely too excited to sleep, so I read for a few hours before drifting off around 3 a.m.

By 6 a.m., I was awake again, and making more noise than was absolutely necessary in a bid to wake my sleeping tent neighbour. Eventually, Faye stirred, we left our sleeping cocoons, I began blasting Christmas songs from my phone and we shared a breakfast of ham, cheese, crackers and orange juice. Really chunky, bitty, fresh-as-it-comes orange juice. Oh, the luxury! Morning messages were sent to loved ones via GPS devices and even the orange-juice-loving Christmas ants were welcomed to the breakfast party.

While munching on brekkie, I thought about what would be going on back at home and, although I wasn't there, I knew precisely how the day would be unfolding in the McNuff household in south-west London: My newlywed younger brother, Jonty, would have stayed the night at my parents' house (because he's a homeboy at heart). He'd wake up to my mum yelling 'Happy Christmas, people!' at the top of her lungs. Despite having been up since the crack of dawn, Mum would have patiently waited until 8 a.m. to wake the household with her Christmas birdsong.

Jonty would then make his way down the stairs, wearing an assortment of clothes from his childhood cupboards, clothes that last saw the light of day in 1997. In the kitchen, he'd find Mum in her Christmas dressing gown, preparing the morning feast of Buck's Fizz, baked beans, eggs, mushrooms and bacon (cardboard-like 'veggie bacon' for Mum). Dad would appear and begin giving a helping hand – he was usually on bacon duty. Post-breakfast, Jonty would sneak into the living room and begin secretly eating all the strawberry and orange creams from the box of Quality Street. Dad would tag team with him throughout the morning, so that by 11 a.m. all that remained were the hard-centred chocolates and a trail of lies and deceit as to who ate the soft-centred ones.

My older brother, Jamie, would then arrive with his wife and kids sometime after 11 a.m., possibly around 1 p.m., but definitely a few hours later than they intended. Those who did not look to be 'busy enough' would be tricked into Brussel sprout peeling duty, and responsible for carving a cross in the base of each sprout so that they would cook perfectly.

A present marathon would begin, followed by the arrival of the parents of my older brother's wife, who are Chinese and Malaysian but embrace McNuff British-family madness wholeheartedly. At 4 p.m., an exhausted Mum would at last emerge from plumes of kitchen steam to present lunch, and it would look and taste SPECTACULAR. Dad would then name the bird (e.g., Gordon) and carve it for the table. Faces would be stuffed, jokes would be shared, and everyone would tuck into Auntie Kate's Christmas pudding (gifted to the family the previous week) with lashings of brandy cream. Except for my older brother, who doesn't eat Christmas pud and would have extra home-made mince pies instead. Over the course of the evening, all hard-centred chocolates would at last be eaten, board games would be played and many, many films would be missed as everyone drifted in and out of sleep on the living-room sofas until bedtime.

On a roadside in rural Argentina, I smiled at the thought of those scenes unfolding some 6,000 miles away. I asked Faye what would be going on in her house that day and enjoyed being guided through a Shepherd family Christmas – which funnily enough shared many of the same traditional events as my own family's. Beyond our chat about the festivities back home, I was watching Faye closely that morning, checking for signs that she really was okay after events of the previous day. Even though I felt like we'd started with a clean slate, that didn't necessarily mean that Faye felt the same. But it was so far, so good – there were no signs of any lingering upset.

After finishing breakfast, we set about packing up camp. I stuffed my knitted Santa and snowman under the straps of my handlebar bag (so that I could look at them all day and not for one moment forget that it was Christmas) and we rolled out, headed for the wild swimming hole. It was only 8 a.m. but it was already warm as we wound up and over the first mountain pass, swooping into grey canyons on the other side, before passing tall green cacti set in beds of deep red rock. After two hours of cycling we arrived at a small gap in the crash barrier at the side of the highway.

'This is it,' said Faye with a grin, pointing to a dirt track that led away from the road and disappeared into the bushes.

We wheeled our bikes down the track as far as we could, before locking them to a tree and continuing along the trail on foot. Nearing the wild swimming spot, I realised that I could hear voices. At first that seemed odd. Who would be out here on Christmas Day? I wondered, and then I realised that if I lived near a wild swimming spot in Argentina, I might just go and visit it on Christmas Day too. One last shove through the bushes and we popped out into a clearing. There were a group of three women sitting on the edge of a green-blue river, which wound its way slowly through surrounding tall grass and reeds before meandering out of sight.

On either side of the river were tall yellow-brown cliffs with matching yellow-brown boulders on the ground. Just upstream from where we were standing, I could see what we'd been aiming for since leaving Chilecito: a 5-metre-high waterfall which cascaded over one of the larger boulders and plunged into a tidy pool at the bottom. The locals already at the pool smiled and bid us a good morning as we surveyed the water, which was deep aquamarine in colour and, as we soon discovered, icy cold. We stripped off our T-shirts, left them on the rocks and eased into the pool until we had both managed a full-body dunk. I revelled in the rude awakening of every weary body cell and enjoyed chatting to the pond-skating insects that darted across the surface around us. 'Merry Christmas,' I whispered. 'To you, and you… and you.'

Bodies now fully awake, we clambered up the side of the pool and lay side by side on the rocks like lizards in the sun. From our lizard lookout, I glimpsed another group of people, sitting in picnic chairs and cooking up a feast on a barbecue in a clearing just beyond the tall grass on the bank. We sat there for 30 minutes, watching the locals go into the pool and splash around, as wafts of their bush-side barbecue sauntered up our nostrils. Oh, how I wished that my Spanish was better and that I could pluck up the courage to chat with them in the hope of being thrown a rogue rack of ribs.

'Ahh, this is lush,' said Faye, flat out on her back with her eyes shut.

'It is,' I replied, enjoying the double dose of warmth, from the rock and the sun, on my skin.

'I suppose we'd better get going now, though,' said Faye.

'Yes, we should,' I replied, making no effort to move.

'How far do we have left today?' she asked.

'Err… about fifty miles.'

'That's quite a way.'

'It is.'

'Five more minutes?'

'Five more minutes.' I smiled.

Thirty minutes later we were back on the road, riding away from the swimming spot, refreshed by our Christmas morning dip. It was approaching midday and starting to get very hot: a sticky, itchy kind of heat that wrapped itself around me like an unwanted goose-down jacket. We turned off the main tarmac road and onto a rubble trail leading towards the centre of Talampaya National Park. Soon the temperature began to soar. I checked my watch to find that it read 40°C. Crikey O'Riley. I looked down the road ahead. It was a mix of yellow and orange rock, with small trees dotted along the roadside every now and then. The air was thick and soupy, forming a constant haze over the horizon, and the surrounding sand seemed to be reflecting heat onto me from every direction. I decided that this was what it would feel like to ride a bike in a blast furnace. It was so hot that the palms of my gloves had started to melt onto the handlebars, creating a gloopy webbed mess, and giving Spiderman a run for his money. On top of that, my black brake levers had become almost too hot to touch, I was inhaling hot air and the salt stains on my clothes were starting to look like a moving modern-art installation.

Our bikes were still heavily laden with food and water, so the going was tough and slow. Over the next few hours, the water in our bottles reached an obscene temperature and threatened to change the shape of the plastic bottles around it.

'What is going on?!' Faye said, both of us completely baffled as to why it felt so much hotter that day than on any previous days. We'd coped with this kind of heat in the Yungas after all, but out on the rubble and sand of Talampaya; it felt unbearable.

As the afternoon wore on, I began to struggle, and I mean really struggle. I watched as Faye moved further ahead of me, her usually sharp silhouette now a blurry mess a few hundred metres up the hazy road. I had learned that with smaller wheels on my bike and thinner tyres, I was always slower than Faye over the rough surfaces, but this was getting ridiculous and I was getting frustrated. She seemed to be streaking effortlessly into the distance, while I went backwards. I looked down at my legs.

'Come on,' I said softly, but really I knew that they weren't the problem. The problem was that I felt sick. My head was throbbing, I felt like my cheeks were going to explode and I knew I needed to cool down. Faye must have noticed that the distance between us was bigger than usual because she stopped and waited for me to catch up.

'You alright, mate?' she said as I pulled alongside her.

'Err, alright. Is it just me, or is this really hard today?' I asked, embarrassed at how slow I was going.

'Err… I mean, yeah, it is hot,' said Faye, eyeing me closely, and I could tell that she wanted to say that she wasn't finding it difficult at all. In that moment, I concluded that I had gone soft. Come on, McNuff, put a bit more effort in, I thought.

Perhaps I was just being lazy. All that Christmas cheer and nice food for breakfast had distracted me from the task at hand. I just needed to focus and get my head back in the game.

After a long slog along the rubble, we hit paved road again but, instead of feeling better, I felt worse and went even slower. I'd drunk eight litres of water since leaving the swim spot (way more than I should have done, according to our rations), but on account of the sun beating down on our water bladders, most of that liquid had been like sipping on hot tea. All I seemed to be achieving by drinking water was warming my insides while the sun's glare warmed my outsides. I confessed to Faye that I needed a sit down in the shade and asked for a rest under a small tree at the roadside.

Pouring some hot water over my head, I hoped that it would cool me as I pedalled. I then got back on the bike and wobbled onwards towards the final miles of the day. At the national park entrance, I was surprised to see two guards standing there. They obviously didn't get Christmas Day off and went above and beyond by looking extremely official and letting us know that we couldn't wild camp in the grounds of Talampaya. Instead, they said we must head to the official visitor centre and camp there. It's not what we had in mind. I love wild camping. We'd wild camped for 61 nights of the 77-day trip so far and something about an official campsite felt restrictive. Faye interrupted my train of thought.

'They might have cold water at the campsite, Anna?' she said. I thought about that for a moment, imagining what it might be like, not drinking another drop of my lukewarm, plastic-infused water and instead swapping it for something icy cool. It sounded like heaven. The Talampaya campsite it would be.

Some 10 miles later we arrived at the visitor centre. Making our way into the air-conditioned building, I began chatting to the man at the counter (I say chatting, mainly I was swaying and nodding) when I suddenly felt faint and sick. I turned around and mumbled something vaguely coherent to Faye before stumbling to the table and laying my head on it. There I stayed for 30 minutes. I could hear Faye encouraging me to drink cold water as I drifted in and out of sleep. I raised my head a little and glugged from the already unscrewed bottle in my right hand, before returning my face firmly to where it belonged on the tabletop. I know that it's customary to succumb to unplanned bouts of narcolepsy in the afternoon on Christmas Day but this wasn't how I'd expected it to play out.

'I think you might have heat exhaustion, mate,' said Faye, and I agreed. I had overheated, and I was very grateful for the air-conditioned visitor centre. Over the next hour, I drank as much cold water as I could and did a small pee (which looked like liquid gold) in the visitor centre toilets before finally summoning the energy to head outside and begin the process of setting up camp and making dinner. There was no one else around except the two of us and the visitor centre attendant so we had our pick of the camping spots in the dusty pen next to the main building.

I got halfway through pitching my tent before feeling faint again, so I took another short nap on a picnic bench under the shade of a wooden shelter. I pulled out my phone and took a video to send to Jamie. It was Christmas, after all, a time for sharing things with your loved ones. In the video, you can see that there are dark circles around my eyes, which are in stark contrast to my whiter than white face. I am slurring my words and lifting my arms up briefly before letting them slump back down by my side and onto the floor. My mouth is dry and my teeth are sticking to my lips as I try to talk.

'I'm lying here, willing the sun to go away. I've decided I don't like the sun anymore. I'm over it. The sun is so 2015… I mean 2016 because it's now nearly 2017… It needs to go down.'

(Pause.)

'Bring back the rain. I like the rain.'

(Delirious giggle.)

'No. I don't mean it. I'd like just an hour of rain per day, please. And less heat. Who's taking the order here?' I said, looking up at the sky.

After peeling myself away from the picnic bench to finish pitching my tent, I managed to join Faye for a small dinner and a lot more cold water, before crawling into bed. As I drifted off to sleep, I thought back over the events of the past 24 hours and all that had happened since we'd left Chilecito. There had been surprises, smiles, joy, copious amounts of liquid consumed and an afternoon nap. It was certainly Christmas, but not as I'd ever known it.

16

False Hope and Unexpected Cake

Distance cycled: 2,238 miles
Metres ascended: 59,327

I, Anna McNuff, do solemnly swear that I will make it my life's mission to never grow up. At times, that mission is a difficult one but, on other occasions, the opportunity to behave like a child presents itself so beautifully. Thankfully, our journey through the canyons of the Valley of the Moon in central Argentina fell into the latter category. It had been a few days since my heat-induced delirium; we were back on the road and back up to full speed. Santiago was now less than 10 days' riding away. That thought alone spurred me onwards as we rolled into yet another national park, where we began ducking in and out of man-made road tunnels. Tunnels which were just long enough to offer up a shot of adrenaline, but short enough to be safe for two cyclists without lights.

When we were deep inside the first tunnel, I felt like a kid who was afraid of the dark. I wrestled with my imagination and, just at the point where it got so dark that I could practically *see* the boogie man, a sliver of light appeared at the other end and my fears evaporated. Having whizzed through a couple more tunnels and gotten used to the thrill of each short ride through, I began to look forward to each one. And when that anticipation took hold of the two of us, we started whooping and cheering as we cycled through the darkness, listening to our voices as they ricocheted off the walls. Soon, we were really beginning to push the boundaries and had progressed to making whale noises (because whale-song echo sounds just fabulous off concrete walls). It was an act that made us descend into fits of giggles every time.

Our whale songs antics must have worked to summon any nearby living creatures, because the road beyond the Valley of the Moon turned out to be a wildlife extravaganza. By 11 a.m., we had a live snake sighting under our belt, and I was deep in a lyrical exchange with a Shania Twain album, when I spotted the second creature of the day.

'Mega spider!' I shouted at Faye, pulling to a halt to get a closer look.

We inched closer to the gigantic arachnid that was sitting in the middle of the road. It looked like it could be a tarantula but I couldn't be sure. My spider research in Argentina had been on a par with the scorpion research in Bolivia. Read: zero. The traffic was light, so we had enough time for a good stop and stare, noting that all eight hairy legs, bulbous torso and beady eyes were entirely intact – and that it was dead, thank goodness. It was a mid-road GCSE biology lesson waiting to happen. We prodded the spider for a few minutes before taking some pictures, and I shuddered at the thought of having not long left our camp spot. I had some vague recollection (from a *Blue Peter* episode I'd watched as a kid) about tarantulas not being able to inflict too much harm, but this fella was huge! *What would we have done if one of those had come wandering by in the night?* I wondered. Just then, Faye got the fright of her life.

'Oh my god! It moved!' she shouted, leaping backwards.

'Did it?!' I said, leaning in to get a closer look.

'Waa! There it goes again!'

'Ha! That's just the wind. Look.'

We watched as another gust of wind blew one of the tarantula's giant hairy legs up in the air and waggled it around. Faye breathed a sigh of relief, delighted that the spirit of the spider had not escaped the underworld and come back to haunt her. We pedalled off, leaving the spider on the road, legs akimbo.

At the next snack stop, we did some googling and discovered that we had, indeed, happened upon a tarantula. I know. A freakin' hairy-bodied, chunky-legged, I-thought-they-only-existed-in-fairy-tales tarantula. Jeepers.

The game of biology bingo continued long into the afternoon, and we continued to call out to one another whenever we saw exciting living things.

'Butter hopper!' I shouted, pointing at a bug we'd been seeing most days for the past week, which looked like a giant grasshopper when still, but like a blue-winged butterfly when it flew.

'FOX! I mean RABBIT... I mean... WHATTHEHECK-ISTHAT?!' Faye shouted as a creature the size of a small dog bounded out from the bushes and across the road, followed by another, and another until we realised there was a whole gang of them, all bouncing around at the side of the road, like caffeinated ping-pong balls with legs. After googling the words 'Animal Argentina looks like cross between rabbit and deer with pig nose and black bum', I discovered that we had just seen a group of Patagonian cavies. Well, I never.

Wildlife spotting was one of the things I had come to love about adventure. I wasn't much one for paying attention in school when things were written on pages or laid out as pictures in books, but when I was in it, up close to whatever I was learning about, everything was so much easier to take in and much more exciting, too. I'd already learned so much on the journey and we'd answered many questions that I didn't even know I wanted to ask.

***

Beyond the tunnels and the roadside wildlife, the days leading into Santiago began to run long. We were now both anxious to get there, and to get there on time. Sometimes we managed to keep our nerves hidden from one another and other times they bubbled to the surface in the form of minor disagreements about things like: where to set up camp; whether I should wear earplugs while sleeping (which made Faye afraid that I couldn't hear her if she needed me); and, as was the case in the city of San José de Jáchal, whether we would make it to the supermarket before it shut. None of these things really mattered, of course, but as is always the way with trivial disagreements, it was less about the *thing* that we were discussing and more about our general frustration. When you're eager to move on quickly, every day can seem painstakingly slow. Our journey to Santiago had become like a watched pot, and it refused to boil.

To help with a sense of slow progress, I'd learned to break days into manageable chunks. It was a tactic I'd used on many an adventure in the past. When contemplating total mileage was just too overwhelming, I would focus on one small section at a time. Sometimes it was 5 miles, sometimes it was 10 miles. Sometimes it was more about landmarks and the people I thought I was going to encounter along the way. In rural Argentina, where the distances between towns were long and the temperatures were scorching, it had become about the next road junction, the next town, or, if we were lucky, the next shop and an ice-cold soda hit – Fanta for me, Sprite for Faye.

The trouble with using potential soda opportunities as milestones was that we would engage in a dangerous dabble with false hope. All too often we arrived in a town where we had expected a shop, only to find an empty patch of dirt where the shop should be and then an empty void in our stomachs where our ice-cold sodas should be. Whether or not there actually is a real live shop when you make it to a place might not seem like a big deal in normal life. But on our journey, when we were frequently tired and all miles were hard won, those little nuggets of hope became our reason to keep cycling. They distracted us from the miles we still had to make and kept us anchored in the present.

One particular morning, I began the day in an excited state. I was excited because we had reason to believe, nay, we were sure (because it said so on our map) that there was a small town and a shop at the end of the day's ride: a place called Niquivil, a mere 60 miles away.

By 4 p.m., we had made it to Niquivil and I spotted three teenage boys hanging out on stone steps on a street corner. I wasted no time in going over to them, whipped out my limited Spanish, and asked if there was a *tienda* nearby. The boys looked confused. '*No. No tienda,*' one said, and my heart sank. I wanted to clasp his face between my hands, to fall at his feet and weep dramatically at the loss of my beloved, long-awaited, ice-cold soda. I was reaching a 10-point-zero on the screw-the-world-o-meter when the boy interrupted my train of thought. He said the word *kiosco* and pointed to a house opposite with a small faded Coca-Cola poster on its outer wall. I perked up immediately.

I had gathered, during the past week, that words that work in one Spanish-speaking country did not always work in others. For example, lemon meringue pie in Chile is *pie de limon*. In Argentina, you can throw your phrase book out the window, because it is 'lemon pie'. Trust me, I've eaten many a pie in Chilean and Argentinian towns in the name of linguistics research. And so, here in Argentina, from what I could gather, small shops in people's homes were *kioscos*, not *tiendas*.

I caught sight of a woman carrying a baby on her hip, going into the house that the young lad had pointed at. I left Bernard the Bike at the side of the road and chased after her, with Faye in hot pursuit. I summoned my best Spanish to ask if we could buy food and drinks from her home. '*¡Sí!*' she said, before disappearing inside and shutting the door. I waited outside, like a prize lemon (pie) and felt confused. There was some faint shuffling and the sound of something heavy being dragged across a floor, followed by the distinct sound of a bolt being unlocked. A second white door to my right swung open and behind it was the same woman, with the baby still on her hip and, now, two more children at her feet.

Faye and I went through the white door into a small room, which I could now see was next to the kitchen. Sitting at the kitchen table was a woman who, I assumed, was the grand-mother of the family. It felt odd to be in their family home, as if we were intruding on something private. Both Faye and I smiled and bid the older woman '*buenas tardes*' before beginning to survey the snack landscape in the *kiosco*. While we searched for supplies, the young children looked on and I noticed that the toddler was transfixed, his unmoving dark-brown eyes like a world of galaxies, watching intently as we rummaged around on the three small shelves that made up the shop.

Having selected some wafers, biscuits, crackers and an odd-looking vegetable which neither of us could identify, Faye asked the woman if she had any water. We'd been sipping on filtered river water that day and, although the bacteria had been removed so that it was safe to drink, it still tasted unmistakably of donkey arse.

'¿*Agua*? ¡*Sí!*' said the woman, lifting up the top of a large freezer and pointing inside.

We peered in and were surprised to find an unidentifiable dead, skinned animal in there. The woman shoved one of the frozen animal's legs aside and pulled out a large bottle of water.

'¿*Más agua*?' (Any more water?) we asked. The woman thought for a moment, before rummaging further underneath the carcass and presenting us with a large bottle of grapefruit juice. She seemed proud to have found it. I looked at Faye, who shrugged, and we took it, noting that we should clean the outside of both bottles thoroughly before drinking the contents. I was sad, of course, that there was no Fanta in the giant freezer, but carcass-flavoured grapefruit juice would do just grand as a close second.

Thanking the woman profusely, we paid for our goodies and moved outside to sit on the curb at the side of the quiet suburban street. Five minutes later, the woman appeared again, this time from the main door, and she was carrying a large plate. On the plate were two slices of cake. It was cake for us! As the cake neared, I could see that it had a vanilla sponge base, with cream around the edges. Each slice was triple layered, stuffed with jam, mango and then banana. It was surely a cake of champions – moist enough to make Mary Berry proud and packed with enough flavour to make *Master Chef*'s Greg Wallace give an almighty 'Phwooooaarrr'. The woman went back inside and left us sitting on the dusty curb, happily munching on the cake of champions.

'I tell you what,' I said to Faye, pieces of sponge falling from my mouth.

'What?' said Faye, catching a wodge of moist mango before it slipped off the plate and putting it in her mouth.

'Argentinians are so ruddy lovely,' I said.

'They really are,' said Faye.

17

Girls! Do Not Go Down that Road!

Distance cycled: 2,607 miles

Metres ascended: 61,586

I had always been excited about making it to the Argentinian city of Mendoza. Largely because I knew that Mendoza was a region famous for its vineyards, and I was a big fan of vineyards, or rather the wine they produced. I can't drink a huge amount – one or two glasses is all I can handle – but that does put pressure on those one or two glasses to be extra-special.

The original plan for Mendoza had been to take a day off the bikes and visit a few local vineyards to sample the wine. But, after cycling 2,600 miles, I decided that I hadn't the money, the time or the inclination to go on a vineyard tour. I had lost my Mendoza mojo. It was buried deep in my panniers, under my dirty socks and sweat-encrusted cycling shorts. Instead, my sights were fixed firmly on Santiago as the next place to relax. With that in mind, I was happy to just pass through Mendoza and make a promise to myself to come back one day. Faye, as a non-drinker, was happy either way.

Having paused only briefly for a coffee in the city centre,

we were standing over our bikes at a crossroads on the outskirts of the city. I watched as a man in his late twenties on a white and green moped diced with death and swerved around on-coming traffic. He was waving one arm wildly, and it was only as he got closer that I realised he was waving at us. I looked on in horror as he put himself at the mercy of the surrounding cars, narrowly missing their bumpers in his bid to make swift progress towards us. I wondered what on earth could be so urgent that he needed to cross the traffic like that.

'*¡Chicas! ¡Chicas! No se vayen por ese camino! ¡Es peligroso!*' (Girls! Girls! Don't go down that road. It's dangerous!) he shouted in Spanish, and pointed to the road which led straight on, over the traffic lights.

'Er… hola!' I said, smiling, if a little confused, as he pulled up next to us. The man continued to repeat '*¡Peligroso! ¡Peligroso!*' (Dangerous! Dangerous!) before going on to explain in Spanish (at least to the best of my understanding) that we should not go through the traffic lights and down the dirt track we intended to take, because (if we hadn't already got the message) it was dangerous.

When deciding on our route from Mendoza to the next town, Uspallata (oos-pie-ya-ta) – I spell it for you only because, phonetically at least, it includes the word 'pie' – we had two choices. Option one was to go via the rough and ready Route 13, which would lead us up to 3,000 metres and over two remote mountain passes on what was rumoured to be challenging dirt-track terrain. Option two was to follow Route 7, the main highway that skirted the mountains. We'd cycled on Route 7 into the city and, if that was anything to go by, it would likely be crammed with heavy trucks and fast-moving cars, which zoomed passed within a cat's whisker of our bikes. We suspected that Route 13 would have less traffic on it so, in our mind, Route 7 was the more dangerous option between the two. Plus, Route 13 sounded a darn sight more adventurous.

Using the international language of hand signals and phone maps, we explained to Juan, the nice man on the moped, what we were doing, that we'd cycled there from La Paz in Bolivia and that we were headed for Uspallata. Juan continued to insist that we *must* go left through the city and back onto Route 7. We thanked him for his concern, told him that we understood, smiled, took selfies and did the Argentinian cheek-kiss goodbye thing (this is similar to French cheek kissing, but you must do it with South American flair). We watched Juan ride off on his moped, before I turned to Faye and said, 'We're still on for Route Thirteen, right?'

'Yep!' said Faye, not looking up from her phone. 'I'm just waiting for him to get out of sight.'

Now this might sound like madness. Why-oh-why would we go against the advice of a local man who warned us off our intended route? Because, in our experience, people often told us we 'can't go that way' or 'it is too far for you on bikes' or, my personal favourite, 'it is not possible'. In the minds of those who drive cars, the off-road routes were dangerous and scary, while the paved roads were safe. The reality is that, for cyclists, it's often entirely the opposite. And besides, this was an adventure! We were there for some gnarly Andean rock 'n' roll, not an easy glide past sights that could be seen from a car window.

Juan had now whizzed out of sight, so we moved across the traffic lights and started down the dusty trail. A minute later, we heard the unmistakable noise of a moped engine, and then some shouting. There he was again: Juan was razzing down the trail behind us.

'Oh crap,' I said to Faye.

'Busted,' she replied.

We slowed to a stop and I prepared my best 'we didn't understand' routine. Although there was something about his persistence that was starting to sow a seed of curiosity in my mind, and perhaps we didn't quite understand after all. On this visit from Juan, there was also an extra element that seemed unusual. Following behind him was a navy-blue and white car. As Juan pulled up next to us, so too did the car. A woman in the driver's seat wound down her window. She looked at us sternly and said, in broken English, 'Girls. You must not go this way.' Just then, I spied a badge on her arm. It read: Policía de Mendoza.

Lola, a member of the Mendoza Policía, was strikingly pretty, with a round face, cat-like hazel eyes and jet-black hair, which was fashioned into a neat plait down her back. I couldn't help thinking that she looked like she might be a lovely human, despite her stern tone. Once she'd finished giving us a firm telling off for ignoring Juan's advice, her manner softened. She got out of the car and continued in broken English. Her English was on a par with our Spanish and so, flipping between the two languages, we managed some semblance of a conversation. Juan looked on nervously as we tried to get Lola to explain what it was, precisely, about our intended journey on Route 13 that was so dangerous.

'Bad people. Very bad people,' she said. 'It is not safe for you, for tourists.'

Ah. Okay. Now perhaps that *was* something we should listen to. Much as I like to believe there aren't any bad people in the world (only bad deeds), I know that's mostly a happy little bubble I choose to live in. And I do appreciate that tourists can wind up in sticky situations when they wander into the wrong neighbourhood. I started envisaging what lay ahead on Route 13: Bandits? Drug smugglers? Human traffickers? I acted each of these things out to Lola in an elaborate game of roadside charades, trying to understand exactly what it was that we were attempting to ride into.

We were open to listening now, so I asked Lola about alternate options for cycle tourists who wanted to travel to Uspallata. She said that she didn't know enough about that, and instead suggested that we follow her back to the local station where she could call the 'tourist police' (yes, they have tourist po-po in Argentina).

'They can advise on the way to Uspallata,' Lola said. Faye and I were very excited about the prospect of a trip to the local police station, wherever it might lead us.

'Would you like to ride behind the car, in convoy?' Lola asked.

'Yes, we would,' said Faye, grinning. And I grinned back.

'This is so cool,' I mouthed.

Before following Lola back down the trail, we turned to a relieved-looking Juan and apologised to him for ignoring his original advice. We dished out more flamboyant Argentinian cheek kisses and waved him off (again), before following Lola to the station, riding slowly behind her police car for a mile and a half through the city streets. She had her lights on the whole way, and I wondered if she did that just because she'd taken a shine to us. Faye and I chatted as we pedalled, riding side by side, the blue and red flecks of police lights reflected on our faces and dancing across our bike frames.

Once we made the station, Lola stopped briefly to chat to her husband, who was also a policeman, before getting straight on the phone to the tourist police. We were each given a bottle of water by another nice police lady and then sat on chairs outside the main office. As it turned out, this was a police cavalry station, so all around us were green grassy fields, with horses grazing here and there. It wasn't a bad place to pass some time, so we waited patiently. A few minutes later, Lola emerged from the office and said that if we could stay until 5 p.m., someone from the tourist police who could speak English would come by and explain everything.

'Great!' we said in unison. It was 4.30 p.m. by then and Faye and I were only too happy to spend 30 minutes ogling all the police stuff going on in the office and watching the horses trot around outside.

Ten minutes later, a man in a black T-shirt appeared. He was accompanied by one of the police officers. Strolling up to us, he said in perfect English, 'Hello. I'm Marcus. How can I help?' *Ah great, the tourist police had arrived early!* I thought. We nattered back and forth with Marcus about the proposed route and he explained that, at the traffic lights, we had been heading for the dangerous Mendoza neighbourhood of San Martín. He took us into the office, said something in Spanish to Lola's husband and then pointed at a map of the city on the wall. He traced around an area of it with his finger. It was less than half a mile square in size, but Marcus said that it was a 'red zone' and that tourists really shouldn't go through there.

At last the penny dropped. Route 13 wasn't the problem; it was just the route we were taking through the city to get there. Marcus confirmed that we'd come to the right conclusion, but there was still a short debate about whether we'd be able to cope with the tough conditions along the route, namely with a lack of water and the mountainous terrain.

'I'll give you the number of the tourist police, just in case,' Marcus said. This seemed a bit odd, given that I was sure there wasn't going to be any phone reception up in the mountains, but I accepted the number anyway. Marcus then asked if we had various things, such as spare tubes, water and chains, all of which I assured him we had. He then asked, 'Do you have a light?'

'Oh yes, we can make a fire to keep us warm,' I replied, trying to curb his kind concern for our safety.

'No, I mean a light for a cigarette,' he said, holding up a cigarette.

'Oh, sure,' I said slowly, as Faye moved off to get the lighter from her bag. I thought his question was a little unprofessional for a tourist policeman. And then it dawned on me that he had arrived a little early.

'You're not from the tourist police then?' I asked Marcus.

'Me?! Oh, no. I just play the drums in the police band and I can speak English, so they called me over.'

Brilliant. After Marcus the drummer had lit up and taken a few puffs, a phone call was made to the real tourist police to inform them that we couldn't wait any longer and that we were heading into the mountains. At last, we were free to go. We left the station, took a one-mile detour to avoid the rough neighbourhood of San Martín, and set off on the same route we'd been heading for almost three hours earlier. Route 13 was a go, and it already reeked of adventure.

***

After a night spent camped just a few miles outside the city, beside Route 13, we left our camp spot in high spirits, and with good reason. We were now less than a week from making it across the Chilean border and into Santiago. As long as British Airways' strikes didn't scupper plans, Jamie (aka the most wondrous boy on the planet) was going to fly to Chile and so was Faye's mum (one of the two most wondrous mums on the planet, my mum being the other, naturally.) Their arrival would mean two weeks off the bikes for Faye and me. Time to drink, eat, sleep, and catch up with those we love. That was definitely something worth cycling over a few more mountains for.

During the coming days, we knew that we would have to drag both our bodies and our bikes from 650 metres above sea level up to a high point of 3,200 metres. Having spent two weeks below 1,000 metres, our lungs had been living in luxury and we were eager to get some altitude back into them.

I had taken three pedal strokes away from our camp spot when I noticed my rear tyre was flat. It was a blow but, in the grand scheme of things, it was no biggy. I let Faye know and started the process of unloading all the bags from the rear rack to fix the puncture. Ten minutes later, we were off again, riding along a track that started out as lightly rocky and descended into full-on bump 'n' hustle.

We were now a good 10 miles from the main road at Mendoza and, although the track was still wide enough for a car, we hadn't seen any cars since leaving the city. As we continued on the track, I couldn't help but think how superb it was to be riding on Route 13, going where the cars could not. I smiled an inward smile and gritted my teeth, shoving hard on the pedals to get Bernard up and over the uneven rocks.

A few hundred metres further up the climb, water began to trickle down the road and, before long, the road had turned into a full-blown stream. I'd run along many riverbeds during my time in New Zealand but I'd never had the pleasure of cycling up one. It turned out to be a great workout for the abs and a novel way to clean my increasingly feral-smelling bike shoes.

Unfortunately, I couldn't ride up the river for long: the rocks were too slippery and, try as I might to grip the handle-bars tightly and keep inching forwards, Bernard's tyres slipped and slid around, and I fell off, many times. Soon Faye and Gustavo's big tyres began to struggle too, so we got off the bikes and started pushing. It had been a while since we'd had to walk with the bikes, but immediately there was sense of a familiarity about it.

A mile further on, the road river disappeared as swiftly as it had arrived. Now, with dry rocks under foot, we were able to get back on the bikes but, for some reason, I was really starting to struggle. Faye was streaking ahead but my wheels seemed to be sinking more than usual into the shingle and sand. Then I realised. 'Faye!' I moaned. 'I've got another puncture.' I laid Bernard on the ground, took all the bags off (again) and set about repairing the flat.

Punctures on a long bike ride are always a battle of wills because there is never a 'good' time to get one. We still had a long way to go, on rough and rocky terrain, and the last thing I needed was for it to happen again. Frustratingly, we couldn't locate the puncture, which meant I couldn't patch the hole up as I'd hoped and instead was forced to use my last spare inner tube.

'I'm sure it'll be fine,' I said to Faye, and off we went again.

Optimism was clearly a poor repair strategy because, a few hours later, I was slipping and sliding around on the gravel with the third flat of the day. Poor Faye. Her face was the epitome of patience when I broke the news.

'Faye, I've got another flat,' I sighed.

'I think we need to check that back tyre out properly this time,' she said.

'I think you're right,' I replied.

This time around, I went full mechanic on the tyre's ass. I couldn't afford to get any more flats and no stone was to be left unturned in the tubular investigation. I sat in the middle of the road, pumped up all the old tubes and, with detective-like precision, I began to look for any kind of pattern in the puncture crimes against humanity.

Faye took a picture of me at that moment, and her photo turned out to be one of my favourites from the whole trip. In the picture, I am sitting on grey gravel, smack bang in the middle of the trail (because we knew that there wouldn't be any passing traffic). I'm wearing a grubby pink T-shirt, which stands out against the grey river that's winding away from the camera, on a gentle slope around a bend and toward some hazy green-black mountains in the distance. Strewn around me on the ground are various items I'd taken off the bike or emptied out of my panniers in a bid to make the repairs. Instead of seeming separate from the surrounding landscape, I am a part of it. My arms are deeply tanned by the sun's rays, my cheeks look battered by the wind, and my leg muscles have been sculpted by the many metres spent climbing mountains. A short flop of blond hair has fallen across my face as I stare intently at the tyre, locked deep in a mission to get us back on the road.

'Ah hah!' I shouted, looking up from the tube in my hand. 'They're in the same place! All the punctures are in exactly the same place.'

'Ah! It must be the tyre then,' Faye said, and I agreed. I spent five minutes searching the tyre for signs of what might be causing the repeated punctures but I found nothing. At a loss, I decided to use an older tyre I was carrying, just to be sure I wouldn't get a puncture again. Except... that tyre had a deep gash in it, which was the reason I had taken it off in the first place, back in San Pedro de Atacama.

I summoned my inner Girl Guide (because she is resourceful and brave and practically a superhero) and thought about what I had in my possession that could potentially plug the gash in that tyre to make it usable. Then I remembered someone once telling me how strong toothpaste tubes are. So I rummaged in my bag to find my tube of toothpaste. I squeezed its innards out by the side of the road, noting how they looked like a neat pile of white dog poo. I then used my first-aid scissors to open up the tube, cut out a rectangle and fashion a makeshift lining for the inside of the tyre. I accessorised the new lining with some electrical tape to make sure that the toothpaste tube sat flush against the tyre wall and sat back to admire my handiwork. Even I was impressed. Closing the tyre back up, I fitted the inner tube and loaded Bernard up again, ready for the road. It was then that I checked my watch.

'Err, Faye.'

'Yep?' Faye replied.

'It's half past four.'

'What?! No way.'

'Yes way.'

'What time did we start?' she asked.

'Half past nine.'

'And how far have we come?'

I checked the GPS app on the phone. 'Thirteen miles,' I said.

'Thirteen miles?! Oh, my goodness. You've got to laugh,' she replied.

'I think we're gunning for some kind of slow-speed record. Fewest miles and longest day,' I smiled.

'Shall we?' she smiled back, motioning down the trail,

both of us determined to make the top of the 3,200-metre climb before nightfall.

By 8.30 p.m., we were just shy of the top of the pass and had been pushing and pedalling uphill for 11 hours, but we weren't quite done yet. The final incline steepened, and steepened, and steepened until both of us were wedged into the hillside, like frozen statues, feet slowly sliding downward in the loose gravel, doing all we could just to stop our bikes from tipping backwards and landing on top of us. I was trying a new strategy to make progress, which involved resting for 10 seconds, before taking three steps and trying my best not to wet myself under the strain of it all. Alas, that soon became futile. The bike skidded sideways, and I slipped and landed in a heap on the ground with the bike and bags on top of me. I lay on my back and stared up at the sky.

'Arrrrggggghhhhh!'

'You alright, Anna?!' came a distant call from Faye, who was by then a little way above me on the slope. I didn't move, I just sighed and lay there wondering what the heck I was doing. I seriously considered investing some time in creating gravel angels in the dirt and perhaps just falling asleep where I was lying.

'Yeah,' I shouted back to Faye. 'Grand thanks, just losing my shit down here. Business as usual.'

In the end, I accepted that I could not push the fully loaded bike any further. My arms and back were screaming at me and, in the words of *Star Trek*'s Scotty, 'I just did n'y have the power!' Instead, I settled for an extreme version of PE-lesson shuttle runs. I took my bags off the pannier racks, and ferried the bags and bike up the slope separately. At one point, Faye, who had managed to push her bike all the way to the top already (because she is strong like a BULL), came back down to help me with my bags. Why? Because we were a team and, in that moment, I had never felt it more keenly.

Working together, we managed to reach a small plateau and flopped onto the ground to rest for a while before taking on the final, equally steep, section of the climb. Faye turned her head sideways and looked at me. She did a double take.

'Oh god, mate.'

'What? Whassup?' I slurred in reply.

'You look ruined. I've never seen you so white!'

'Well, if I look even half as bad as you do, we're in big trouble,' I retorted. We burst out laughing. All we could do was laugh. Delirious, exhausted, sweet laughter.

For the final ascent, we hatched a cunning plan. This time we would both work together to push just one fully loaded bike up the slope at a time. Bernard went up first, followed by Gustavo. The bikes felt floaty light with four arms pushing them as opposed to two. Cresting the top of the hill with Gustavo, we were greeted by a majestic scene. We were, at last, 3,200 metres high. The sun hung low in a pale blue sky, its rays shooting off in a hundred different directions like a recently exploded firework. Mountains upon mountains were silhouetted against the warm evening glow. Some were nearby and intimidating, others were just ghostly outlines in the distance. And then there they were: two gigantic condors – black-bodied, huge wings – just floating, right above our heads. Our jaws dropped. We looked at one another and smiled and then looked back at the birds. It was as if those two condors knew. As if they'd been watching us struggle all day through the punctures, rocks and rubble, and had popped out for a late-evening flight on Route 13, especially for us.

18

Switchbacking to Santiago

Distance cycled: 2,664 miles
Metres ascended: 65,027

At the town of Uspallata, our journey along Route 13 came to an end. We rejoined the main highway and the previous days of hard-won solitude felt like a distant dream. Back again were the honking cars, the minimal cycling space and the heavy, articulated trucks. Streams of them, all heading towards the Argentinian-Chilean border, just as we were.

Faye and I soon became a finely tuned, two-up, women's time-trial team. We zipped along the smooth tarmac on Route 7, tucked tightly up against the other's wheel as we passed through a steep-sided canyon. Whoever took the front was responsible for pointing out potholes, dead animals or any other potential bike-stopping hazards, and whoever ended up as 'tail-end Charlie' was appointed chief safety officer. The primary responsibility of the chief safety officer involved checking behind frequently for any approaching trucks, and double-checking behind for approaching trucks if there was oncoming traffic. If a situation had the potential to be dicey, the chief safety officer would shout at the other person to pull off the road and let the motorised monsters be on their way without squashing us.

As Faye had developed a faster cruising speed than I had on the flat roads, I was often up front, dictating the pace so that we could stay close together. So it was me who spotted it first on the second day, along the road towards the border.

'Faye, look!' I said, pointing through a gap in the surrounding cliffs and towards a sharp, granite peak covered in snow off to our right.

'Is that…?!'

'A-con-cag-ua,' I said, slowly, purposefully, letting every vowel roll around for an extended period of time before it left my mouth.

'Wow,' said Faye, both of us now staring wistfully at the peak.

Reaching 6,962 metres into the sky, Aconcagua is the highest mountain in the southern hemisphere. Originally, Faye and I had discussed making a side trip to climb the mountain, but the trek to the top takes an average of 20 days. We'd have needed a chunk of extra time, a more clearly defined schedule and a bucketload of spare cash to do it. So we had decided to leave it for another time. We both loved mountains and Aconcagua was up there with the best of them.

There are many different explanations of where the mountain gets its name but my favourite is that it comes from the native Aymara tribe of the Andes for whom Aconcagua means 'white ravine'. Looking out on the mountain, I could see one of its three glaciers set clearly against a backdrop of blue sky.

Still within view of the peak, we stopped for a snack break in the shade of a roadside tree.

'We'll just have to come back one day and do it,' I said to Faye, chewing on a piece of tortilla wrap.

'Yeah, I'd like that,' she replied.

'Shall we make a pact?' I asked.

'What's that?' she said.

'That we won't climb Aconcagua without the other one?'

'A mountain pact,' Faye said, turning the idea over in her mind.

'I mean, it might be in fifteen years' time or something. We might have kids and responsibility and all that jazz, but shall we make that deal?'

'I would love that. You, me and Aconcagua. It's a deal,' said Faye.

***

A few mornings later, just shy of the border with Chile, Faye looked up from her phone. 'We have eighty-eight switch-backs to take on today, Anna! Eighty-eight!' Her eyes were aglow with all the wonder of a child on Christmas morn.

When researching the border crossing between Argentina and Chile, we'd discovered that we had two choices. Our first option was to pedal up to the start of the two-mile-long Paso Internacional Los Libertadores tunnel, which funnels motor vehicles across the border. From reading various blogs online, we'd learned that cyclists aren't allowed in the tunnel itself and so, if we chose that option, we should expect to be stopped by the mythical 'tunnel police'. The tunnel police (rumoured to be half-man, half-donkey) would then ferry us through the tunnel themselves in their police chariot or arrange for a truck to stop to take our bikes through. If we didn't fancy a run-in with the tunnel police, option two was to take the old road across the border – a winding dirt track that went via Paso de la Iglesia, and up and over a mountain. Now then, which option do you think appealed the most? I'll give you a clue: it started with 'up the' and ended in 'freakin' mountain'. Hooray!

We wound our way back and forth along the red and dusty road to Paso de la Iglesia. It was a quiet road because most motorists would have taken the tunnel option, but a few brave drivers had chosen to come over the pass too. Every 10 minutes or so, a vehicle would go by. Some were camper vans, some modern cars and others were clapped-out old bangers, sporting rust around the wheel arches and on the bonnets. The drivers beeped and honked their horns, giving us a thumbs up for 'doing it on bikes'. Many of them were tourists who spoke English with a European accent, but some shouted in Spanish, '*¡Chicas bravas! ¡Chicas bravas!*' and we smiled and waved back. It was nice to be sharing a mountain with others for a change, and they seemed to be enjoying the thrill of the zigzag climb as much as we were.

Halfway up the pass, we stopped for a water break and to take in the view. Beyond the red-grey rubble of the road, to our right, jagged granite peaks shot up from the ground and stood tall and proud against a steel-blue sky. Pockets of snow were nestled in the darkest corners of the peaks, and a white glacier peppered with grey snaked between the two largest mountains in the distance. Despite the coating of dust on our arms and the frequent inhalation of car fumes, everything up there felt fresh. Crisp. Clean. Just as mountain air should be.

It took us an hour to reach the top of the pass at 3,900 metres, and it was only as we pedalled onto the small plateau at the summit that I realised how blinkin' freezin' it was. Despite having cycled past snow on the way up, I'd managed to get a nice sweat on and so was still clad only in shorts and T-shirt. But now, out of the shelter of the mountainside, the windchill at the top was something else. A stiff gust of wind sent an icy blast right through to my bones. My teeth started to chatter. I looked around on the summit. There was a dusty grey car park, two small cafes, a modest gift shop, an information centre (which looked more like a railway-station waiting room) and, beyond the car park, a 10-metre-high bronze statue of *Cristo Redentor de los Andes*, keeping watch over the mountains. I'd only ever seen pictures of the Christ the Redeemer statue in Rio, Brazil, but this one seemed smaller, with one hand reaching forward and the other holding on to a large cross.

'Bloody hell, it's nippy up here!' I shouted at Faye as we rolled into the car park and closer to the statue.

'Shall we get some clothes on?' she asked.

'Yep!'

'Then maybe a hot chocolate?'

'I'd say a cheeky *choco caliente* is definitely in order, Faye-Bomb. I like your style.'

'I knew you would,' Faye smiled.

Despite her smiles, I had noted that Faye seemed subdued that day. It might have seemed that she was as happy as Larry, but she was quieter than usual, and I suspected that she was feeling jaded. Perhaps I'd noticed it more because I was feeling jaded too. In Faye's eyes, I saw my own weariness reflected back at me. Just a few more days, I thought. A few more days and we'd have some time off the bikes in Santiago. Some time away from the incessant need to keep moving. Some time to sit in coffee shops, to eat pie and just be. If only for a little while.

We piled on all of our clothing and (once I had six layers on my top half and three on my bottom) grabbed a quick *choco caliente* from one of the small stalls at the top. Post-hot-choc-inhalation, we decided that it was too cold to pose next to the huge Chilean flag and, more importantly, we couldn't be arsed with standing in line waiting for the other tourists to take their turn, so we began the descent of Paso de la Iglesia in earnest.

Once over the plateau, we got our first real glimpse of the track down the other side of the mountain and it was a beauty.

Snaking its way down to the valley floor was a dirt road with switchback after switchback. I counted 28 of them, in fact. The track looked like a ride you might see at a fairground – not quite a helter-skelter but some kind of elaborate water slide, one that you would happily queue for a good few hours to have a go on. In contrast to the grey road we'd followed to the top of the pass, the colours of the landscape on this side of the mountain were bolder. The orange-red dirt of the valley, the granite of the mountains surrounding it, a few small patches of snow and then the blue of the sky. It was a work of art.

We followed a man on his mountain bike down the pass. He was carrying just a small backpack, so we expected him to streak away from us towards the valley, but we were delighted that he wasn't actually going much faster than we were. Months of bouncing over loose rock and gravel had made us nimble while descending on loaded touring bikes. It was a tall order to keep our speed up and cling on around sharp bends but I only fell off once, which was pretty amazing considering that my total fall count now sat at well over 30. As always, Faye somehow remained upright through the whole descent, despite me telling her that it's good to fall over as an adult once in a while. Adults don't fall over enough, you know.

There were no cars on that side of the mountain and, aside from the man on the mountain bike, we had the descent entirely to ourselves. After 30 minutes of switchback-swooshing, the dirt track came to an end and spat us out onto tarmac once again. We nipped through a few more tunnels on the way towards the official border, stopping at the start of each one to perform the newly developed tunnel-safety ritual.

'High-vis vest on?' I said to Faye.

'Check,' she replied in military fashion.

'Lights turned on? Front and back?'

'Check… and check.'

'Sunglasses?'

'Oops!' said Faye, removing her sunnies from her face and sliding them into her bar bag. 'Check.'

If you've ever made the mistake of trying to ride through a long dark tunnel with sunglasses on, it's a mistake you only make once because pedalling into a wall of blackness at 15 mph is terrifying. Despite enjoying the tunnels of the Valley of the Moon, I was nervous about going through the ones near the border because they were longer and there was more traffic. Now that we'd rejoined the main road, we were once again surrounded by huge trucks. So I was grateful that some of the tunnels were short or had gaps on the sides that allowed beams of sunlight in so that we could be seen by the passing traffic.

I approached each tunnel with trepidation, breathing hard or singing to myself to keep calm as we passed through it. The tunnels didn't seem to bother Faye so much but they made my imagination run wild as I calculated just how many ways an adventure cyclist could be squished by a gigantic truck.

At last we arrived at the official border. Technically, we'd crossed into Chile at the top of Paso de la Iglesia, but evidently there wasn't space for a full-blown immigration outpost there, and I could see why. At the official border crossing, there were thousands of people spilling out of a white and green building, which looked like an airplane hangar and was almost as large. We pulled on our brakes and ground to a halt in a sea of tour buses, cars and lorries. As we'd come to expect in South America, it was in no way clear where we should go, but the bonus of being on a bicycle was that we were often waved to the front of any line – although, on this occasion, we waved ourselves to the front of a line that we liked the look of. We took great care to maintain an expression that was a mixture of confusion and intent in a bid to ward off any questions from those waiting patiently in line in their cars.

The immigration shed turned out to be a challenge that would put even the toughest gladiator to the test. In a battle of wit and wills, we spent two hours standing in many different queues but finally we emerged, bemused and triumphant. Boasting a new set of stamps in our passports, we set off into Chile.

The switchbacks of Paso de la Iglesia were merely a warm-up for the wiggle fest that followed, and soon we reached what was billed as the highlight of the day.

'It looks like a giant plate of spaghetti down there!' said Faye, looking out over a jumble of tarmac below.

I had seen this road once before, in a picture online. I hadn't believed it then, and I couldn't quite believe it now that I was standing at the top of it. As much as a road could be, it was beautiful. Back and forth, the ribbon of tarmac flowed – never going in a straight line for more than 100 metres before turning 180 degrees back on itself – soft curves of light grey, swooping down the valley, all the way to the foot of a grey-green wall of rock in the distance. Dotted along the road were cars and trucks and, from where we were standing, many of them looked tiny. I liked the brightly coloured blue and red vehicles the best. Not only because they stood out on the light grey road but also because they looked like the Micro Machines I used to play with when I was a kid. I felt like I could reach out my hand, pick one up and zoom it further along the tarmac if I wanted to.

As we began the descent, I noticed that there was a sign at each corner that let us know just how much fun was still to come: '*Curva* 29… *Curva* 28… *Curva* 27…' they read – on and on and on. I couldn't stop smiling and I noticed that Faye was grinning from ear to ear too.

'This is ridiculous!' I shouted as I caught up with her on a bend.

'Ridiculously AWESOME!' she shouted back.

Having switchbacked our way since 8 a.m. that morning, eventually the curves ended. The road flattened out in a granite valley and we continued to descend towards the bottom, albeit less dramatically. The number of buildings lining the road increased. There were more cars, more noise, more people, and I began to realise that it might be difficult to find a place to sleep. We spent an hour looking for a suitable place to pitch up, before squeezing through a fence into a disused truck yard and, after moving a few concrete blocks out of the way, we set up camp in quite possibly the ugliest 'wild' camp spot so far. Luckily, the noise of the adjacent river went some way to drowning out the hum of traffic on the main road, but we were still treated to the toots of bemused truck drivers who, from their higher cabins, could see two girls cooking up pasta on a concrete patch next to the highway. We were both exhausted, so where we slept that night didn't really matter. In fact, it mattered even less because the following day we would be riding into Santiago. Safe in the knowledge that only 56 miles stood between us and a few weeks of R & R with loved ones, I drifted off to sleep.

The next morning, we were up and at 'em early, streaking away from our camp spot and down a busy but direct route into the city. Faye needed to stop and send a message to her mum, who was about to board the plane to Chile. We stopped 'briefly' after just 6 miles, at a cafe where we could get some phone signal. The cafe turned out to be serving the most splendid hot dogs, sprinkled with onions and all kinds of exciting saucy things. I ordered one while I waited for Faye to have a message exchange with her mum. Naturally, Faye experienced hot-dog envy and got one too. Then I became envious of Faye eating her hot dog when I had finished mine, so I ordered a second hot dog, which led to Faye getting a second one too. We could have played that game all day but an hour later, we finally left the cafe and got back on the road.

Fuelled by hot dogs, we were making steady progress towards the city, and the usual two-woman-team time-trial formation was keeping us safe from passing trucks. Just then, I spotted a sign at the side of the road with some width-restriction instructions on it. Alarm bells started to ring in my mind because experience had taught me that there was normally only one reason for width-restriction instructions on South American roads. I then saw the words '*Por túnel*', which confirmed my suspicions. Oh, bugger.

'Err, Faye,' I shouted over my shoulder. 'Can we stop and check the map? I think we might be headed for a tunnel.'

We pulled over and checked the route. Sure enough, when we zoomed in on the map (which was something we had failed to do earlier), I could see that we were pedalling right into the unforgiving jaws of a mile-long road tunnel. Faye let out a deep sigh. I could tell that she was feeling tired and just wanted to get that day's riding over with. We started discussing our options. We could go around the tunnel, via a side road that looked like it would add 6 miles and would take us up and over a nearby mountain. It was hot that day, pushing 35°C, and our legs were tired from a week of climbing over 7,000 metres. All we wanted to do was make it to Santiago. We'd even hoped to make it there in the early afternoon so that we could begin to relax before dinnertime.

'I'm sure the tunnel will be fine,' said Faye. 'I think we should just go for it.' I fell silent. I really didn't want to do the extra miles over the mountain but I also really, really, hated tunnels. Granted, I hated tunnels more than Faye did and my fear wasn't always rational, but this was a tunnel with a width-restriction sign, advising wide vehicles to take an alternative route, which meant that the tunnel must be narrow. And a narrow tunnel was not a place for cyclists. That said, I considered whether I was being overly cautious.

'Okay, hang on, let me think,' I said to Faye. I went back and forth in my mind but eventually it was my gut that made the decision. I just couldn't do it. It felt like a risk that wasn't worth it. The alternative route over the mountain would be longer, harder and hillier, but we'd be safer.

'I'm really sorry, mate, I can't go through that tunnel. It's just not worth the risk.'

Faye let out a sigh and then fell silent. I could tell she was pissed off. In that moment I felt terrible for stopping her taking the route she wanted to but I had to be honest. I wasn't comfortable with it. We calmly chatted it out for a few more minutes and at one point I even suggested that we could split up and go separate ways, which, in hindsight, seems like an odd thing to have said. I didn't want to split up but, equally, Faye was her own person. I resolved that I could tell her how I felt and what I'd like to do, but ultimately what she wanted to do was up to her.

'Don't be silly. We're not splitting up. Let's just go around,' Faye said wearily.

We rode off and for the next 30 minutes Faye didn't say much. I began to wonder if we'd inadvertently had a falling out. Maybe I'd been patronising in laying out the risks of going through that tunnel, maybe I was being stubborn in not being willing to do it. I caught up to her and called forward.

'Faye.'

'Yep.'

'Are you annoyed with me?' I asked.

'What?' she said.

'Are you pissed off? You seem pissed off.'

'No, I'm not pissed off with you,' she replied.

'But you are pissed off?'

'Yes.'

'But I haven't upset you?'

'No… I'm just really tired. And I just want to get to Santiago.'

'Ah, okay. I get it. Thanks.'

I was relieved. At that moment, I wanted to crack a joke. To burst the bubble of exhaustion so that we could go back to our default light-hearted state. But it wasn't the time for that. Faye was exhausted. I could feel the slow creep of tiredness start to darken my mind too. Let's just get over that mountain and into the city, I thought.

The mountain road actually turned out to be a pleasant surprise. From the outset, it had a smooth surface, with yellow lines down the middle that snaked towards straw-coloured hillsides dotted with green shrubs. Signs at the side of the road warned us of 'dangerous curves' and 'strong gradients' but, in our new more upbeat state, Faye and I concluded that we possessed some dangerous curves ourselves (oh, yeah), and we were now very much up for some strong gradient action.

By 1 p.m., we'd made the top of the climb and could see the main highway thundering on through the valley below. I was glad we weren't down there, fighting for space among the trucks and the cars. The temperature had hit 38°C but, now over the climb, we took off like two women possessed, whooshing down the other side to rejoin the main road, with just 40 miles to ride to Santiago. Once back on the highway, we had a wide 3-metre shoulder to ourselves and we went into full-on mission mode. Legs pumping, lungs burning, over the next four hours we stopped briefly to drink some water and have a nibble on a banana, but, otherwise, there was quite literally no stopping us. By 5.30 p.m., we were on the outskirts of the city, winding through the backstreets.

'I hope this gets a bit better,' Faye said, nervously, eyeing the broken shop windows and graffitied walls. I reassured her that these were usual things to be seeing on the outskirts of a big city, and that riding into big cities is always an ugly affair.

The torch of weariness had been passed back and forth all day and, by 6 p.m., I was clutching it tightly. I had taken over directing us through the city streets, but I had chosen a bad route in. Faye spotted the faux pas and suggested a new route, which (in my tired state) I took to be an attack on my attempt to help, so we exchanged some angry words. I then threw a small huff and snapped at Faye. She snapped back. We paused at a road junction and stood over our bikes. There was tension in the air. But the tension was cut by a homeless woman with one tooth who approached us and offered to sell us biscuits. She was very insistent but I had no idea what she was saying. It also looked like she had already eaten half the packet of biscuits and was trying to do us a deal on the second half. We thanked her politely and then I looked at Faye. She smiled. I smiled. This was ridiculous. I took a deep breath and apologised. Faye apologised too and within two minutes of both of us having become ratty with the other we were back on track. Quite literally, thanks to Faye now doing the navigating.

The increase in frequency of these smaller disagreements was a sure sign that we were both in need of a rest. A rest from the road. A rest from one another. Just a rest. At 6.30 p.m., we arrived at a hostel in the southwestern suburbs of Santiago, stinking, sweaty, exhausted and with the hunger of two… hungry horses. It felt strange to be stepping off Bernard the Bike outside that hostel, knowing that I wouldn't be getting back on him for two weeks.

The following day, at a packed terminal in Santiago Airport, part one of our adventure drew to a close. Jamie and Faye's mum had inadvertently managed to book the same flight, so Faye and I waited together for them to appear in the Arrivals hall. I'd spent the morning making Jamie a brightly coloured sign that read, 'You are the sunshine of my life.' Which was true. I hadn't seen him in three months, I'd cut all my hair off and lost a good five kilograms, so I wondered if he might just walk straight past me. But he found me in the crowd. He didn't quite seem real for the first few minutes. Having been a voice on the phone or a face on a screen for so many months, to see Jamie in the flesh was surreal. It was a strange thing that someone I knew so well should seem so unfamiliar.

As we left the airport, Faye arm in arm with her mum, Jamie and me hand in hand, I thought how odd it was going to be for Faye and me to be separated for a few weeks, although the thought of being off the bike, with no particular place to be for a while, felt wonderful. The past few months together had been a steep learning curve. We had scaled mountains and volcanoes together, we had marvelled at wildlife and been fed through the kindness of strangers. We had suffered altitude sickness, saddle sores and dents to our pride. We had pushed our bodies to the brink of exhaustion and our friendship to breaking point.

Beyond Santiago, to the south, the wilds of Patagonia lay in wait. A land ravaged by wind and rain but rumoured to be one of the most beautiful places on the planet, filled with glaciers, snow-capped mountains and swift-flowing, crystal-clear rivers. The thought of riding out into the elements made me feel exhausted. Right now, I needed a break. But I knew that by the time we got back on our bikes for the rest of our journey to the end of the world, we would be ready. Ready for whatever the second half of our Andean adventure together would bring.

PART II

Santiago to Puerto Montt

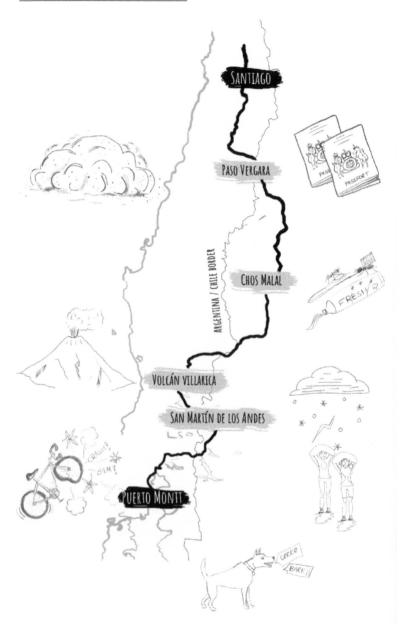

Santiago

Paso Vergara

Chos Malal

Argentina / Chile Border

Volcán Villarica

San Martín de los Andes

Puerto Montt

19

Piglet 'n' Pooh

Distance cycled: 2,832 miles

Metres ascended: 70,128

'McNuff! There are four boys in our room, and they smell!'

It was 10 p.m. and I was making my way home across Santiago when a message from Faye came through on my phone. I had spent a large chunk of the past two weeks with Jamie in the quirky coastal town of Valparaíso, sleeping, eating (delicious things), drinking (delicious things), going running and doing the final edits for a book about a previous running adventure in New Zealand. After three months of cramming in late-night book editing, with my head propped up on my sleeping bag in my tent, it was a novelty to be sitting upright at a table in front of my computer. And I had sat at many tables, in many local restaurants, slowly becoming addicted to the Chilean delicacies of ceviche and pisco sour, along the way.

I was reassured by just how easily things had slipped back to normality for Jamie and me. It felt nice to do 'normal' things together, like go for walks, cook on a proper stove and spend hours drinking coffee. I remembered how much I enjoyed the simple act of cutting up vegetables on a chunky wooden chopping board. The satisfying clunk as the knife moved through the stems of a head of broccoli. I had missed knowing that I was about to eat something fresh and nutritious, not to mention having the time and space to prepare it.

The studio apartment where we stayed in Valparaíso was rented to us by a woman who lived next door. She'd gone away for a few days while we were there and had said that we were welcome to go into her home, sit on her balcony and drink wine, whenever we liked. We took up her offer one evening, lying side by side on sun loungers, clutching large glasses of Chilean red wine. The air was warm, still 20°C in the evening but with the addition of a cool breeze from the South Pacific rolling through. I shut my eyes and listened to the sounds of Chilean suburbia. I could hear chatter from nearby neighbours, the dull throb of music from somewhere downtown, and dogs barking in the street. From the balcony, we could see the whole of Valparaíso, stretching out like twinkling tea lights floating on an ocean of black, while dark, cobbled alleyways and crooked stone steps glowed silver where the moonlight hit.

I didn't see Faye during those two weeks, but we'd kept in touch via messages and I knew that she'd spent the time with her mum exploring locally and further afield. They'd had a whale of a time, going for hikes, eating lunches out and as Faye told me 'non-stop laughing'. I knew just how much Faye had missed her mum and it made me happy to know that they were on their own mini adventure together.

The transition from life on the bikes with Faye to a sedentary break with Jamie had been easier than I'd expected. It was like a flick of a switch, as I stepped out of one set of routines with Faye and into another set with Jamie. Somewhere in the corner of my mind, our journey to Ushuaia had been put on pause. Ghostly outlines of Faye and me were suspended, mid cycle, in a bizarre dream world until we decided that we were ready to hit the play button again. That time had now come. Jamie had flown home and Faye and I had reunited at a downtown hostel. We'd spent a couple of nights there and, after a day of gathering supplies for the road ahead, I was on my way back to the hostel when Faye's message about the invasion of the four boys came through to my phone. I hit reply.

'Oh, cripes, I knew having the room to ourselves was too good to be true. How smelly are we talking here? On a scale of one to vomit-inducing?'

'I'm retching!!' she replied.

Being on a budget and spending a few days longer in a city that we usually would have, Faye and I had opted for two beds in a six-bed dorm room in a hostel. I had wondered for a moment if, at 32, I was too old for hostel life, but we'd been lucky enough to have the dorm room to ourselves for two whole nights. But that night, our final night in the city, was set to be another matter entirely. I sent another message to Faye.

'I'll be there in thirty. Hang on. Be strong.'

As I entered the dorm room, I was met by what can only be described as a perfumery of body odour. Armpit musk had collided headlong with lingering fart and was now dancing wholeheartedly with wafts of cheesy feet. The saving grace was, perhaps, that a lethal amount of deodorant had been dusted over the top of it all. It was a warm night and the room had reached furnace temperature. If ever there were a case for spontaneous human combustion, the conditions that night were perfect.

Faye informed me that 'the lads', who were in their early twenties, had gone out for the night, so we snuggled into our beds and waited for the first inevitable wake-up call. At midnight, two of the boys returned. The lights went on, there was a loud conversation and they left again. I got up and turned the lights off. Fifteen minutes later, all four of them returned. The lights went on, the boys stood around chatting for five minutes and departed again, leaving the lights on.

This game of disco lights continued until 1.30 a.m., at which point all the boys were now in the room, and in their beds. This was, of course, the cue for boy number one in the bunk opposite me to begin playing music on his phone. I heard Faye mumble something about 'being too old for this shit' and I couldn't help but agree. Only, the music didn't seem to be bothering boy number two in the bottom bunk. He had started snoring so loudly that the walls shook around our ears.

To top it off, the couple next door were at it again. In the three days we'd been staying at the hostel, the pair in the room next to ours had been having loud sex every hour or two. They did this with great gusto and with the small windows above their door wide open, so that all the other inhabitants of the four-bedroomed hostel could enjoy the auditory show. Every now and then one of them emerged from the love cocoon – to buy snacks, fetch a pizza or have a shower – before promptly resuming the romp-fest.

The resumption of the lovemaking was the final straw for Faye; she had had enough.

'I'm sleeping in the hall!' she announced. After dragging a pillow and bed cover out of the room, she inflated her camping mat and bedded down in the hallway. As I helped her with the move, I discovered that there was also a male snorer in bedroom number three, possibly even louder than the one in our room. His snores filled the hallway and swirled around Faye's ears. I decided that any attempt to sleep was pointless and so, instead, I did my best to turn frustration into creativity with a few hours of writing. My plan was to continue until I was so tired that I no longer cared about the surrounding noise.

So, there I sat at a table in the hallway at 3.30 a.m., Faye tossing and turning a few metres away, moans and groans (and the odd '¡*Oh, sí!*') coming from the room down the hall, and two thundering, albeit slightly harmonious, snorers doing their best to recreate the noise of an orchestra in the Sydney Opera House. Through bleary eyes, I smiled and thought about just how much I was looking forward to getting back on the bikes again the following day. To be headed for the solitude of our tents pitched in the wilderness once more.

***

Thanks to my new friend Mr Pisco Sour and his accomplice Mrs Chilean Wine (middle name: delicious), when the time came to ease my Lycra cycling shorts over a now slightly larger derriere for the first time in two weeks, they felt uncomfortably tight. Taking the first few pedal strokes away from the hostel and through the bustling streets of suburban Santiago, my body began to protest. My knees were especially grouchy. They resented being dragged from what they had assumed was to be an early retirement.

Left knee: Oh, bloody hell, not again. I was all settled here and midway through season three of *Breaking Bad*…

Right knee: For goodness' sakes. Will this woman never learn?!

When researching a route to take us out of the city, I had decided that all attempts to select a 'good route' were futile. If previous cycling adventures had taught me anything, it was that all roads in cities tend to be ugly. Therefore, you might as well just pick any old route out of town, and crack on. So, shortly before leaving, I traced my finger in a southward direction over the mapping app on my phone. I left a wobbly red line in my finger's wake, and off we tootled.

Despite the immediate protests from various body parts, it felt great to be on the move again. There's always something so soothing about forward motion. I enjoyed the familiarity of slow progress through an unfamiliar landscape. The simplicity of it all. The rush of blood through my veins and the air passing over my skin. Eat. Sleep. Cycle. Repeat. I looked across at Faye and I knew that she was glad to be on the move again too, despite being sad about leaving her mum.

'How you feeling, mate?' I asked.

'Good,' she smiled, as if affirming it to herself. 'It's weird, isn't it? Like we never left the bikes.'

'It is.'

'Well, except…'

'Except?' I pressed.

'I feel a bit unfit. Is that possible? I mean, can you get unfit in a couple of weeks?' she asked.

'Nah, I don't think you'll have lost much fitness. Maybe it's more of a feeling?'

'Yeah. You're right. And I have a feeling I drank one-too-many *submarinos* since we got off the bikes,' she laughed.

'I feel your pain! Me too. Except my vice was the vino.'

'My name's Faye Shepherd and I've got *submarino* problems,' she said.

'I'm here for you, Faye Shepherd. Whenever you think about dunking a chocolate bar in milk, call me instead. I'll talk you round,' I grinned.

'Thanks, McNuff – you're a true friend.'

Those two weeks apart with our loved ones had given us

a chance to take a step back and put everything from the first three months of the journey into perspective. We were heading out of Santiago not only with a better understanding of what to expect from the road, but also what to expect from one another. On my part, there was none of the anxiety I'd felt when we first left La Paz. There was no second-guessing what Faye might be thinking, because if I wanted to know, I would just ask. And I knew that I couldn't hide any emotions from her – she understood me too well for that. We knew what we needed to do, so we just got back to doing it, and with ease.

Much as we did our best to avoid it (often by taking longer, unpaved side roads), we soon had no choice but to spend time pedalling down Ruta Nacional 5, an activity that we affectionately dubbed 'fun on the 5'. The RN5 runs almost the entire length of Chile. It's the main, often only, route through the country for northbound and southbound traffic. Think of it as equivalent to the UK's M1 and you get the picture. Although the traffic moves swiftly on national highways like the RN5, I never felt unsafe. Because with big roads come big shoulders to cycle on, so Faye and I glued ourselves to the outer edge of a 3-metre-wide piece of RN5 tarmac and claimed it as our own. Feeling safe and at ease on Ruta 5 didn't necessarily make for a pleasant riding experience however, and each afternoon I would grow weary with the incessant noise of the passing trucks and cars.

One afternoon on the RN5, while firmly engrossed in 'the fun of it', I began to notice that lots of cars were flying Chilean flags. They were stuck out of windows, flapping on poles and jammed into truck doors. In fact, now that I'd noticed it, one in every five vehicles that passed us that day had a flag on it somewhere. Some flags had the words '¡*Fuerza Chile!*' scrawled on them. I also noticed that, if it was an open-back truck flying the Chilean colours, there would be various household items piled up on the back, like chairs, blankets and mattresses.

That spring, the most savage forest fires had raged through Chile. They'd begun back in November and were still going strong two months later. After our first day on the RN5, I read about them online and learned that there were over 100 blazes reported over an area of 1.35 million acres, which had so far left 2,000 homes destroyed, 8,000 people homeless and 11 dead. Egged on by unusually hot weather and strong winds, the forest fires had officially become the worst in the country's history. The news reported that the response from Chileans unaffected by the fires had been phenomenal, with many people heading south to help clear up the devastation and donate anything they could spare from their own homes. The fires were to the east of our planned route south, but if they continued to spread, they could easily cross our path, so we needed to keep an eye on them. One of the blazes was just 50 miles from where we had camped that very night. Over dinner, a message came through to my GPS device. It was from my mum.

'Wild fires getting worse in southern Chile, Petal. Are you two going to be okay?'

I hit reply right away. 'Yes, thank you! We've seen them. Our route doesn't go near, but we'll keep an eye on them in case they spread more. Promise. Hugs and kisses xxx'

Suddenly I felt foolish and useless, to say the least. There I was, on a jolly old adventure, and people were losing their homes in the small communities nearby. I thought back to the line of vehicles with flags, and my heart was warmed at such a display of unity. What we'd seen that day on the RN5 was everything I had come to believe about the human race. When push comes to shove, people will sling a load of mattresses on their truck, proudly display their country's flag and razz it down the motorway to look after others who are in need. Just because they can.

On the fourth day south of Santiago, we unzipped our tents to find that the skies were shrouded in a murky smoke-filled haze. It was a hot and humid morning and both of us confessed that we were finding it hard to get going. There was an underlying lethargy lingering in my bones. I couldn't stop yawning, and everything felt... flat. I told myself that it was understandable. That it might take some time to get back into the groove after a few weeks of rest, after all, but I couldn't help but feel that the smoke was playing a part in my low mood. That morning was like the dark winter days back home, when you look out of the window at a cloudy sky, and feel a little cloudy inside too.

Having left the busy RN5 and headed into the country-side, we were moving back towards the spine of the Andean mountains and towards the Chilean-Argentinian border. By mid-afternoon, we had sanctioned ourselves a roadside lunch stop on a grassy bluff above a river. The smoke seemed to be lifting gradually and, with each mile that we put between us and the main highway, the landscape had become ever more beautiful. It was as if a giant camera lens was being adjusted on the world around us and, despite the blanket of haze, the surroundings seemed in sharper focus. Swathes of granite rock shot up from the ground on either side of the country road, the trees seemed taller, and the river swifter in its meanders.

After eating lunch, we lay down on the ground, resting our heads on our helmets and staring up at the smoky sky. The earth had absorbed much of the day's heat and was acting as a hot-water bottle for my back, making the grassy bluff a very comfortable place to be. I watched strong gusts of wind bend the surrounding trees to and fro, and I shut my eyes. Gone was the hum of cars and the honking of horns. All I could hear now were the rustle of tree leaves and the thunderous roar of the river down below. I kept my eyes closed and began to doze off, lulled by nature's chorus.

Faye must have dozed off too, because it was 30 minutes later when I woke up and checked my watch. We had gone well beyond our usual one-hour-sanctioned lunch break. The drill sergeant who lives in the back of my mind started to bark at me.

'Cycling cadet, McNuff. Get yerrr butt off that grassy ground and get back on that bike, you lazy son of a gun! Those miles aren't going to make themselves,' he said. But the orders fell on deaf ears.

In stark contrast to the sluggish morning, it was turning out to be such a lovely afternoon. I had stopped fighting the lethargy and, instead, chose to embrace it with open arms. Besides, after our race to make Santiago on time, we were back to a looser daily-mileage schedule. Faye began stirring next to me and seemed to have read my mind.

'Anna?' she said, breaking our doze-induced silence.

'Mm huh?' I replied, opening one eye.

'I like that we don't have to be anywhere today,' she sighed.

'I like that too,' I said with a smile, and shut both eyes again.

In that moment, Faye was Winnie the Pooh and I was Piglet. We had gone down to the river for a picnic, or so it felt, and as Pooh once said, 'Don't underestimate the value of doing nothing, of just going along, listening to all the things you can't hear, and not bothering.' In that moment, we were both excelling in the art of not bothering, and it was glorious.

Two hours after we first lay down, we dragged ourselves away from the lunch stop and carried on up the valley. The road paving ended – a sure sign that we were heading into the boonies – so we continued on a familiar brownish rubble. We passed men, waist deep in the river, fishing; families chatting on the rocks beside clear plunge-pools; and friends gathered around tents, the smells from their roadside barbecues tormenting our nostrils.

'Ooohh, I could nail a burnt sausage right now,' I said to

Faye, inhaling deeply. Even though we'd just had lunch, there was always space for barbecue food in my belly.

'Mmm. Me too. Or a slightly blackened burger?' she replied.

'Heavy on the onions, light on the ketchup, soft squishy bun,' I dribbled as we rode on by.

At 5 p.m., we stopped by the riverside again, this time just briefly to fill up our water bottles. With crystal-clear river water, it was nice to know that we needn't worry about purifying it before we drank it. We could glug freely from nature's water fountain, something that felt reassuringly primal. The families, their barbecues and the fishermen were a long way back and we were now entirely alone. It was still early for a day of riding and, with the sun setting at 9 p.m. at that time of year, we could potentially have ridden on for a few more hours.

After taking a drink from the river, I looked longingly at the flat patch of grass at the side of the road, which came complete with river view. We'd only camped a few times by a river so far in the journey. It was a real luxury that meant we got a wash, a drink, and a swim all in one. Again, psychic Faye was already one step ahead of me.

'I'm screwed,' she said.

'Me too!' I chirped back. There was a long pause, and then Faye uttered the two magic words.

'Tent time?!' she asked.

'Yes! Tent time!' I cheered, in firm agreement that we

should stop for the day and just camp there.

Within 10 minutes of making the decision, I was butt naked and waist deep in the Río Teno. I ventured a quick full-body dunk in a small pool at the edge of the river and emerged with an excruciating brain freeze. It was icy cold. After a follow-up bits 'n' pits wash, I scrambled back up the bank, put on some fresh clothes and parked my tired heiny on a large rock, dangling my feet in the water. I looked down at my pasty white feet, bobbing around under the distorted surface, before shifting my gaze to the right and watching two white birds swoop above the bluff opposite. I took note of the power of the water as it surged over a giant boulder in the centre of the river and shut my eyes to better feel, on my face, the tiny droplets that were flung upwards as water collided with rock. The sun was getting low in the sky and just upstream, where the river flattened out, I could see rays of golden light begin to catch the surface, making it shimmer. I sighed. A long, deep sigh. As clunky as the first week back on the road had been, it was good to be on the move again. Back out there, among the trees and the birds and the rubble roads, where we belonged.

20

The Vanishing Visa

Distance cycled: 3,002 miles
Metres ascended: 72,749

A week after leaving Santiago, we prepared to cross the spine of the Andes for the fourth time. Although this time, we would make the crossing at the civilised height of 2,500 metres above sea level, an altitude that felt more than manageable after a month above 4,000 metres.

We began a long rubble-tastic slog, away from the river-bed and towards the top of Paso Vergara (which we naturally kept calling Paso Viagra). An hour into the climb, and still an hour shy of the summit, we reached the Chilean border. Pulling over at an official border building, we were greeted by five guards in uniform who were standing outside the immigration building. It was a friendly and straightforward border-crossing experience. Despite having the facilities to, the guards didn't make us go through the pointless 'put your bags through the scanner' ritual and, instead, we had extra time to chat politics and weather with a man who spoke good English because his dad was from Miami, Florida. After 10 minutes of form filling, Miami man handed us back our passports. We shook hands with all five guards, thanked them for the kind farewell from Chile and resumed the wobble up to the top of the pass, towards the Argentinian border.

We had learned that passing from one country to the other tended to happen in two stages. First, we must be stamped out of one country, then some miles later, stamped into the other. I was never entirely sure who owned the land in between the two. I wondered if the countries shared it and perhaps used it for inter-country picnics or polo matches on weekends? I could only hope. The road leading away from the Chilean border post was flanked by modest hillsides, carpeted in green and straw-coloured grass. Where the slope of the land had become too steep and a chunk of it had given way to gravity, the grass had slipped off, leaving the rocky innards of the mountain exposed, weather-beaten and raw. Large volcanoes loomed beyond the dusty greens of the nearby hills. They were reddish-brown, with rivers of white rock cascading from peaks and ridges, both of which cut a sharp line across the cloudless blue sky.

After 12 miles of riding through no-man's land, we made it over the top of the pass and began a well-earned zoom down the other side. Nearing the bottom of the mountain, I spotted a large group of people sitting in the shade of a lone white building, with the Argentinian flag flying on a tall metal pole out the front. There were men of all shapes and sizes, clad in matching kit: tall ones, tubby ones, lean ones, grey ones, smart-looking ones and unshaven ones. When they spotted us riding towards them, the men got to their feet and clapped and cheered until we were right in front of the building. '¡*Chicas bravas! ¡Chicas bravas!*' shouted one. 'Girl Power!' shouted another. After dismounting our bikes, we began a hugging-and-cheek-kissing frenzy – quite the feat of endurance with a group of 20 people.

Using a mixture of broken English and broken Spanish, we gathered that the cheering men were camping at the border that night and they soon decided that we simply *must* join them for dinner. One of them was midway through asking me whether we eat 'just vegetables' or 'meat and vegetables' when a stern-looking man in a white polo shirt appeared behind Faye and tapped her on the shoulder. In all the chatting, cheek-kissing and cheers, we'd completely forgotten to get stamped into Argentina. In fact, right at that very moment, we were illegally standing on Argentinean soil.

The stern officer motioned for us to follow him and turned swiftly on his heels. He was a young lad with shiny black hair, dark brown eyes and a strong jawline, and he wore a very serious expression. As we entered his poky little office, I decided that he could potentially be quite good-looking, if he only smiled. We handed over our passports and he disappeared with them into another room. A minute or so later he returned and placed my passport on the desk, indicating that all was well, but he said that there was a problem with Faye's.

'*No hay visado de salida,*' said the man, explaining that Faye had no exit stamp from Chile.

'What?!' I said out loud. I mean, I knew Faye was a pro at

losing things, but losing a permanently inked exit stamp from the inner pages of her passport would have been quite the achievement. The man thrust Faye's passport back towards us and I began frantically leafing through the pages. It had to be there, I thought. We had both been stamped out of Chile, except… now I couldn't see the exit stamp anywhere at all. How could we miss something so crucial?! I wondered. And then I remembered Miami man at the Chilean border. He was so full of life and full of chat that perhaps we had been distracted. I tried to reason with the human in the polo shirt. Surely he could see that this was a simple mistake.

'She came over the border with me, I mean, we're together, a two.' I mimed handing over, stamping and getting the passports back. The man stared blankly back at me, then shrugged.

'Can you make a phone call to the Chilean border?' I asked, to which he sat back in his chair, crossed his arms and shook his head.

'No,' he said, and I sighed. He seemed very insistent on telling us what we couldn't do, so I wondered what we could.

'What can we do?' I asked.

'You must go back,' he said.

'Back over the mountain?' Faye asked.

'Yes,' he replied. 'Back over the mountain. Stamp. Come back.'

This was ridiculous! The thought of completing a 24-mile

round trip, over a 2,500-metre pass, to get stamped out of Chile and come back again, although adventurous, did not appeal in the slightest.

'And you definitely can't make a phone call?' I asked again, thinking that it would take five minutes for the Chilean men to confirm that two British women had indeed come through on their bikes a few hours earlier.

The man shook his head again, but he did at least get up and head into the back room to double-check with another man, who I assumed to be his boss. The door was shut firmly behind him, and we heard a mumbled Spanish conversation.

'I can't believe he can't make a phone call to the Chilean guys?' I whispered to Faye.

'He can make the phone call, he's just being a knob,' said Faye and, as ever, she was spot on. I mean, seriously, what did he think I was trying to do? Smuggle a 6 ft 1 in. redhead into Argentina? I knew redheads were rare out there, but I wasn't sure that Faye would go down well on the black market (she's priceless anyway).

A few minutes later, the door swung open and the polo-shirted guard reappeared. He looked at us and shook his head. I let out a sigh and resigned myself to the fact that we would have to cycle back to the Chilean border. I watched the guard as he sat down again at the desk and took one more idle flick through Faye's passport. Just then, something entirely unexpected happened – a smile began to creep across his face.

Ever so slowly, he rocked forwards in his chair and placed Faye's passport down on the table, extending his index finger over a small area in the middle of one page. Faye and I took a few steps towards the desk and leant over the passport, squinting.

'*Vi-sa-do*,' the guard whispered. And right there, partially obscured by two other more vibrant stamps in the middle of a page, was the faintest Chilean exit stamp I had ever seen!

'Yes! There it is!' shouted Faye.

'*¡Visado! ¡Visado!*' I chanted, as we both began dancing around the little office.

Crisis averted. Although, before emerging from the suffocating immigration building into the bright sunlight outside, we made a mental note to always check in future that our passports had actually been stamped. We regaled the group of adoring male cyclists with our tale of the vanishing visa, and they all thought it was hilarious. Which, of course, now that we didn't have to cycle back over a mountain, we did too.

After thanking the biker gang for their invitation to dinner (with or without meat, and/or vegetables), we decided that 4 p.m. was too early to stop for the night and that we should push on for a few more hours. There was more hugging, a tornado of double-cheek kissing and a hefty round of 'good lucks', before we pedalled away from the border, into Argentina proper and towards the towering volcanoes beyond.

Our hard-won, slightly bumbling battle to re-enter Argentina was well worth the effort. We'd been reliably informed by the bikers at the border that the Valenzuela Valley, at 2,400 metres, was '*muy lindo*' (very pretty) and it didn't disappoint. Within 10 miles of the Argentinian immigration building, the landscape had changed from golden brown to lush green. The whole place looked like a fairy garden, patches of spongy moss leading away from the edges of the rubble road and parting to reveal small, sapphire pools. It was the kind of place where you'd want to slip off your shoes and wander around barefoot, sprinkling glitter as you went.

Over the days that followed, we continued to trace the path of the upper Río Grande. I could see the brown-red, snow-spattered summits of the Calabozos to the west – a collection of peaks that make up 70 of Chile's biggest and most active volcanoes. At first, it seemed strange that the valley could be so green when the mountains beyond it were so barren, but we soon discovered the source of such an explosion of life: glacial meltwater. Waterfalls tumbled down the hillsides, veins of white running over slick black rock and feeding the pools. The waterfalls closest to the road were modest in size, so we would stop to drink from those, holding our sweat-encrusted faces under the icy cascade for a few moments, just long enough to allow the cool water to trickle down our necks and onto our shoulder blades.

Every now and then, we'd come across a ford, where the meltwater had chosen to cross the road on its way to one of the pools. Faye and I amused ourselves by careering through the fords at breakneck speed, hoping that we'd make it out the other side. One night, we set up camp just beside a meltwater pool. After a hearty dinner of mashed potatoes, sausages and cheese, I spent longer than usual sitting outside my tent, looking up at the stars. I decided that the Valenzuela Valley was a place where I truly felt alive. It was a world of opposites, of extremes. Out there, dust from the road covered my arms and legs, burning rays of yellow-white sun beat down from above, and the air was harsh and dry. But then there was the soft moss, the perfectly circular pools and the cool, fresh water. It was the best of nature, and the worst of it, all together as one.

21

Temper… Temper…

Distance cycled: 3,122 miles
Metres ascended: 73,760

'Err, Faye… what in the world is THAT?!'

I was standing outside my tent, midway through brushing my teeth, when a distant rumble distracted me. A mile or so further down the mountain track, I could see people on horses. They were surrounded by plumes of dust and silhouetted against the early morning sun. They were carrying flags, banners and all manner of brassy things, which held rays of dawn light captive for a brief moment before reflecting them into the valley. The rolling thunder of humans and hooves continued towards us at a steady pace over the next five minutes and, for a moment, I wondered if I was still asleep and this was all a dream. It looked like so many cowboy movies I'd seen as a kid, where the cavalry appeared *en masse*, over the brow of a hill. Were we about to be attacked? I was rooted to the spot with my mouth wide open, and Faye had now come to stand beside me.

'This is so cool,' she whispered.

'I know,' I whispered back. 'Where do you think they're

going?'

'Maybe they ran out of milk and they're headed to the shops,'. Faye replied with a smile.

'I think you could be right… say, why are we whispering?' I asked.

'I don't know. I'm scared. I'm hoping they don't see us.'

'I think it's too late for that,' I said, breaking from a whisper and into a normal voice.

Just then, two green military trucks appeared around the nearest bend. They stopped close to where we were standing and three men dressed in military uniforms hopped out of each truck. The colourful procession was just a few hundred metres behind and the men nodded in our direction, as if finding two tall white women in their pyjamas at the side of the road in the middle of nowhere (mouths open, toothbrushes in hands) was a perfectly normal sight. Once out of the trucks, the men began setting up a video camera on a tripod.

Oh, how I longed to ask them what the Dickens was going on. It was a Tuesday morning in late January and I wondered what kind of special occasion it could possibly be. Was it someone's birthday? An Argentine bar mitzvah? I did consider testing my Spanish on one of the men setting up the tripod, but they looked rather… hardy. Especially the man on the main camera – he had accessorised his outfit with a cigarette and a soft khaki cap. So neither one of us said a word, we simply grabbed our own cameras, bid the military trios a good morning with a brief nod and sat ourselves down on a pair of large boulders, ready to enjoy the show.

It took a few more minutes for the horse parade to reach us. A few minutes during which I actually thought I might pee my pants with excitement! I could not get over how freakin' cool it all was! It was imposing sight, with the clatter of hooves and grunts passing so close to where we were sitting. I had always been amazed at how powerful horses look, the bulge of muscles where legs meet torso especially. In fact, as someone who has only ridden a horse a handful of times, I'm often terrified by those muscles. But that day, there was a majesty to them. I felt no fear, only awe.

Some of the horses were a deep chestnut brown with black manes, some were grey with flecks of white and some were jet black, with sandy-coloured manes. Whatever their colours, they all looked awe-inspiringly strong – closer to stocky mules than lean thoroughbreds. The men riding them were sitting on rugs that looked like they were made from llama fur. Just like the men with the cameras, almost all of them were in uniform, with only a couple in civilian clothing.

At the front of the group was a man on a black horse, carrying a metal-tipped wooden pole with a scarlet red flag. The flag was metal too and it didn't flutter in the wind as flags usually do. It was rectangular on one end, with a fishtail cut into the other, and featured a cross, a horse and an eagle. It was a flag fit for a king. Perhaps the man carrying it was royalty?

We smiled and waved as the procession passed, wishing all

of them a '*Buen día*' and taking photos and videos so that we wouldn't think that we'd imagined the whole thing. One of the civilians, in a blue denim shirt, called over to us from his horse, in perfect English: 'Where are you from?'

I told him proudly that we were from England, and then Faye pushed for some extra information.

'What's going on here?' she shouted.

'This is a celebration of the crossing of the Andes,' he said. 'It is very important to the people of the region!'

Naturally, I had no idea what that meant at the time. Faye's blank look hinted that she didn't have a clue either, so we both just said, 'Oh fantastic!' and smiled. But later on, we did some diligent googling. That day, as it turns out, one Tuesday morning in January 2017, was the two hundredth anniversary of the 'crossing of the Andes' when, in 1817, Chilean exiles and Argentinian soldiers joined forces to invade Chile and liberate the country from Spanish rule. Led by a cool cat called José de San Martín and accompanied by his lieutenant, Bernardo O'Higgins, the crossing was one of the most important events in Chile's attempt to regain its independence from the Spanish. It was noted, at the time, that San Martín and his men aimed to enter into Chile along 'unexpected pathways'. So I felt proud that, 200 years later, Faye and I were on one of those unexpected pathways between the two countries ourselves.

After breakfast *avec* horse parade, we continued to snake our way southwards, skirting the foothills of the Andes to our west and the green-brown waters of Río Grande to the east.

We descended slowly over the following few days to 1,200 metres, entering the province of Neuquén. Gone were the lush greens and aquamarines of the Valenzuela Valley and instead we were surrounded by a landscape of brown. I'd never thought about how many shades there might be on the spectrum between yellowish-brown and dirty tan but, as the week wore on, and as all other colours faded from view, I saw them all. Straw-coloured earth led to mustard-coloured mountains. The grey tarmac road was also coated in a fine layer of sand, so that even the road appeared light brown. It was a real Wild West kind of place: the sun did its best to sneak a few rays through the sandy haze, but even the sky didn't look blue. The sand got everywhere. It nestled on our eyelashes, clung to our eyebrows, took up residence in our hair and settled on our forearms. I gave up washing that week because water simply served to attract even more sand to my skin.

One evening, we were forced to make camp earlier than usual because a sandstorm blew through. It was terrifying to see it approach from the horizon, an ominous plume of dark-brown cloud thundering down the valley. And yet there was something exciting about being out there, in nature's way, with no option but to hunker down and hope. We took shelter under a small patch of trees, pitching our tents in record time and crawling inside just before the storm hit.

'This is nuts!' Faye yelled from inside her tent, a comment that I could just about hear above the roar of the wind.

'It is! I reckon we'd have had lovely smooth skin if we'd

stayed outside though,' I yelled back.

'You're right. They should sell this as some kind of spa experience!' she replied.

For the week that followed the sandstorm, it was back to the good old days. Riding for hours with no one and nothing except one another and our thoughts for company. I'd given up on learning any more Spanish via podcasts after we passed through Santiago, largely because I got disheartened that whenever I tried to speak Spanish in the city to a shopkeeper or waitress they would reply in English. It was a poor excuse to quit but as the trip wore on, I was less inclined to challenge myself mentally. Instead, Faye and I both indulged in audiobooks. We further cemented our status as similar to that of a married couple by listening to, and then recommending, books to one another. On one occasion we were both listening to Jennifer Saunders' and laughing out loud on our bikes at the same time. In turn (although not in unison) we also worked our way through the memoirs of TV presenter Davina McCall, comedienne Sue Perkins and Hollywood star Drew Barrymore, patiently waiting until the other person had finished the book so that we could discuss the parts we'd enjoyed and connected with, or the few parts that we hadn't. The books and the shared laughter eased what were long, dusty days through mid Argentina. There was a fair distance between towns out there, sometimes as much as 60 miles, and most had a population of fewer than 100 people. After the madness of Santiago, there was a sense of tranquillity to being a lone duo again, laughing and creating memories with the turning of pedals. Memories that only Faye and I would share in the years to come.

***

After 420 miles of sand, scrub and audiobooks, we prepared to cross back into Chile. Zooming down a long hill towards the border, we screeched to a halt in front of a smartly dressed female Argentinian guard, who was standing next to a white and orange road barrier. Making our way into the neat wooden guards' building, we found three more female border workers sitting at desks. How refreshing, I thought, delighted to have happened upon the most *femme*-friendly of country crossings so far. The young woman sitting at the desk closest to us looked up. She said hello and asked the most taxing question of that day so far: 'Where are you going?'

Faye and I looked blankly at one another and blew out our cheeks. In all the riding into nothingness of the past week, our brains had turned to mush. And, as is the way with long-distance travel, the town names all merged into one. Neither one of us could remember the name of the Chilean town just across the border which we were headed for and so, instead, we just stood there, like two chimps, scratching our heads, pulling faces and making a few sounds.

I ventured some jumbled vowels and went up at the end of my sentence. '*Vamos à… ¿Mooopuko? ¿Melanomu? ¿Melipectra?*', hoping that the look on the woman's face would change from confusion to understanding when I happened upon the right combination of letters. After a minute of insufferable stupidity, the border guard took pity and snatched victory from the jaws of defeat:

'Chile?' she asked. '*¿Van a Chile?*'

'*¡Sí! ¡Sí!*' We shouted, throwing our arms into the air. 'Chile! We are going to Chile.'

It then became apparent that the guard was simply enquiring which direction we were travelling in and which country we hoped to enter into. As we had just walked into the building from the road, for all she knew, we could have been crossing the border into Argentina rather than out of it. I apologised for our blunder and made the internationally understood sign for 'crazy' with my finger, swirling it at the side of my head. The guard then turned to say something in Spanish to her colleague and they both burst out laughing. I can only presume she said, 'Silly tourists. They don't know if they're coming or going.' And she would have been spot on.

That day was beginning to feel like a journey through the Crystal Maze. The mental challenge of the Argentinian border complete, it was off to the Red Zone (Chile) to complete a physical task. The laws of both Argentina and Chile state that you may not carry fruit in any form across the border. Despite this being our fifth border crossing, we had forgotten this detail and our hearts sank when we remembered a recently purchased cocktail of fruity things hidden in our panniers. We duly fessed up to the border guard that we had in our possession three bananas, two apples and an orange. We were CRIMINALS.

A male guard tried to prise our fruit hoard from our grasp there and then, but we protested. This was precious, delicious, fresh produce! We were not about to give it up to the bin! So Faye and I proceeded (much to the guard's disgust) to inhale all the fruity items before his very eyes. I felt sick as I crammed the final banana into my pie hole but I could, at least, rest easy that my five-a-day had been reached in one fell swoop.

Bellies bulging and vitamin levels rocketing, we were at last granted entry into what we believed would be Chilean utopia: the Lake District. After poring over the map in our tent one evening, we'd become entranced by the intricate web of small roads just over the border in Chile, weaving their way in between large patches of blue. Being a planner, I instantly formulated an image of the area in my mind. I fell in love with the idea of what was to come – deserted wild camp spots on the edge of glacial lakes, rubble trails running between tiny villages, and a few local people dotted here and there, all of whom would smile and wave at us as we glided by because it was such a novelty to see tourists in the area.

Having imagined all of that, I was taken aback by how busy it was. I reasoned that things would quieten down as the week wore on but, as we cycled deeper into the countryside, we soon learned that this area was where every family in southern Chile and Argentina came to spend their holidays. In place of the solitude we'd expected, we found bustling towns, traffic jams and many (many) opportunities to purchase inflatable flamingos. As it turned out, the Lake District of Chile was about as deserted and peaceful as a football stadium on match day.

Busy as it was, the landscape was as beautiful as I'd hoped for, and we were able to enjoy it from the comfort of satin-smooth tarmac roads. One evening, we took great joy in camping among a jumble of monkey puzzle trees, which were perched precariously on rocky outcrops above ski-slope-worthy sand dunes. We wound onwards through the region, past evergreen forests that fringed vast expanses of turquoise water, admiring the snow-capped Volcán Villarrica, which kept watch over lone kayakers who paddled, carefree, under skies sprinkled with marshmallow clouds.

After a few days on what we had by then dubbed 'tourist tarmac', we found some familiar dusty tracks once again. Perhaps, the area was about to quieten down, I thought. But, sadly, that wasn't the case. To top it off, the dusty tracks were the dustiest we had ever encountered. They were dustier than Dusty Springfield, dustier even than Dusty from *Three Amigos*.

The combination of still traffic-heavy roads and rubble tracks proved a new challenge. Car upon car would plough past and cake us from head to toe in a fine grey mist. Every now and then, I would run my tongue over the surface of my front teeth and find there was enough dirt clinging to them for a three-course meal. Occasionally Faye, who was riding in front of me, would disappear entirely in a puff of road smoke. When one particular car drove by and kicked up the usual dirt cloud, I honestly thought she'd been swept under its wheels and dragged out of sight. Straining my eyes, coughing and spluttering, I couldn't see her for love or money. At last I glimpsed the reflective panels on her panniers and breathed a huge sigh of relief.

At first, the beautiful scenery and smooth tarmac in the Chilean Lake District made up for the throngs of tourists. But soon the abundance of people, the need to pay for camping at cramped sites and the constant stream of cars coating us in dust ground me down. By the time we rolled into the small lakeside town of Puerto Fuy, I was beginning to feel irritated. We were due to cross back into Argentina again, but this time we had opted for the most exciting border crossing we could find – via ferry across Lake Pirihueico. I couldn't put my finger on why I was quite so angst-ridden that day – but the sensation was there, bubbling beneath the surface. I wondered whether it had anything to do, yet again, with the change from blissful solitude to being surrounded by so many cars and noise. I had pinned my hopes on a quiet ferry journey across the lake, so when we rolled into Puerto Fuy to find it brimming with people, that was another blow.

'They don't have any space,' said Faye, emerging from the ticket office on the lakeshore. I looked up from my phone.

'What? No space? Just for two people with bikes?!' I gawped.

'Nope. She said we can get the ferry at seven tomorrow morning, I think. I didn't really understand…'

'Okay. Did you get tickets for tomorrow then?'

'No. She says we can't buy them until tomorrow, I think. Again, I didn't really understand…'

'What?!' I said, feeling frustrated that we wouldn't be guaranteed passage out of the surrounding bustle.

'I know, it sucks. Do you want to go in and try? I could have misinterpreted everything.'

And so, armed with my best friend Google Translate I went in and spoke to the lady behind the desk. I say 'spoke'. She mainly talked very fast, and I mainly flashed her a variety of words from my Google Translate app, which, when turned sideways on the phone, automatically made the words ten times the usual size. So I may, at points, have appeared to have been shouting at her, via the medium of CAPITAL LETTERS. Still, it did the trick and I managed to confirm that Faye was right. We couldn't buy the tickets in advance, and we needed to arrive before 6 a.m. the following morning to make sure we got a spot on the first ferry.

I emerged from the ticket office and broke the news to Faye with a sigh. I was pissed off. For starters, I didn't want to be still that day; I wanted to keep moving. After cycling day in, day out for eight hours at a time, exercise had become a drug. On top of my physical restlessness, I was struggling mentally. My mind felt as crowded as the lakeshore. I had enough self-awareness to know that I needed to be in a non-crowded place to unpick the tangled web of thoughts and feelings. Everywhere that week had been crowded, and so my mind had remained crowded too. If we could just get across the lake and back into Argentina, perhaps we would have some roads to ourselves again, and perhaps I could work out what was bugging me. That day, I felt trapped and I could feel my frustrations starting to creep into my conversations with Faye. Do you ever catch yourself behaving like a person you don't recognise, and don't want to be? That was me on the lakeshore that day.

'Sorry, Faye. I'm just irritated,' I said as we sat on a wooden table outside a cafe.

'Am I irritating you?' she asked.

'No, no, not at all, you're being great. It's nothing to do with you. I'm just… restless.'

'I can see that,' she smiled, and I smiled back. Just the simple act of saying it out loud, of sharing the struggle without necessarily knowing what the solution was, had helped.

'It's nothing to do with you,' I said.

'Good. Then you can be as miserable as you like,' she smiled.

'Thank you.'

It was times like that when I was grateful for how much the relationship between Faye and me had grown. Me being in a huff could easily have created an air of tension and, perhaps, at the start of our trip we might have headed that way. But now, four months into the journey, we both understood that it was impossible to be on tip-top form all the time. We'd learned that when one of us was acting strangely, the best course of action was to give her some space. Faye was patient with me that afternoon. She didn't try to talk me out of it; she just let me be.

A friend who will watch you throw a huff and hold a space for you until you're ready to transform back into a decent human being again is a good friend, indeed.

Post temper-tantrum, we spent the evening camped by the lake, and guess what? It was lovely. In the end, I was glad that we'd been forced to spend a night on the lakeshore, and we'd even managed to find a spot with just a few other people around us. It was a pleasant place to pass some time. I went for an icy swim in the glacial waters and we took advantage of a little 3G connectivity to check in with friends and family. I video-called Jamie from the lake to show him where I was. He told me that it looked 'Beeaawwtifuwl' (in his thick West Country accent), a comment that helped me to appreciate the surroundings, even if I was finding it difficult to be there. I hung up the phone and spent some time sitting in the porch of my tent. After watching the sun tuck itself in for bed, next to the silhouette of the mountain opposite, I turned in for the night myself.

The following morning, we made our way in silence back to the terminal building. Faye ventured some Spanish to buy the tickets and we rolled onto the Hua Hum Ferry across Lake Pirihueico. It was freezing cold as we pulled away from the dock. I could see my breath on the air and the tip of my nose began to go numb. I watched as the sun started to rise, casting a striking orange glow across the lake. We floated through rags of early morning mist, gliding silently past low-hanging clouds wrapped around steep grey cliffs, and into Argentina again.

***

A few days later, away from the hustle of the lakes, we'd managed to get some quiet days of riding under our belts, but I was still struggling. And something now felt distinctly odd. By this point in the trip, I had developed a well-honed wake-up routine. My eyes would ping open, I'd have some vague recollection of a vivid and bizarre dream (usually involving a castle and a dragon) and I'd immediately swing into action. Reaching behind me, I'd unzip the tent a little and let some fresh air in (and perhaps the odd pasta fart out). I'd then sit upright, unpack the clothes from my makeshift pillow and stuff them into dry bags. Next, I'd remove myself from the sleeping bag, stuff that away in its little sack, let the air out of the sleeping mat (enjoying the ride down to earth as it deflated) and begin to get dressed for a day of riding. It was a routine that I had performed on autopilot every single morning. Usually, it was completed with a little smile, or with not much going through my mind at all. That morning, things were different.

I opened my eyes and stared at the ceiling. I let out a long deep sigh. My limbs felt like lead and seemed reluctant to any kind of motion and, worse than that, there was a fog on my brain. A brain which said: 'Do I have to?' That morning, I was missing home. The sparkle of passing the halfway marker in Santiago had well and truly faded. Plus, I'd had a message from my mum earlier in the week, letting me know that she'd mashed up her knee in a skiing accident. She'd torn a cruciate ligament and chipped a thigh bone and, even though I knew that she'd have already worked out how to bench-press her body weight without hurting the knee, it was at times like these that I just wanted to be at home to deliver a strong daughter hug. Instead, all I could do was send a few short messages. It was also the start of an eventful week for Jamie. He was launching his first book that day, something he'd ploughed his heart and soul into. For a man who is dyslexic, writing 80,000 words had been no easy feat. I was beyond proud of him and wanted to be by his side that day. But, instead, here I was in my tent in a forest, thousands of miles away.

I tried to pin down the dull throb of melancholy so that I could get a closer look at it and, perhaps, understand where it was coming from. I'd recently been reading Lois Pryce's book about motorcycling through Iran and realised that she summed up the feeling perfectly by referencing *Fernweh* and *Heimweh* – two German words which describe the longing for the road and the longing for home. I knew full well that it was part and parcel of any adventure to be caught between the two, and that day I was firmly stuck in the middle.

It wasn't a dramatic, throw myself at the side of the road and burst into tears kind of feeling – it was just a numbness I'd been experiencing for the past few days. Every minute on the bike felt like an hour. I wanted to stop and sit. To stare into space all day and just be, but the world kept turning and I had to keep my wheels turning too. I knew the feeling would pass, or at least I hoped it would.

Over an early breakfast I confessed to Faye that I was feeling a little fuzzy inside. I wanted her to know that my unusually quiet demeanour wasn't anything to do with her. Then I spent the day in quiet reflection, running through the things I had to be grateful for, of which of course there were hundreds. I was actually amazed that I'd made it four months into the trip without having a day like this one. That, in itself, was a triumph and something to be grateful for. Faye understood the feeling well – she'd had her own collisions of *Fernweh* and *Heimweh* over the past few months. As only good friends can, she knew what I needed better than I did. She struck the perfect balance between efforts to cheer me up and just letting me be. Making it to our camp spot that night, I sent the usual 140-character GPS messages to loved ones. I pulled on my new favourite Elmo hat Jamie had given me in Santiago and immediately felt a bit better. I reminded myself that I was a very lucky girl and fell asleep with the assurance that the peaks and troughs of life will always roll on at will. Tomorrow was a new day.

22

Frieda's Dream

Distance cycled: 3,627 miles
Metres ascended: 84,989

It was early morning in the uber-chic ski resort of San Martín de los Andes, when Faye made an important adventure announcement.

'I'm going to wear my non-see-through shorts today,' she said, holding a handful of black Lycra and brandishing a grin that indicated she was feeling very proud of herself. I paused for a moment and wondered whether to be a killjoy.

'Err, Faye-bomb. I hate to break it to you, but all of your shorts are now see-through.'

'Are they?!' she gasped.

'Yes. But each of them to varying degrees so I'm delighted that I get a choice as to precisely which section of your behind I have the opportunity to stare at all day.' I grinned.

Faye's cycling attire – well, the bottom half of it at least – had been in a state of increasing degradation for the past month. It began with the gradual thinning of just one pair and, in my role as chief (and only) friend in South America, I had taken it upon myself a few weeks earlier to confess that I could see 'the Great Divide'. I did think about delivering the news via a rendition of Mark Morrison's lesser-known hit 'Return of the Crack' but, instead, I opted for plain honesty. At one roadside lunch stop, I took a deep breath and said, 'Mate, I can see your arse.'

Faye found the revelation rather embarrassing and apologised profusely for the skin show. I, on the other hand, found it hilarious. And the more embarrassed Faye got, the funnier it became.

Since that day, Faye's two other pairs of black Lycra shorts had followed suit, seemingly taking permission from their now translucent colleague to reveal a rump area of their choosing. One pair of shorts favoured the right cheek. The other had developed a bare patch on either side of the Shepherd Canyon, and the original culprit had gone for a 'take-no-prisoners stripe down the middle of the bum' approach. On the ride into San Martín de los Andes, the shorts situation had gone critical, when Faye's buttocks (presumably after months of Lycra oppression) had finally broken free and created an actual hole in the original pair of offending shorts. That pair was now destined for the bin, but Faye was under the illusion that she still had one decent pair – the pair she was holding as she sat on her bed and made her important adventure announcement.

By 1 p.m. Faye had slipped into her least-tattered pair of shorts and, after exchanging a high-five in the hostel car park, we pedalled out of town. The high-five was to congratu-late ourselves for such an 'early' departure. Over the past few weeks, with the miles being covered more easily and the rid-ing becoming increasingly predictable, we'd become slapdash with the cycling portion of our days. Often, we would aim to leave towns at 10 a.m., but end up rolling out at 4 p.m., arriv-ing at camp around 8 p.m., just as the sun went down. The more comfortable we were in towns, with amenities and coffee shops and food on tap, the harder it was to find the motivation to leave. We had certainly never wanted to just 'hang out' for the day in parts of Bolivia, where the wind savaged our faces and food and water were scarce. They say that comfort kills ambition and it had massacred ours. So, all in all, we took that day's lunchtime getaway as a huge triumph.

Pedalling away from the traffic, restaurants and cafes once again, we wound our way along the shores of Lake Lácar. It was now late February and unseasonably warm, even for that part of the Southern Hemisphere. I looked at my watch and saw that the temperature was 38°C. Although I hadn't enjoyed the heat in the Yungas at the start of our journey, I had learned that Faye really loved the heat, which is unusual for a redhead. As my experience on Christmas Day in Talampaya National Park had reminded me, I was not the heat's biggest fan. I reach optimum heat-appreciation at around 26 degrees. Even better if there's a cool breeze with it. Anything beyond that and I find it all a bit unnecessary. The fact that I hated the heat and Faye loved it likely came down to the amount that each of us sweated. Faye isn't much of a sweater, whereas I could win the

National Sweat Championships. In fact, I could likely enter Miss Sweaty Universe and win that too, although there would be a danger that I might slip right off the winners' podium, on account of the pool of sweat I would have no doubt created at my feet. Excessive heat for me means sweating out all available body salts and having to drink gallons of water, which I must carry on my bike. See? Heat = Unnecessary.

That warm summer day, we rode past the Seven Lakes of Argentina, a region where there are, wait for it... six lakes. I'm kidding, there are seven. Despite the area being very popular with tourists, the traffic on the road was light and, given our glorious early departure from San Martin, we were taking our sweet time to stop at each of the 'miradors' to look out onto the lakes. The second lake, Nahuel Huapi, was enormous and fringed by forest-covered mountains. The afternoon sunshine sparkled across its surface as a warm wind nudged fluffy clouds across the sky. I watched a boat speed over the violet-blue waters, streaking towards the horizon and leaving a trail of white waves in its wake, like a shooting star across a night sky.

By mid-afternoon, the heat made a hasty retreat and the temperature fell dramatically. At first, I thought it unusual that it could go from hot to cool, all in the space of one afternoon, but then I remembered: we were entering Patagonia, an area famous for its rapidly changing and dramatic weather systems. Dark, bulbous clouds had gathered on the now blue-grey horizon and were rolling slowly towards us. I looked back down the valley, towards San Martín, and noted that it was shrouded in grey mist, a sure sign that it was now raining in town.

'Eek. I hope that doesn't head our way' said Faye, pointing across the lake at the ominous cloud-wall of black and grey.

'Nah, we'll be fine,' I said, trying to remain optimistic. After all, it'd been blue skies and sunshine just 30 minutes earlier. I was sure the weather would perk up again quickly.

Twenty minutes later, I began to feel the light pitter-patter of raindrops on my shoulders. The clouds hanging over the mountains up ahead had now turned purple and a fork of lightning shot out from one of them. There was a crackle of thunder overhead.

'Woah! Did you see that?! That was cool,' I shouted over my shoulder at Faye.

'I don't like it!' she yelled back, and then I remembered. Poor Faye-bomb. She's like a household pet when it comes to storms. She would much rather be inside, snuggled up next to the fire than dancing with potential lightning death. I, on the other hand, find them exciting; there's something about a storm and the power of Mother Nature that humbles me. Just then, the wind began to pick up and my heart rate followed suit.

Little raindrops turned into large droplets and the large droplets got bigger still and soon there were heavy globules of water splashing over our bodies and bikes. Seeing as how Faye was in a strappy vest and I was in a T-shirt, we decided to pull over to put our rain jackets on. Of course, the rain jackets were at the bottom of our panniers, so we had to empty out the contents of our bags onto the road to find the jackets. All the while, the wind was growing stronger and the rain was getting harder.

In that moment, the storm saw its chance. It spotted two overly optimistic, scantily clad Englanders, rummaging around in their panniers with their belongings strewn across the grass verge, and it struck, with vengeance. The heavens opened and we were soaked to the skin within a minute. We thanked our lucky stars that we had both just about managed to wriggle into our rain jackets before the hail started. The first few ice bullets made contact with my head and shoulders and they were a shock to the system.

'Ooo! Ouch! Ow!' I yelped, realising that this was no ordinary hail. This was marble-sized, Patagonian hail. Being in that storm felt worse, far worse, than the time I went paintballing with my friends and decided to 'go over the top' and towards the blue team's trench. A block of ice thudded onto the back of my neck, followed by one on my hand, just as a third slammed into my thigh.

'Ow! Ow! Ow!' I yelped again as Faye and I both began dancing like cats on a hot tin roof. I had a feeling that this attack by Mother Nature was just the beginning of the storm so I took off, running along the road as fast as I could, dragging Bernard with me.

'Where are you going?!' Faye yelled.

'To find shelter! To a tree! To… anywhere but here! Come on!!' I shouted.

I spotted a roadside shrine with a corrugated metal roof and headed for it. Faye followed me and we ditched our bikes most unceremoniously at the roadside and took cover inside the shrine. We had been so consumed with finding shelter that we hadn't noticed what was going on across the road. Two cars had pulled over under a line of trees, and we watched a third one stop abruptly behind them, also taking shelter under the roadside branches as the monstrous hailstones smashed into their windscreens.

We stood under the flimsy metal roof of the shrine for 10 minutes, struggling to talk to one another, our words drowned out by the deafening sound of ice colliding with metal just inches above our heads. The hail got harder and grew larger until the road was carpeted in white marbles. Both of us began to shiver. The icy rain had made it through to our base layers and reached our skin.

There was another flash of lightning, swiftly followed by a low rumble of thunder, which sounded as if it was immediately above us.

'Err, Anna!' Faye hollered.

'Yeah?'

'It's right overhead. What are we supposed to do in lightning? Are we safe here? Are we going to get struck?' she asked, and I thought for a moment.

'Well, umm… we're lower than the trees around us… But we are under a metal roof…' I replied.

'I don't think metal roofs are good, are they?' asked Faye.

'I'm not sure… I don't think so… But I read something once about getting low to the ground. Shall we mushroom?'

'Yes!' said Faye, already starting to move into a crouched position. 'Let's mushroom!'

And so, like two, cold, wet, wild fungi, we crouched on our heels. We hugged our knees to our chests and hoped against hope that the lightning wouldn't choose our shrine sanctuary for its passage to earth. Ten more minutes passed and eventually the hail turned back to rain. We both breathed a small sigh of relief and slowly uncoiled from our mushroom positions. We were 12 miles short of our planned mileage for that day but we were beginning to get cold and agreed that we didn't fancy cycling on through the rain.

'We could just call it a day and camp somewhere nearby?' I said to Faye, feeling somewhat guilty for suggesting we cut the day so short.

'Yeah, I think we should,' said Faye.

'Great. Let's find somewhere.'

In that moment we both turned to look at a flat patch of grass, just behind the shrine.

'Here?' Faye said.

'That'll do!' I grinned. It was far from the most glamorous camping spot, right next to the road and on slightly soggy ground, but that night, it was paradise.

***

Over the following few days, the weather was kinder as we pedalled between the lakes of southern Argentina, passing through landscapes that fell part way between the dramatic grey gorges of southern France and a Venezuelan cloud forest. One morning, I watched Faye cycle off down the road ahead of me. She looked so small out there, just a tiny human among the granite giants of nature. The mountains around her were covered in dense forest, a layer of dark green going some way to soften their sharp peaks and ridges. Wisps of cloud gathered around small summits, fusing and then dispersing against a backdrop of satin blue. I was standing astride a yellow painted line on the road, which rolled away from my feet in gentle undulations. From there it looked as if Faye was riding directly into the mountain ahead of us – that perhaps, if this was a fairy tale and she was the heroine, the great curtain of forest on the face of the mountain would part and offer a gateway to another world.

I was amazed that, even though we were now four months into the journey, I was still being surprised by the ever-changing South American landscape. Here, at the edge of Patagonia, the weather continued to change too. Patches of stormy weather blew through and each day we rode in sticky heat that was often swiftly followed by cool rain. We got used to the rhythm of things. The idea that nothing would last forever. If it was sunny when we woke, it wouldn't stay that way for long. There was an unexpected beauty in that. A serenity to be found in accepting whatever the day decided to throw at us, in embracing the impermanence of it all – and in knowing that, if it was tipping with rain one minute, we would likely soon be riding in brilliant sunshine. When the sun shone, we hung our sopping clothes off the back of our bikes to dry and, when it rained, we pulled our rain jackets up around our ears and retreated into our own little worlds. At night, we wild-camped wherever we could, drinking from cool glacial streams and gorging on wild blackberries.

One afternoon, we'd not long left a lunchtime break on an Argentinian lakeshore when we spotted a lone female cycle tourist at the side of the road, standing next to a golden-yellow bike. Cycle touring etiquette dictates that you should always, at the very least, stop for a hello, so we pulled over. The woman looked to be in her early sixties. She was of a strong build, had short grey hair and calves that you could crack walnuts on.

Seeing as we never knew which country other travellers were going to be from, it was always best to start with a greeting in Spanish and go from there. After a couple of Spanglish sentences, I detected a German accent, and the lady must have detected our English accent too.

'Ah! You are English,' she said. I was hurt, of course, that my Spanish was so bad that she could tell so quickly but, now speaking in English, I asked her where she was going.

'Well, I'm going into Chile, but I was thinking I might stop here and hitch a ride. I haven't really got enough food, and there's no shops or anything for a while along this road,' she said, gesturing ahead. We were carrying the bare minimum of supplies for this stretch and I hadn't got any spare food to give her, but I reached into my front handlebar pouches and pulled out two toffees.

'Have some toffee power!' I said, holding them out.

'Oh, thank you!' the woman replied, immediately unwrapping a toffee and beginning to chew on it. 'It's a big mountain to get over, you know,' she added between chews and motioned to the road ahead. I knew, from looking at the map, that she was talking about Paso Cardenal Antonio Samoré, a significant 1,314-metre lump on the horizon, which straddled the border between Argentina and Chile. 'I don't think I can do it,' she continued.

'You know you could do it if you really wanted to,' I said, before trailing off, thinking I shouldn't get all preachy on this woman I hardly knew. 'But at least you're on a good road to get a ride,' I continued, remembering that I'd seen a few big trucks go by in the last hour, each with space enough for a woman and her bike.

'I'm not so sure. I've been here for thirty minutes and seen nothing!' the woman replied.

We chatted for a while longer and learned that our new roadside friend was a teacher on a one-year sabbatical. She explained that she had a husband back home in Germany, and two grown-up kids.

'That's pretty cool that your husband is happy for you to

go off exploring!' said Faye.

'Yes, well, he doesn't like to travel so much, so I say okay, I just go alone.'

As the conversation came to a natural close, we started making a move to leave, at which point the woman began to put her cycling helmet on.

'Well, maybe I will see if I can keep up with you two for a bit, and go a little further along the road?' she said.

So, just shy of the start of Paso Cardenal Antonio Samoré, we welcomed a third member into the McNuff-Shepherd peloton. I began to pull away from the roadside before realising that, if we were going to be cycling with this woman, there was one crucial piece of information missing.

'What's your name?' I called over my shoulder.

'Frieda!' the woman shouted back. And off we went. Freida, Faye and Anna, a trio of spinning gears and whirring tyres, moving through the mountains of southern Argentina.

Frieda had originally said that she would pedal just a few miles with us and then stop to hitch a ride over the pass, but 12 miles further up the road, and now well into the climb, she was still by our side. We were about to cross the border again, so we pulled over at the Argentinian immigration building to get stamped out of the country.

'I'll definitely hitch a ride from here after I get stamped,' Frieda said. And we nodded. 'I surely cannot make it up a 1,300-metre pass,' she continued. And we nodded. There was a long pause, before Freida looked wistfully down the road and said, 'But I would be so proud of myself if I crossed the Andes.'

After getting our passports stamped and leaving the customs building, Faye and I saw our chance to distract Frieda with some chatting. We continued to go through the motions as we talked. Moving back to the bikes, putting away our passports and getting ready to ride off again. Before we knew it, Frieda was on her bike too, not even having mentioned the option of getting a lift from a passing truck. It was a further 25 miles to the Chilean border post, so we rode off into no-man's land, slowing the pace and putting Frieda at the front of the peloton to make sure she didn't get left behind. She huffed and puffed up the climb, a determined look on her face, half-grimace, half-smile, locked in a silent battle with Cardenal Antonio Samoré himself. The road was quiet and no cars had passed us for a while, so Faye and I moved alongside Frieda. The conversation between us naturally petered out as the pass steepened, so we continued the climb in a line of three in silence.

Two and a half hours later, I saw the top of the pass come into view.

'That's it, Frieda, that's the top!'

Frieda looked up from the crossbar of her bike, which she had been staring at for the past hour. There was a look of pain etched across her face.

'No! Is it? That is the top?' she said, looking at Faye for

confirmation.

'Yep,' said Faye, as a broad grin spread across Frieda's face.

'The top! The top of the Andes! I am going to cross the Andes!' she shouted.

At the top of the pass, we pulled into a small car park, next to a sign that read 'Paso Cardenal Antonio Samoré – 1,314 metres altura' and Frieda was elated. She couldn't quite seem to comprehend what had just happened and stood for several minutes, just staring at the sign and the surrounding landscape. We hugged and high-fived and hugged some more, before deciding it was getting late and we should really make it down the mountain before dark. There was a chill in the air and the sun had begun to drop behind the surrounding grey peaks so we pulled on all our layers and descended as fast as we could.

At 8.05 p.m., we rounded the final bend before the border and were greeted with a 10-ft-high metal gate and a sign that read: 'Frontera cerrado'. Bugger! We'd missed it! We could still see people milling around just beyond the gate so we guessed that the border must have been closed at 8 p.m.

There was nothing for it but to set up camp and wait for the border to open in the morning. Frieda opted for a small patch of grass just off the side of the road. Faye ducked down under a canopy of dead wood and bush, into a ditch, and pitched her tent on some kind of bog (complete with frogs), and I did the same in a separate (albeit slightly less boggy) spot just a little further along. Tents up, we reconvened to cook dinner together, deciding to eat right in the middle of the road, because, well, how often do you get to do that? In the fast-fading light, trapped in no-man's land, cooking up a mixture of noodles, rice and sausages, it all felt surreal, like some kind of Mad Hatter's tea party. Over our modest dinner, we reflected on the day and once again congratulated Frieda on her first crossing of the Andean mountains.

'I just didn't think I could do it,' she said, shaking her head and spooning rice into her mouth.

Faye and I looked at one another and smiled, before saying in unison, 'We did.'

23

Crash. Bite. Wallop.

Distance cycled: 3,708 miles
Metres ascended: 85,370

Patagonia is a region famous for savage winds, awe-inspiring glaciers, snow-capped mountains and endless stretches of nothingness. If we were ever in any doubt as to who was in control on our journey through the Andes, ourselves or Mother Nature, Patagonia provided the answer. There, Mother Nature reigned supreme and, worse still, she was restless. We were at the whim of her moods but I couldn't help but be drawn in. As Bruce Chatwin wrote in his memoir In Patagonia, 'Patagonia! She is a hard mistress... An enchantress! She folds you in her arms and never lets you go' – and Faye and I were being held tightly.

It had been three days since we'd crossed into Patagonian Chile and it had rained for most of that time. We'd parted ways with Frieda soon after the border and had become a two-woman team again, heading south under stormy skies towards the gateway to Patagonia proper, the town of Puerto Montt. Cold rain hammered down on us all morning and, by mid-afternoon, I couldn't feel my fingers or my toes. I had resorted to making circular motions with my legs, using my thigh muscles, in the hope that they would somehow be dragging my feet on the pedals behind them. I was also steering and breaking 'by sight', because I could no longer feel whether or not my hands were in contact with the handlebars or brake levers. Still, we were making steady progress south and that was a good thing.

After a few days of camping on small patches of land just off the side of the road, everything we owned was sopping wet. Each morning, we shuddered as we eased on sodden clothes, inch by inch, over our already shivering skin. This was all part of the adventure, I reminded myself. And it was only right that we should be exposed to all the Patagonian elements. If we got to revel in the bright sunshine and blue skies, then we must endure the pouring rain too. A love for Mother Nature is unconditional, after all. And besides, I had recently invested in a bright-pink rain-resistant poncho. I called it my 'Poncho of Power' and every time I pulled it on it cheered me up no end. Despite doing our best to remain chipper, we decided, on the third soggy morning in a row, that it wasn't going to be a fun day to be on bikes. So, instead of taking the scenic route, we opted for the more direct road into town, via the main Puerto Montt highway.

Taking the main highway had some advantages. We had a wide shoulder to ride along the edge of the road, we would make it to town faster and, as an added bonus, we were able to make new friends at every highway toll booth. I enjoyed the first few awkward moments as we arrived at each one: the surprised look on the face of the attendant in his little booth-shack. One attendant had boldly paired a high-vis jack-et with a floral shirt and all of them waved us through without charging us anything, maybe because they hadn't yet worked out the tariff for soggy cyclists. When we pulled away from the final booth, we saw a sign that read 'Puerto Montt 2 km'. We whooped at the prospect of transporting our sodden, shaking bodies to somewhere warm and dry at last. After zooming past the sign, we began a small descent. I was travelling at around 20 mph and was midway through shouting at Faye.

'Not far now, Fay—' when, THUNK! The front end of my bike dropped suddenly. There were two loud cracks as first the front wheel and then the rear wheel disappeared down a pot hole the size (and shape) of Tasmania. My rear tyre emit-ted a loud bang and I felt like I had just collided with a brick wall. I let out a yelp and grasped the handlebars tightly, swerv-ing left and right as the rear of my bike jack-knifed and I tried to remain upright. Then everything seemed to unfold in slow motion…

I pulled hard on the brakes and managed to regain my balance, before hearing a scream from behind me. I looked over my shoulder just in time to see Faye's front wheel buck-le and her body catapulted forwards from her bike. Arms outstretched in a bid to break her fall, she slammed into the concrete. I pulled harder on my brakes to bring my bike to a stop and threw it on the ground. Running a few paces back to Faye, I found her lying in a crumpled heap. I could see that the hoods on her bike bars were bent and she and the bike frame were tangled up as one. She began to move and immediately clutched her right elbow as a look of pain spread across her face.

Gathering Faye up from the ground, I led her to the crash barrier at the side of the road.

'Here… sit here,' I said, easing her onto the metal barrier. Her face was white as a sheet and, immediately, my Girl Guide first-aider brain swung into action. I knew it wouldn't be long before she went into shock. For the next five minutes, Faye kept trying to get up from the barrier and I kept gently sitting her back down. She had hit the ground really hard and I was trying to work out how badly she'd hurt her elbow. I began asking her questions, but anyone who knows Faye also knows that she is permanently concerned about the well-being of others, often above and beyond her own well-being. Therefore, our conversation went as follows.

Me: Faye, are you alright?

Faye: Are you alright?

Me: I'm fine, Faye. Where does it hurt? Are you okay?

Faye: Are you alright?

Me: Yes, yes I'm fine. Is it your elbow?

Faye: You alright?

(Faye tries to get up again.)

Me: Faye. I'm fine. I stayed up. You hurt yourself, you crashed into the ground. Now just sit still will you?!

Faye took a deep breath. 'Sorry,' she said. 'I think I'm in

shock.'

'No shit, Sherlock!' I laughed, relieved that she had now recognised that she was more hurt than I was.

After a joint assessment of Faye's cuts and scrapes and some tentative moving of limbs, we worked out that she was just beat-up and bruised and that nothing was actually broken. Gustavo was pretty mashed up too, but it could have been a whole lot worse. I set about repairing my exploded back tyre as Faye tried to bend her brake hoods back into place and, 15 minutes later, we were on our way again. There was a notable reduction in speed and conversation as we pedalled through the streets of Puerto Montt to our hostel. I felt defeated by the day, and I could tell that Faye felt the same.

Sitting on our beds an hour later, warm and dry once again, and listening to the rattle of rain on the windowsill, I watched as Faye inspected the patchwork of reds and blues that had begun to appear on her right arm as the bruising took hold.

'I think I might need to take a day off the bike tomorrow,' she said, rubbing her arm, and I couldn't have agreed more. In fact, we decided to take not one but a few days off in Puerto Montt. Partly to give Faye some time to recover from her bumps, bruises and scrapes, and partly to wait for a package from the UK. The package contained new pairs of cycling shorts for both of us, and we hoped it would arrive soon. We had 1,600 miles left to ride to Ushuaia and two months to get there and, after some quick schedule calculations, we decided that we could afford a couple of days' rest.

During our stay at the hostel, we grew fond of the owner, Corina. She was a whirlwind of a woman – all smiles, dark hair, and rosy cheeks. Although she was only 5 ft 2 in., she had a personality that made her seem 6 ft tall. Most days, she wore a burgundy-coloured dress with a cream-coloured pinny tied around her waist.

Corina's hostel was more like a home than a hostel. The floors were carpeted in a regal red, the cream wallpaper was fresh out of the 1980s, and each room felt like a journey back in time to my grandparents' house. Corina often had family visiting in the mornings, so Faye and I would sit at the breakfast table, trying to catch scraps of conversation in speedy Spanish. In Patagonia, the Spanish wasn't anything like the language we'd learned in Bolivia. The words were clipped and cut or run together in one breath and spoken very quickly. Corina couldn't help but laugh as we tried to keep up. Every now and then she would pause and ask us, *'¿Entienden?'* (do you understand?), to which I'd pull a face and make a hand gesture that said 'Sort of, but not really.'

'¡Hablamos muy rápido!' Corina would laugh, before continuing the conversation with her family at breakneck speed.

We passed our rest days hanging out at the hostel or sitting in coffee shops – but often apart and in our own company. It's not something we talked about, but it had become a natural development when we were in towns, which we were rolling into more frequently as we travelled south. During the day, we did our own thing. I caught up on emails and wrote blogs and social media posts. In the evenings, we met up for dinner. It was strange to have to ask the other person how her day had been. Dinner was always an early affair and, afterwards, we would return to the hostel and sit in Corina's communal kitchen. From there, we could look out over a small bay on the Gulf of Corcovado, watching the inky fingers of night claw at the amber of dusk until it was pitch black beyond the window and the city lights danced across the water.

On the third morning in Puerto Montt, we began packing up our things to leave. Faye was feeling better and her cuts had healed from the crash. Unfortunately, there was no sign of the long-awaited package from the UK. We'd decided to give up on its arrival and went to bid farewell to our new friend, Corina. She seemed surprised that we were leaving.

'You are going today?!' she asked.

'Sadly, yes. We have to get going,' said Faye.

'But the plane that brings the mail will arrive tomorrow,' Corina replied.

'Will it?!' I gawped. This was news to us and, possibly, something that had gotten lost in translation during the previous days' thrilling and repetitive 'are the packages here yet?' chit-chat.

'Yes, the mail plane comes in on Wednesday each week,' Corina confirmed.

Faye and I looked at one another. After three full days off

the bikes, cabin fever had well and truly set in. Although I had gone running along the lakeshore a couple of times, my body was craving more movement. I was like a caged (cycling) tiger, and I couldn't wait to hit the road again. But in light of the new news about the mail plane's imminent arrival, it seemed foolish to leave. Especially when just one more day of staying put and a shiny new pair of shorts would save Faye's butt from its naked fate.

'Okay,' Faye said to Corina. 'Can we stay one more night, please?' Corina broke into a broad grin. 'Of course! Of course!' she said, and so we went back to 'our' room and began unpacking our bags. I let out a sigh as I sat down on my bed.

'I know it's right to wait for the package, but I just need to warn you that I might go nuts in the meantime,' I said to Faye.

'I know, me too. It feels so weird not to be cycling all day. Actually, we could…' she trailed off at the end of the sentence.

'We could what?' I asked.

'We could go for a little cycle this afternoon?'

'A cycle without our panniers?! You, Faye-bomb, are a maverick! Let's do it!'

There was a whiff of the illegal about heading out the door for a two-hour ride on completely unloaded touring bikes. It had started to rain again but that didn't bother us in the slightest. The feeling of blood pumping through our veins and fresh air filling our lungs was enough to spur us on. We rode along the lakeshore, passing quaint towns and fishing boats bobbing out in the bay. After 30 minutes, we arrived at a particularly industrial-looking section. There must have been some kind of fish factory nearby, because the smell of 'the sea' was so overwhelming that it seemed like someone had shoved a fish up each nostril. The salty air made me gag, but the views across the glassy water and onto the surrounding green mountains were a wonderful distraction.

After an hour of pedalling away from the hostel, we turned around and began the journey back to Puerto Montt. We were gliding down a small hill when I spotted a sandy-coloured dog on our side of the road. There were three large trucks coming up the hill in slow procession and the dog was going crazy at them. I'm talking totally lost it, gone full-blown Imma-gonna-bite-your-wheels-off crazy. It was barking and snarling at the passing trucks, chasing them and narrowly avoiding being run over. Of course, a dog going nuts at the side of a road is not an unusual sight in South America. Over the course of four and a half months, we'd been chased by hundreds of dogs. Some had tried to bite our tyres, others ran alongside us for a mile or so, and a few would lunge straight for our ankles. It scared me from time to time but, for the most part, we were able to get the dogs to back down using one of a few different strategies we'd developed. Sometimes we'd squirt water at them. Other times we'd try to out-pedal them. But by far the favoured strategy, especially if there was just one dog, was to stand astride the bike and shout at the dog as loudly as possible. To go alpha on it and let it know that you could be damn scary too. Rather than chasing you, the dog would usually back down and you could be on your merry way.

Faye had just run the snarling-pooch gauntlet with this particular canine and it was my turn next. It was still going bananas as I approached and had moved right into my path. I pulled to a halt and shouted at the dog, just as I had done dozens of times before. The dog stopped dead in its tracks, looked confused for a moment, then retreated a few steps, beginning to move out of my way. I was so fixated on the dog in front of me that I didn't spot a second one bounding from the house on my right. Out of the corner of my eye, I caught sight of a light-brown shape on the move. I spun my head to see a stocky mid-sized Staffie, with a square jaw and eyes filled with rage. Before I had a chance to think, the second dog lunged at my right leg, clamped its jaws around the front of my shin and bit down, hard. It felt as if my shin bone had been put in a vice. A wave of excruciating pain surged up my leg. In a flash, the dog released me, before retreating a few steps but continuing to bark and snarl. I stood stock-still in the middle of the road, in complete shock and unable to compute what had just happened.

Fighting off nausea, I looked down at my leg. I wanted to see if the dog's bite had broken the skin, but I was surprised to find that there wasn't any blood. Instead, there were just four white puncture marks where the dog's canine teeth had gone in. But, as I looked again, I noticed one of the teeth had gone deeper than I'd originally realised. The hole it had made then filled with blood, before a flow of warm viscous red liquid started to trickle down my leg. I brought myself 'to' and wondered what the hell I was doing, still standing opposite the damn barking dog, so I began to hobble down the road towards Faye. Thankfully, neither dog seemed interested in following me; they stayed where they were, barking in front of the house.

Once I was a few steps further down the road, out came the tears. I am always amazed, in such situations, how we are reduced to our most basic human selves. How evolution takes over and we have seemingly no control over our behaviour. I certainly had no control over mine as salty tears began tumbling down my cheeks and my chest started to shake. The pain in my shin was unbearable and I couldn't get over how powerful the dog's jaws were. But, above all else, I was in shock.

Faye rushed back up the road and asked if I was alright. I began babbling at her, repeating the same things over and over again in between sobs. 'I didn't see it. I didn't see it… I just didn't see it,' I said. And all the while, I was trying to get back on my bike. I just wanted to get out of there. Away from the barking dogs and away from the pain. I felt like a complete idiot for not seeing it coming, and on top of all that, I was beginning to think about the dreaded R word: rabies.

24

The R Word

Distance cycled: 3,828 miles
Metres ascended: 86,865

There aren't many things I take seriously in life but potentially fatal diseases are one of them. Luckily, I had had pre-exposure rabies injections before I left the UK. The jabs don't prevent you from getting rabies, but they will slow the spread of the virus so that you have longer to make it to a hospital. Unluckily, and in some kind of sick fascination with one of our few modern incurable diseases, I had recently read a whole book about the history and mythology of rabies. I had learned how it is unlike any other virus; how it makes its way into your nervous system and travels undetected for anything between a week and a year, up the spinal cord until it reaches your brain. By the time the symptoms appear, it's too late. All cases of rabies symptoms being reported in humans have ended in death.

'We need to get you to a hospital and get you some jabs,' said Faye, and I knew she was right. I nodded and wiped the tears from my cheeks. I knew that it was important to wash the wound with water as soon as possible (although not to rub it), so we poured water from our bottles over the four places where the dog's teeth had broken the skin, giving the most attention to the deepest wound.

As we started the pedal back to town, the rational and irrational parts of my brain collided and did battle. It was likely that everything would be fine and that the chances of that particular dog carrying rabies were slim, but there are few things scarier in this world than not being 100% sure that you're not going to die of rabies. And I was anything but sure.

Back at the hostel, a concerned Corina directed us to a local clinic, just down the road. There, we were bussed from pillar to post, grappling with our limited Spanish to work out who I needed to see and where I needed to be. The medical centre looked run-down; many of the walls were a murky yellowish-cream and the furniture dark brown. It had a whiff of the 70s about it, but then again, I supposed I couldn't expect small medical centres in Chile to look just like they do back home.

I was grateful not to be alone in the waiting room, and Faye had to be one of the best people to have there with me. In times of crisis, she is cool, calm and collected. And at least, this time, she could ask me repeatedly if I was alright and it was a valid question. Faye struck a much-needed balance between discussing the practicalities of getting treatment and making jokes about our luxurious surroundings, which brought a smile to my tear-stained face.

After a 20-minute wait, I was seen by a nurse. Unfortunately, she didn't seem overly concerned about what had happened. She was nice enough, but she might as well have slapped an Action Man plaster on the wounds and given me a lollipop, such was the level of care. I wasn't satisfied and so, after doing battle about me not having the right 'papers', I managed to get seen by a doctor. I hoped that the doc would at least entertain a discussion about getting a post-rabies jab. The doctor spoke good English, which made everything easier, and all in all he seemed like a nice man. I put him in his mid 20s. He was clean-shaven, with a friendly smile and a flop of brown hair – he wouldn't have looked out of place in a boy band.

'Do not worry,' he said, smiling at me and Faye. 'Rabies is a real public health issue here in Chile. We are very aware of the procedures.'

Phew, I thought. This man knows what he's doing. What a relief. After some initial reassurance, the young doctor then introduced another, older man who had appeared. He was dressed in non-medical clothing, a green sweater and a pair of jeans, and seemed to be advising the younger doctor, speaking in rapid Spanish. I couldn't work out what was being said, but his attitude was dismissive and I didn't much like his tone. He was all tuts and hand gestures with some shoulder-shrugging thrown in for good measure. If I'd been asked to sum up what was being said through his body language, I would have boiled it down to, 'Foolish British women, what are they worried about?'

After listening to the man in the corner for a minute or so, the doctor turned his attention back to me and Faye.

'If you have had a vaccination in the UK, this is okay. You cannot get rabies here in Chile. You have the antibodies to fight it,' he said.

Well, that sounded wrong to me, not to mention at odds with what both Faye and I had read online during the 40 minutes of waiting outside his office. But perhaps things had changed recently. Perhaps the young doctor and his jeans-clad advisor were at the forefront of medical expertise. My default position in life is always to trust people and to trust in their knowledge, so I remained open-minded as the doctor continued to speak.

'And besides… we have not had a case of canine rabies in Chile since 1970. It is now only bats that carry rabies here.'

Okay, I thought. Now that does sound like some local knowledge I could go with, and I felt somewhat reassured. The doctor seemed eager to please and eager to give me something to take away, so he moved over to a cabinet in the corner of the room and rummaged inside it.

'To be safe, I am going to give you some antibiotics,' he said, handing over a cardboard box of pills. I turned the box over in my hands and began to read the label.

'Do not be concerned that they say 'clinical trial' on the packet.' He smiled 'These are good drugs. Except they may give you diarrhoea. Do not worry about that either.'

That night, while icing my swollen and throbbing leg, I couldn't bring myself to touch the antibiotics, and I was even less encouraged when I discovered that each pill was the size of my head. More than that, I couldn't shake a feeling in my gut. Something didn't add up. The more I read, the more I began to doubt the Chilean doctor's knowledge. Reading online that evening, I discovered that there had in fact been three confirmed cases of humans dying of rabies in the past six years in Chile. One of them was a case earlier that year in Valparaíso, not far from Santiago, where Jamie and I spent some time. A young woman had been bitten by two dogs from a pack of strays and she had gone on to contract rabies. It wasn't the specifics of the deaths that concerned me so much, but more that the doctor didn't know about the cases. If he didn't know about the cases, then what else didn't he know? Alarm bells started ringing in my head.

I called Jamie back home to talk things through but I still felt uneasy as I crawled into bed, and I had a fitful night's sleep wondering whether I was merrily lying around while the rabies virus crept up my spinal cord toward my brain. The following morning, the feeling in my gut was still there so I decided that I should get a second opinion, just in case. After packing up a small bag, I was all set to hobble the 2 miles to the main city hospital.

'Do you want me to come with you?' Faye asked.

'Nah, don't worry. There's no point in two of us hanging around at the hospital. I'll be fine,' I replied.

'Okay, well, just message me if you need anything… promise?' said Faye.

'Okay, Dr Faye-bomb, I promise.'

The moment I clapped eyes on the hospital building, I heaved a sigh of relief. In contrast to the cedar-panel walls and 70s decor of the downtown medical centre, this was the Shangri-La of hospitals – a large modern facility, all bright jade greens and sparkly whites. Thanks to some clear and helpful signage, knowing where to go and whom to ask for was far easier, too, and I was soon seen by a lovely female Colombian surgeon called Dr. Moreno. I decided not to tell Dr. Moreno that she was my second opinion so I simply relayed the events of the previous day to her as if for the first time. Even though she spoke great English, I wanted to try my best to explain what had happened in Spanish.

'Un cerro me mordió' I said confidently.

'¿Un cerro le mordió a usted?' she smiled.

'¡Sí… sí… oh! No, I mean *un perro!* A dog,' I said, putting my head in my hands at the fact that I'd just informed her that I was bitten by a hill. Cerro… perro… it's an easy mistake to make. I've never been great with details.

In a bid to prevent the consultation from lasting all day and me mistakenly announcing that I had been bitten by any other natural landmarks, we switched to English from that point on. Dr. Moreno began to ask questions about the dog itself, where I was bitten, what it looked like, if it was near a domestic home, and so on. These were all pieces of information that would help establish whether the dog was rabid or not and were questions that the doctor at the medical centre should have asked.

'Okay. You must have the post-exposure rabies injections now,' she said, and I felt another wave of relief.

'Yes! Great, thank you,' I replied.

After calling an infectiologist for additional advice (because she was thorough like that), Dr. Moreno prescribed two post-vaccine injections for that day and said that I would need to find another hospital in Chile to have a follow-up injection in a month's time. She also prescribed a short dose of antibiotics, which I was delighted to see were in non-clinical-trial packaging. As an added bonus, she reassured me that the antibiotics wouldn't make me poop my guts out.

On the hobble home from the hospital, I relaxed at last. The events of the past 24 hours had made me even more grateful for the NHS in the UK. I appreciated how easy it was to get treatment back home and the luxury of being able to trust the advice given. I dropped a message to Faye to update her.

'On my way home, mate. I'm drugged up and good to go.'

'Phew! What a relief. Let's get out of here before anything else tries to take a bite out of you.'

'Agreed. Although I am pretty darn tasty.'

'Better than the finest pedigree chum.'

'You know it. See you in 30 mins.'

That afternoon we packed up for a second time and finally

left the hostel. The package with our shorts still hadn't arrived but we were both beyond caring. Staring at Faye's semi-naked bum was preferable to sitting it out any longer and, having been stationary for four days, we were eager to start our journey deeper into Patagonia. As I tentatively turned the pedals and we cycled away from town, I thought back over the events of the week. A week that had begun with Faye crashing in torrential rain and had ended with me being bitten by a potentially rabid dog. Adventures: never a dull moment.

Puerto Montt to Ushuaia

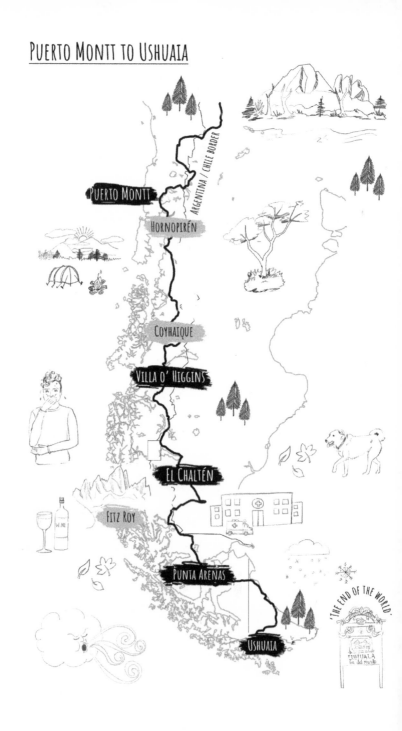

ARGENTINA / CHILE BORDER

Puerto Montt

Hornopirén

Coyhaique

Villa o' Higgins

El Chaltén

Fitz Roy

Punta Arenas

Ushuaia

"THE END OF THE WORLD"

25

The Wall Between Us

Distance cycled: 3,842 miles
Metres ascended: 87,042

Carretera Austral. These were two words neither Faye nor I had heard until we began cycling in South America. But everywhere we went, and from every cycle tourist we met who learned of our route south, the question was the same: 'So you're going to do the Carretera Austral, right?' Many people would take a trip of between one month and six weeks to cycle the Carretera. Just like the Camino de Santiago, the Pacific Crest Trail and other well-known routes around the world, it was 'a thing' on the bucket list of many adventure travellers. Especially those who liked to travel by bike.

We soon learned that the Carretera Austral, which means 'the southern way', is a 770-mile-long road that starts at Puerto Montt and ends at the tiny town of Villa O'Higgins, joining the Chilean Lake District with the heart of rural Patagonia. Part of the appeal of the Carretera is that much of it is only accessible by taking a ferry. In fact, if you choose to do the entire Carretera from end to end, you'll take three ferries, dancing between lakes and along small inlets of Pacific Ocean. The Carretera is rumoured to be one of the most beautiful roads in the world and, in the words of Lonely Planet, will lead you into 'a land of dense forests, snow-tipped mountains,

339

glacial streams, islands and swift-flowing rivers.' Ooh la la. How could we possibly resist all that?

After all the drama around Puerto Montt, we decided to take a conservative approach to the start of the Carretera. I still had antibiotics pumping through my veins and Faye was nervous about another crash in the wet conditions, so we opted to take it steady for the first few days. The wound in my leg caused me grief from time to time. It was still swollen and bouncing around on the gravel roads south of Puerto Montt was painful. I decided to take my mind off my leg by focusing on the scenery and noticed that the landscape had begun to fit neatly into three colours. Grey roads. Green mountains. Blue skies. (Although sometimes the skies were grey too.)

It rained for much of the first few days on the Carretera, which was frustrating at first, but I soon began to feel thankful for all that rain. It could only look so lush and green in Patagonia because of the continued watering from the sky, after all. I was grateful that the land around us was getting a good dousing as we passed through, so that it might look just as lush for those who followed us in the weeks to come.

In between icy deluges, and when we could see beyond the ends of our noses, we glimpsed giant glaciers nestled amid the surrounding mountains – rock and ice side by side beneath a sky of thunderous cloud. Even though the glaciers were way off the road and up in the mountains, we could see them clear as day, a mix of blue and white, inching their way down the mountainside, just like I'd seen on National Geographic.

The rain would clear up most evenings around sunset. Faye and I would shove our bikes off the road to a sneaky camp spot in a forest or on the shores of a lake. We would cook up dinner while watching the sun snuggle into the mountains on the horizon, tucking itself up for the night and leaving behind wisps of purple and tangerine. Those evenings seemed to stretch for hours and there was always a sense of timelessness to them, a feeling that the sunset might exist just as long as we wanted it to. At those dusky dinners, with bellies full of cut-up cold hot dogs and warm buttery instant mashed potato, Patagonia felt like a very special place to be.

As our journey along the Carretera continued, we began to meet more and more cycle tourists. One afternoon, we met two guys from Sheffield, one of whom was a real character. He looked like he'd just been picked up from the streets of East London and plonked down on a road in South America. His bike was similar to those that London couriers might ride, with skinny tyres and straight handlebars. His outfit was a fully branded cycling kit paired with smart gentlemen's cycling shoes and a thin-peaked cycling cap, which he wore with the peak turned upward so that I could see the words on its underside that read: 'My ride. My rules.' We had a short exchange about a shared love of dulce de leche (an Argentinian delicacy of caramelised, condensed milk) and spoke about life back home in the UK. We also touched on the amount of roadwork going on along the Carretera, something I'd noticed over the past few days. The boys said that the Chilean government was looking to turn all the rubble roads to tarmac eventually, and

I couldn't help but feel that it would be a shame if this once peaceful part of Patagonia became as busy as the Chilean Lake District. When the conversation with the lads turned to dyno hubs, gearing ratios and tyre choice, Faye and I decided to make a swift departure because neither one of us cared much for the finer details of our bikes – they had wheels and names and that's all that mattered to us.

Another morning, we chatted briefly with a Chilean student who was taking a month's break to cycle the Carretera. He was like an excitable puppy, all dark curly hair, stubble and wild gestures, telling us how it had been his dream for many years to cycle the Carretera and here he was, finally. Such was the power of his energetic gesturing that I cycled away feeling excited for him.

It was while waiting at one of the ferry ports along the route that we met our favourite couple of the journey so far – Meg and Gordon, two friends who were cycling the length of South America. Meg was Canadian and Gordon was a Scot – nationalities that predisposed them to being good eggs. Our conversation flowed easily and I loved their laid-back vibes and the injection of good old-fashioned sarcastic humour. Faye and I were travelling at a similar speed to theirs so we crossed paths with Meg and Gordon every now and then, leapfrogging one another on our continued journey south.

We were 150 miles and two ferries along the Carretera when we met the German couple Anja and Radko on the roadside just outside the Chilean village of Chaitén. Anja had wisps of blonde hair escaping from her cycling helmet, bright eyes and an even brighter smile. She had a warm, friendly air about her and immediately began putting us to shame with her near perfect English. Radko had opted for a more traditional unshaven 'adventure look' and was sporting a well-worn, and no doubt much-loved, bright yellow long-sleeve top with three black stripes down the arm and a small black eagle on his chest.

The four of us sat around chatting for a good 10 minutes and we soon learned that they were on a round-the-world bike trip. Like us, the Carretera was just a small portion of their overall journey, although their trip would take them at least two years. We got along well, connecting over a shared love of the outdoors and decent food, and all of us confessed to being marginally jaded by the Patagonian rain.

'Do you mind if we cycle with you... for a little bit?' said Anja.

I looked at Faye. Did we? I mean, it would be very awkward to refuse. It was always nice for Faye and me to have the chance to talk to other people and we eagerly embraced any departure from our usual, often staid, conversation. (There are only so many times you can ask one another how well you slept and how your morning poo was, after all.)

We decided to spend the rest of the afternoon cycling with our new German friends. As an awesome foursome, we cruised along the tarmac, riding in pairs past lush green surrounds. The afternoon began to unfold like an on-the-move version of cycling speed-dating: Faye and I would switch between Anja and Radko every 30 minutes or so, taking it in turns to get to know each of them better. On my second stint of riding with Anja, I asked her how she and Radko came to be cycling around the world with one another. She paused before taking a deep breath and I could tell that there was a good story coming.

After six years of medical school and a further seven years of training to be a surgeon, Anja decided that she wanted a change of pace. And what greater way to change the pace of your life than a round-the-world cycle tour? The only problem in Anja's plan was that she didn't fancy pedalling around the world alone, so she put up a post on a German bicycle-touring forum, with an invitation for someone else to join her.

'I received a lot of responses,' Anja said. 'Most of them were from men, and some of them seemed to be a good fit but, when I suggested to each of them that we do a test ride together, to see how we got along, they were never able to make it. They couldn't get the time off work or their schedule didn't match mine. And so a lot of time went by. I still wanted to do this trip very badly but I had no one to accompany me, so then I begin to think, okay, I just go alone.'

Four months passed and, as Anja prepared to head off on her world cycle alone, she logged back into the forum one last time. There she spotted an email from a man called Radko and a message she'd missed the first time around.

'So, I messaged Radko and I said, 'I know that a long time

has passed, but would you still want to join me?' And he replied with a yes! But he said his plans had changed and that he was going to start cycling the Iron Curtain Trail across Europe in a few days. He gave me his number so we had a talk on the phone and I asked if I could come and ride with him in Norway for three weeks, just to see how we got along.'

'So, you travelled to Norway to meet up with a man you'd never met, and to spend three weeks cycling with him?!' I asked, in slight disbelief.

'Yes!' Anja replied, laughing. 'I know it may seem crazy but, to me, it was a very logical step.'

I liked Anja's style. This outwardly 'sensible' surgeon had an inner gung-ho attitude I could really get on board with. At that point in the story, we hit a hill and slowed our pace as she continued to tell the tale between puffs and pants.

'Me and Radko cycled together for three weeks, and it worked really well. I mean, well… we fell in love.'

The hill flattened out and we were on a plateau. Anja got her breath back and sped up her words to match the speed of the pedals: 'And then Radko moved to Berlin for six months to live with me so that we could plan the round-the-world trip, and, well, here we are!'

I sat up from my handlebars and took a moment to process it all. I was head over heels for Anja's story. It had all the makings of a Hollywood movie: boy meets girl, a sliding-doors moment of a potentially missed email, a 'Sleepless in Seattle' style meetup with a stranger whose voice you've only heard on the phone. But there was one crucial piece of information I was missing. I wondered how to put it delicately.

'So, at what point did you think you might fancy the pants off Radko?!' I asked and, for the first time since we'd met, Anja turned shy.

'Well… I had a feeling on the phone when we first spoke. He was different to anyone I'd met before. We just got along so well. It was so easy.'

'And then once you were out there, in Norway?' I pressed on with my questioning.

'Oh, it didn't take very long!' she replied coyly.

'How long? Anja! I want to know when you SMOOCHED!' I yelled. I was now in full-on love-detective mode and I was not giving up on the case.

'Okay, okay! I would say that was ten days in…'

'Yayyyyy!!' I screeched, throwing one arm into the air in triumph. Oh, how I loved to hear of people's first kisses and to watch their faces as they returned to that moment in their mind. It's always such a pure moment. A wistful look crept across Anja's face.

'And that was it. He's the one for me,' she tailed off softly.

We rode for a few more miles with the Deutschlanders before leaving them at the foot of a 700-metre climb. They were tired and decided that they'd had enough cycling for one day.

They packed us off with some 'spare' chocolate (who ever has spare chocolate?!), we exchanged details, hugged and parted ways.

That night, settled in our own camp spot some way up the road, I snuggled deep into my sleeping bag with my favourite Elmo hat on my head and thought about Anja and Radko. A world away from their true home but making a home together in a tent at a new location every night. It was all kinds of romantic, and that made me all kinds of happy as I drifted off to sleep.

***

As the days rolled by on the Carretera Austral, the joy I'd taken from Anja and Radko's love story began to fade and our energy levels followed suit. A tell-tale sign was that Faye and I began to talk less. It wasn't that we'd fallen out, it just seemed that we didn't laugh as much as we had done in recent weeks. I wasn't surprised. There was a familiar sense of being jaded by the journey, as a whole, creeping in. My jadedness had started the day we had to wait overnight to get on the ferry at Puerto Fuy and it continued to wash over me in waves. Now I wondered if Faye had begun to feel the same way. The last thing I wanted to do was put any thoughts in her head about feeling travel-weary, so I opted not to say anything at all, but she did seem unusually quiet.

The dip in our energy levels also coincided with seeing even more cycle tourists on our route. We'd see 20 or so in a day, which might not sound like a lot but, in contrast to crossing paths with an average of zero, it took some adjustment. It felt selfish and spoiled even to think it, but I liked it better when it was just Faye and me out there on the road. And, of course, having lots of people to chat to should be a great thing, but the constant stopping for small talk meant that I found it hard to let my thoughts drift as they had done earlier on in the trip. I felt a need to present myself as a smiley, decent human in those brief exchanges with strangers, when, in reality, I didn't have the energy to chat at all. One night over dinner, I decided to open up the conversation with Faye about whether she had been enjoying the riding over the past week.

'So... what do you think of the Carretera then?' I said, spooning another pile of steaming mashed potato into my mouth. She paused for a moment and I could tell that she was thinking carefully about the words that were about to leave her mouth.

'It's beautiful...' she started.

'Yes, it is,' I agreed.

'But there's a lot of people... other cyclists, I mean. And I'm not sure if I like that,' she continued, a look of nervousness on her face as if she'd just committed blasphemy.

'Me too,' I said, smiling, and Faye let out a sigh of relief.

'Oh, phew! I thought it was just me.'

'No, it's not like Bolivia is it?' I said, and Faye shook her head. 'And another thing... are you finding it all a little...' I paused as I looked for the right word and wondered how to say it without seeming arrogant.

'A little...?' Faye pressed.

'Easy?' I said.

'Yes! Oh my gosh, yes!'

'I miss the big mountains,' I said.

'Me too. I know we hated how hard it was up in the north, but now I miss it. Does that make me mental?' Faye asked.

'Yes, it does. But then I'm mental too. I want to be back in the middle of nowhere, going up one mountain for two days straight.'

'Yes! Me too!'

'You know what I think we need?'

'What?' asked Faye.

'To add a little challenge back into things.'

'You're right. I feel like we're just going to make it to Ushuaia and that's that. I know I can do it now... Cycling sixty, seventy miles in a day isn't a problem. I can't believe I've just said that!' Faye yelped, clasping her hand over her mouth, horrified at herself.

I laughed because it was true, and hark at Faye, Miss Big Bananas, feeling like she's got it easy because she's only got a few 800-metre mountains to pedal up and 70 miles to cycle in a day. We chatted more over dinner, basking in the shared relief of having actually said what we'd both been thinking for the past week. Over a dessert of half a chocolate bar each, we agreed that one way to inject some excitement into the riding would be to get off the bikes and to take some hikes in the mountains. Lots of the cyclists whom we met along the Carretera were doing just that. Patagonia is famous for its mountain trails, not for its roads, after all. But with a flight booked out of Ushuaia in six weeks' time, and our bank balances beginning to look discouragingly unhealthy, going hiking just wasn't an option.

We concluded that our time on the Carretera was shaping up like a mismatched date: on paper, everything seems ideal; the person sitting opposite you ticks all the right boxes. He or she is good-looking, smart and funny, only... two drinks in and you realise there's just no chemistry. And, BY GOD, you need chemistry. Or perhaps your date has just appeared at the wrong time in your life. You're in different places, going different directions. Try as you might to find ways to embrace their apparent perfection – to tell yourself that they are everything you have ever dreamed of – they just don't float your boat. You can't quite put your finger on it. It's not them, it's you. For Faye and me, and at that point in our journey through South America, too many people, too many expensive tourist towns and too much ongoing road-construction meant that we just weren't as enamoured of this part of Patagonia as we should have been. It felt wrong but we couldn't fight it.

With our shared dirty secret out in the open, something in the cosmic cycling universe shifted. The Carretera was what it was; there was nothing we could do to change it. I actually took comfort from knowing that both of us were disappointed, and not just me. The fact that we enjoyed a similar style of travel is likely what had made the trip such a success to that point. We were both happiest when it felt like we had nature to ourselves. Greedy as that sounded, it was true. So we made a resolution to continue to wild camp as much as possible. If we could carve out a pocket of solitude each evening, then that would help to keep the sense of adventure alive.

With that agreement in place, I began to appreciate Patagonia more than I had done earlier that week. Each day, when early evening rolled around and the valleys became our own once more, we enjoyed a different beautiful wild-camp spot. We spent one night pitched in a quiet forest next to Río Baker, the bluest glacial river I had ever seen. It was a deep turquoise and thundering past next to our camp spot. I didn't dare venture more than a foot into the water, such was its speed, but I put enough of my foot in to know that it was absolutely blinkin' freezing! Instead, I just sat on the bank and looked at it in awe – a mass of glacial meltwater, surging through the forest and into the valley beyond.

Gazing out on that river, onto a dozen different shades of blue and green that I had no name for, I realised that things felt different. Since the fireside Carretera confessional, we'd stopped fixating on the elements of the journey that didn't bring us joy and begun to look for the parts that did. Which, of course, were there all along, hiding in the shadows of our disappointment. All we needed to do was keep those shadows at bay until we reached Ushuaia.

***

After the Puerto Montt pooch's attempt to turn my leg into a can of Pedigree Chum, my relationship with the four-legged friends of this earth had become somewhat fragile. The almost-healed hole in my leg had become like Harry Potter's forehead scar. Each time we passed a dog and it (inevitably) began to chase us, the hole tingled with a searing pain, as if the dog version of Voldemort was just around the corner. Still, I did my best to override this sensation using my (naturally highly evolved) front brain, which reminded me that 99.9% of dogs in the world were adorable, loveable things.

Despite having to manage a mild fear of being bitten again, I was patient and loving with many of the stray dogs we met as we continued our journey south. My heart melted especially when we met an elderly black and white mutt by the roadside on the way out of one town. I was understandably nervous as he bounded over to the bikes, tongue out and tail wagging, but it soon became apparent that his only weapon was slobber. He didn't introduce himself, so we decided to name him Alf. Alf clearly had no intention of causing grievous bodily harm so we took a few minutes to pet him. This was our first mistake. As Alf flopped gleefully onto his back, enjoying tummy rubs and behind-ear scratches, an invisible bond was formed.

Alf followed us for five miles that day. He had a limp, the most endearing black, furry face, and a gormless expression.

We fed him lemon wafers as a final treat before doing our best to outrun him on the bikes so that he would return home. Well, I say that 'we' tried to outrun him – when it came to meeting dogs, Faye was the good cop and I was the bad cop, so I initiated the plan to lose Alf. But I genuinely believed the best thing for him was not to run after cycle tourists on a busy road and I was happy when he finally gave up the chase. We met a few more dogs in the days that followed, none of them as friendly as Alf, yet all just as harmless.

After leaving the town of Coyhaique, now 4,500 miles through our overall journey and halfway through the Carretera Austral, we found that our travel fatigue had tipped up a notch. The smallest things were beginning to irritate me and, as had been the case for the past week, I felt like we were simply trying to 'get things done'. That is, wake up, cycle, and move from one hostel or camp spot to the next. We were both knackered and, after our shared dinnertime confession earlier in the week, we weren't chatting much during the day. Instead, we cycled along by ourselves, absorbed in our own worlds, battling our individual demons of exhaustion. We had moved on from solving our mental struggles together and now were firmly settled into dealing with them apart.

As we passed an especially beautiful spot, overlooking a flat plain between two mountains, we pulled into a lay-by to take in the view. As we did, a small, brown dog, not much older than a puppy, bounded towards us out of nowhere. Faye, the dog lover that she is, gave him a cuddle and a pet. The mere thought of this dog following us for a few miles and slowing our progress felt like a lead weight to me.

'You know, if you pet him, he's just going to follow us,' I said, not thinking before the words left my mouth. In my defence, I was tired, and the last thing I wanted was to be dealing with another dog that day. We set off and sure enough, the dog started to run behind us. Faye was up front and I was tucked in behind her.

'He's following us!' I shouted.

'Oh, no!' she replied.

'If we speed up, we can probably outrun him!' I yelled as I sped up and moved onto Faye's back wheel.

Faye didn't say anything more for a while, but I noticed that she had started to look back as we rode along, while at the same time paying attention to the light traffic, most of which was mining trucks.

'I just don't want him to get hit by a truck or anything!' Faye yelled back.

In my mind the best thing for the dog was for us to lose him so that he wouldn't be running in the road, and then we wouldn't have to deal with the worry of him following us. Faye, being the kind-hearted human bean that she is, thought that the best thing for the dog was to keep an eye on him. Of course, neither of us communicated that at the time so I simply kept trying to speed up and Faye kept slowing down. I tucked in close to Faye's wheel, trying to get her to cycle faster, as the dog running around my heels and barking was making me nervous.

'You keep slowing down!' I shouted to Faye over the wind. 'We're not going to lose him if you keep slowing down!'

'Well, I don't want him to get hit!' she yelled.

'He's going to get hit if he keeps following us!' I shouted back.

'If you want to go faster, then you go up front!' said Faye, pulling over to one side and slowing down.

'Fine! I will!' I said, passing her and speeding off to the front.

Faye stayed further back for 10 minutes. I kept looking round and eventually noticed that the dog had disappeared. I slowed my pace to drop back to where Faye was, but I soon noticed that she had slowed hers too. Thirty minutes later, we were still riding apart.

It was nearing 6 p.m. now and high time to find a camp spot for the night, so I pulled over to the side of the road and waited for Faye to reach me.

'I think it's about time to start looking for a camp spot. That okay?' I said, looking at her and checking to see if she was still annoyed or if our little squabble was already forgotten.

'Yep, fine,' said Faye, not looking at me. We had a few more equally short exchanges and agreed on a camp spot, just off the side of the road, down a small hill and hidden from view.

We pulled over in silence and began unpacking our bikes and bags.

'Faye, are you okay?' I asked, leaving my tent and walking over to hers as she was putting the pegs into the ground.

'Yes, I'm fine,' she said, continuing what she was doing.

'Well, you're obviously not fine,' I said. 'So let's talk about it,' I added, and there was a tone of pleading to my voice. I really hated falling out with Faye, and over something so stupid too.

The next few minutes were a tornado of words. We continued the disagreement standing on opposite sides of Faye's tent and, at one point, I remember pausing and thinking that something about us being on opposite sides of the tent wasn't helping the situation. So, I moved over to Faye's side. She stopped what she was doing as we stood looking at one another and there was a long pause.

'Well, I'm sorry,' I said. 'I didn't mean to try to tell you what to do. I was just trying to get away from the dog. I suppose that's the difference – you have more of an affinity for dogs than I do.'

'Okay. I get it,' she said. 'I'm sorry that I got angry. Thanks for bringing it up.'

'Are we alright?' I asked.

'Yeah, we're okay,' she replied.

'Good,' I said, moving in for a hug. Faye hugged me back but it wasn't as tight as her usual squeeze. I'm not sure mine was either. It was a half-hug on both sides.

I went back to my tent to carry on blowing up my sleeping mat and felt a lump well in my throat. I crawled inside the tent so that Faye couldn't see me and I started to cry. Big blobs of tears dropped onto my mat as I tried to blow it up. I didn't want to fight with Faye – she was my rock on this journey, like a sister to me, and I hated falling out with her, especially over something so ridiculous. Right then, I didn't want to be there. I just wanted to be home, I wanted to be with my family, with Jamie. I wanted to be able to call someone and talk to them about what had just happened, but I couldn't.

I was sick of it. Of having no escape from tense situations. I just wanted to be in a normal environment where I wasn't so tired and wasn't fighting about things like a dog chasing us on a bike ride. I felt so alone. So I carried on sobbing as quietly as I could and ate dinner alone in the porch of my tent. It wasn't until some months later that I found out that, just across the way, separated from me by the walls of her own tent, Faye was crying too.

26

Tampons fo' Firelighters

Distance cycled: 4,373 miles

Metres ascended: 96,735

Quickly enough, things got back to normal between Faye and me. I was worried that the disagreement would linger because something about it felt different from those we'd had before. But, in the cold light of day, we'd seen it for what it was. Two tired women on a road in the middle of nowhere, trying to do what was right but royally cocking up on all communication fronts. We were far from perfect, the falling out had proved that, but it had also revealed that the edges around our friendship were more frayed than they had been in previous months. We were both more fragile, and we needed to treat one another with extra care. I made a mental note to think more before I acted over the final few weeks. I didn't fancy any more fallouts before we reached Ushuaia.

There were fewer cycle tourists on the southern end of the Carretera, so we often found ourselves alone again as we wound around the mountains, following the paths of peppermint-coloured rivers into lush green forests. It wasn't long before laughter returned to our daily routine, and one morning the laughter was the result of a technical mishap. Faye's rear rack had been dodgy since the start of the trip. It was held together with a few bolts and an oversized washer, and every now and then a bolt would work its way loose. That morning, I was pedalling behind Faye when her rear rack totally fell off the bike. It looked as if Gustavo had just dropped his trousers – his black back tyre was now naked and exposed to the world. I watched as Faye tried for a few moments to carry on, shoving harder on the pedals, before turning her head to investigate the back wheel. There she saw her life possessions dragging along the ground. The look on her face was one of 'what the hell?' and it was priceless. By the time I caught her up I was in fits of giggles.

'Well, I didn't expect that to happen,' said Faye with a wry grin.

There was no sign of any of the bolts that should have been holding the rack in place (they were presumably scattered somewhere along the Carretera Austral), so we reattached the rack to the bike with a web of cable ties and gaffer tape. It was then that I remembered how much I love having a problem like that to solve. There's something so satisfying about being forced to think laterally, to bodge up a bike and carry on – it filled me with a welcome sense of self-reliance and fresh confidence.

As we set off again, I was still smiling. Although it was only a small incident, it had broken the tension in the air and made us feel like ourselves again – laughing, finding solutions together and ploughing on.

***

A few days later, sitting in a tent just off the roadside in northern Patagonia, I was doing my best not to make any noise. It was early, not even 8 a.m., but I was already deeply engrossed in a top-secret mission: Operation Birthday Surprise. Faye was still asleep in the tent next door as I delicately began unwrapping the sponge cake I had been carrying in secret from a town we'd passed through a few days earlier. Easing it out of its case, the rustle made by the plastic packaging threatened to reach decibel danger level. I winced and paused, listening for any noises coming from Faye's tent, and was rewarded with a light snore – phew. Princess Faye was still sleeping, so the mission could continue.

I set about poking glacé cherries into the depths of the buttery cake, using my fingers, and finished off the sponge sculpture with a sprinkling of hundreds and thousands. I then considered shoving half a banana into the cake to add some 'depth' to my creation but decided that the best artists must know when to leave a masterpiece alone. I left the banana in its skin and opted to offer it up as a side dish, instead. Taking care not to drop the cake and cause a sugary explosion, I eased open the zip on my tent porch and tiptoed over to Faye's tent. The crunch of my bare feet on the gravel seemed deafening in the morning silence but at last I was in position. I inhaled deeply and began…

'HAPPY BIRTHDAY TO YOU,

HAPPY BIRTHDAY TO YOU!

HAPPPPIIEEE BIRTHDAAAAYYY, DEAR FAYE-BOMB,

HAPPY BIRTHDAY TOOOO YOUUUUUU!'

That day, the tenth of March, my favourite red-haired adventure amigo turned 30 years old. It was a landmark day and I felt privileged to be spending it on the road with her. I also felt a sense of responsibility to make sure that she had a lovely birthday because, well, there was no one else out there to do the job.

My angelic singing was followed by Faye's giggles from inside her tent. 'Thanks, McNuff!' she yelled, seemingly having enjoyed the rousing morning chorus. 'You are most welcome,' I said, moving to around the front of the tent as she unzipped the porch. I presented Faye with the bejewelled sponge cake, along with a few cards I had kept hidden in my panniers since her mum smuggled them to Santiago a few months back.

'Err, sorry, they're a bit battered,' I said sheepishly, dusting mud and crusty pieces of cheese off the envelopes as I handed them over.

'Ha! No, I like that they have been on an adventure too!' Faye said. 'They are perfect,' she smiled.

It was not only another year of Faye's life that had come to an end – so too had our journey along the Carretera Austral. Later that afternoon, we would arrive at the Chilean town of Villa O'Higgins, the conclusion of the route through rural Patagonia. Many other cycle tourists would turn around at O'Higgins and hitch rides back north, but we were carrying on. Although it was quite literally the end of the road because the only way to continue south was via a three-hour ferry ride across Lago O'Higgins. From there, we planned to pedal 12 miles and into Argentina on the shores of what was called the Deserted Lake. It all sounded other-worldly and mysterious, and I was very much looking forward to the next phase of our journey, beyond the Carretera.

In our usual relaxed, unplanned style, Faye and I had elected not to research the ferry times at Villa O'Higgins and instead just 'rock up and roll on'.

'It'll be fine,' Faye had said, earlier in the week, when we'd briefly contemplated checking ferry times.

'Yeah. Of course it will,' I had agreed.

The previous day, however, we'd bumped into fellow cycle tourists Meg and Gordon again, and Meg had dropped an in-formation bomb in my lap that threatened to put a large hole in our rock up and ride, unplanned, plan.

'It's a shame the ferry from O'Higgins only goes once a week now,' said Meg.

'Does it?!' I exclaimed.

'Yeah, with winter coming, they're getting into the low season. They changed the ferry schedule last week.'

'What day does it go?!' I asked, thinking that Faye and I

really couldn't stomach a week in the tiny town of O'Higgins, waiting for a boat out.

'Saturday,' Meg smiled.

Phew! Saturday was exactly the day we were hoping to rock up and roll on. The ferry gods had smiled down on us. What's more, Meg kindly informed us that not only could we book our ride across the lake but also, if we paid a little extra, we could visit a glacier too. Given our dwindling schedule, that kind of two-birds-one-stone crossing seemed like the most efficient way to get up close and personal with a chunk of Patagonian ice, so we decided that we'd splash the cash and make a trip to the O'Higgins Glacier for Faye's birthday. Fuelled by cake and cheered by song, we rolled out of camp that morning, headed towards the ferry at Villa O'Higgins.

The following day, Faye and I chatted merrily away with marvellous Meg and her cycling partner Gordon on the three-hour ferry ride from Villa O'Higgins to the tiny port of Candelario Mansilla. There, Meg and Gordon disembarked, and Faye and I carried on for another four hours to make the birthday-treat round trip to the O'Higgins Glacier.

The first portion of the journey had gone well. The gigantic Lago O'Higgins was calm enough, but shortly after we pulled away from Mansilla, heading across the waves in a westerly direction towards the glacier, the first round of chunder roulette began.

Soon I was slumped over the railings on the top floor of the Robinson Crusoe. The boat was rolling from side to side so

I had to brace my legs on the slippery white deck. My stomach felt like a washing machine in spin mode – bile was mixing with the morning's eggs, cheese, bacon and orange juice. Each sideways lurch was transmitted to my stomach contents, which sloshed back and forth with the swaying of the boat.

I tried to concentrate on my breathing. Inhale. Exhale. I focused on feeling the cold wind across the back of my neck and over my bare hands, but it was no use. Squinting through half-closed eyes, I lifted my head to see if looking at the horizon would help. A wave of nausea soon hit the back of my throat and so I quickly stuffed my head back down between my arms. I could swear that I was going to vomit any second now… Why, oh why, did you agree to come on this sodding boat, Anna? I asked myself. You know you always get seasick.

Taking the side trip to the O'Higgins glacier was billed (by us) as a once-in-a-lifetime opportunity and, in reality, that was true. But I'm always nervous about getting on boats, or any mode of motorized transport for that matter, because I get travel sick. Trains, cars, buses, planes – you name it, I have vommed on it.

'Mate, you look a bit green,' Faye said as I scrambled to gather up some warm clothes and head up to the top deck.

I managed to just about deep-breathe my way through the first wave of seasickness and then, after 45 minutes, we crossed into a more sheltered patch and the water in the lake returned to a glass-like state. We were sharing the boat with a large group of French tourists and the excitement began to reach fever pitch as we edged closer to the glacier. The sense of anticipation was aided in part by our very enthusiastic captain, who had elected to give us an X-Factor-style countdown, which included information on precisely how many kilometres remained until 'glacier impact'.

'¡Veinticinco kilómetres!' he boomed over the loudspeaker. '¡Veinte kilómetres! ¡Pasajeros… quince kilómetres!'

Faye and I moved down to the bottom deck to get a better view of the action. Large chunks of floating ice had started to appear in the water around us.

'Iceberg!' Faye yelled, much to the amusement of the surrounding crowd.

We concluded that the Frenchies were on some kind of photography tour as each of them was equipped with a long-lensed, expensive-looking camera. Faye and I looked suitably amateur as we jostled among them for position, armed with only our smartphones. Naturally, we cracked a few jokes under our breath about who was boasting the longest 'lens' and set ourselves apart by trying to photobomb the others' professional shots whenever possible.

'Look at that!' I shouted at Faye, pointing at a chunk of ice on the left-hand side of the ship.

It was an iceberg, but not like any I'd seen before. At one end it was curvy, like a series of waves had collided and frozen, mid crash. In the middle of the berg, slender tentacles of ice reached out as if they were hands grasping for the shore. And at the other end, there were swirls of royal blue and white in an almost perfect spiral, leading into a neat nubbin that resembled a cinnamon bun. As we sailed on, new aspects of the iceberg were revealed, and new shades of colour too. I said to Faye that it looked more like a Mardi Gras float than an iceberg. I was mesmerised by the random, asymmetric beauty.

In the calmer waters surrounding the magical iceberg, my seasickness had subsided, so we messed around for the next half hour on deck, enjoying being splashed by icy waves and pulling on more and more clothing as the temperature began to plummet. The closer we got to the glacier, the cooler it was, in every sense of the word.

At last we arrived at the main attraction. The captain cut the engine and the air was filled with a welcome silence. Now we could hear the creaks and groans of the mighty wall of ice in front of us. I resisted the urge to break the silence by bursting into song about the White Cliffs of Dover, but that's precisely what the glacier reminded me of – one end of it at least. The other end was much less of a solid wall and more like a bleached pile of kryptonite crystals. Huge columns of ice shot upwards, some stuck together, and others entirely alone in their skyward mission from the turquoise lake.

Out of the corner of my eye, I caught sight of an orange rubber dinghy pulling away from the boat. Three men in T-shirts and bright-orange life jackets zoomed off into the distance. We'd heard a rumour that later on we'd be served whisky over a block of pure glacier ice, and I could only assume that this dinghy mission was part of the process. Given that the only other thing that had been served on the seven-hour ferry journey was a single coconut biscuit at 10 a.m., I was a little perplexed by the crew's idea of a healthy diet.

'Ooh, look at them go!' said Faye, watching the men in the dinghy nudge closer to the glacier. The other passengers had noticed the dinghy too and begun to chatter excitedly among themselves.

'I reckon it's all for show you know…' I said to Faye with a wry smile.

'Yeah, I bet they just whizz out there, fanny around a bit next to the ice, come back and get a few bags of supermarket ice out of the freezer,' she replied.

'That's exactly what they do,' I retorted, grinning.

'Silly tourists,' Faye said.

After 20 minutes, the dinghies returned and the ferry's engine kicked to life again. We were handed our tumblers of whisky on glacier ice – most of which ended up in the lake because I hate whisky and Faye doesn't drink. The boat turned around to make the return journey through the 'vomit-zone' in the middle of the lake and, at 5 p.m., we were back on dry land at Candelario Mansilla. We loaded up our bikes again and set off to make camp for the evening, passing through a Chilean border post for the eighth time and camping in no-man's land just shy of the Argentinian border.

After all the to-ing and fro-ing of the day, it was really

lovely to be still at our camp spot just on the edge of a forest. And lovely for it to be so quiet. Most of the other tourists from the glacier tour would be spending the night in simple accommodation near the dock, and none of them were travelling by bike, so we were alone again. Everything was as it should be – everything, that was, except our stove. The MSR WhisperLite stove which had served us so well for the past five months was threatening to die on us.

Next to the stove, our green soup mugs were half-filled with dried mashed potato flakes. Slices of cold sausages sat expectantly on the upturned lids of the mugs, and a slab of cheese had been delicately carved into chunks, patiently waiting to be plunged into a steaming pile of mashed potato. Alas, there sat the water in the pan, cold still, over a flame that simply would not stay lit.

'It's going to go out, it's going to go out, it's going to… Oh, bugger. It's gone out,' I slouched backwards and sighed.

Unscrewing the red petrol canister, we peered inside. There seemed to be rather a lot of black stuff floating around in it and we concluded that the fuel we'd filled up with in Coyhaique must have been of less than ideal quality.

'Aww, I really fancied mashed potato tonight,' said Faye, sitting back and staring at the now defunct camping stove.

'We could just eat cheese and crackers?' I suggested.

Faye's face told me all I needed to know about what she thought of that idea.

'How about a fire? We could probably make a fire?' I suggested.

'Yes!' Faye shouted, immediately leaping to her feet to collect firewood from the forest. Although a fire seemed like a wonderful idea, we knew that it was going to be a huge challenge. It had rained heavily the previous night and most of the potential firewood was just too damp. Still, a girl's gotta eat, so we set about gathering bits of reasonably dry wood of all shapes and sizes and began our attempt to build a towering (or, at least, a small) inferno.

After constructing a small stone circle and then the usual woody wigwam (to make sure we allowed oxygen to reach the flames), we made three attempts at starting the fire but to no avail. On each attempt, where we hoped there to be an abundance of bright orange flames, there were plumes of black smoke instead, which was blown into our eyes, leaving us with tears streaming down our faces and our hair infused with charcoal.

By this point it was 9 p.m. We had been up since 6 a.m., ridden six miles to catch the ferry, spent seven hours on the boat, and cycled a further eight miles uphill to the camp spot. We were exhausted. Perhaps it was time to accept defeat. Next to the charred but not-yet-alight pile of moist wood, we sat back and sighed deeply. I looked again at our camping mugs and the scattered assortment of meat and dairy on the ground around the makeshift non-fire. Suddenly, a thought entered my mind and I sat bolt upright.

'I have a tampon!' I shouted.

'You have a what?!' Faye asked, seemingly confused by my sanitary confession.

'A tampon. And some Vaseline. How about we coat the tampon with Vaseline and use it as a firelighter?'

'McNuff, you are a GENIUS!'

And so, two tampons, a tub of Vaseline, a lot of smoke, and some careful fire-tending later, Faye and I managed to boil some water. We poured it over our dry potato flakes at 9.30 p.m., gleefully mixing in the cheese and sausages before spooning the steaming mass into our pie holes and grinning at one another.

Faye and Anna, one; Nature, zero.

27

This Little Piggy Went to Fitz Roy

Distance cycled: 4,780 miles
Metres ascended: 99,728

Often, on an adventure in some far-flung corner of the globe, I like to zoom out, in my mind's eye. I imagine looking down at the earth from space and seeing myself as a little dot. For some reason, that gives me a sense of calm; it helps me to keep life in perspective; and it also helps me to appreciate where in the world I am at that moment in time.

That March morning, post-battle with the fire gods, Faye and I were two dots on the fragmented fringe of southern Patagonia. As the South American continent curves eastward into the Atlantic Ocean at Cape Horn, the once-hard line of its western edge shatters into hundreds of inlets and islands, and the watery fingers of the South Pacific stretch into the most beautiful glacial fjords on the planet. We were now camped on a patch of land that lay at the transition between the dusty, windswept plains of the east and the fjords of the west. There were no roads where we were, south of Villa O'Higgins, and we felt as if we'd broken into a secret garden, a place that was reserved solely for us. We hadn't seen anyone since leaving the

Chilean border post the previous afternoon and we hoped that kind of solitude would continue for the rest of the morning.

'It's only four miles to the next ferry!' Faye called over as she entered the final throes of her morning-packing ritual.

'Brilliant. We'll be there in an hour, tops!' I shouted back, continuing to stuff my own sodden mess of tent back into its bag. Bikes packed and ready to roll, we both thanked our camp spot (as had now become a tradition before leaving) and set off up a dirt track, headed for a place called the Deserted Lake.

While researching our route for this section of the ride, I'd read a few blog posts that said the trail to the lake was going to be muddy. But I now questioned whether I'd mis-interpreted what I'd read. So far, all we'd experienced was a wide, albeit steep, rubble trail through the forest. It had been tricky to negotiate but it was rideable, and certainly not mud-dy. After a couple of miles of pedalling through damp woods and over shallow crystal-clear streams, we reached a sign that said '¡Bienvendo a Argentina!' It was a sign that seemed lonely, out there in the middle of the forest, but it was nice to be wel-comed into Argentina for the seventh time, all the same. It was only then that we saw the mud.

'Oh wow,' said Faye, peering down the track into the bushes. In front of us was what could only be described as a quagmire. A thick layer of slimy, wet earth covered the narrow single track, banked on either side by dense bushes. It looked just about wide enough to get a bike through, but I couldn't be sure.

'Ready?' Faye asked, her foot already clipped into one pedal, poised to launch herself along the trail and through the narrow gap in the bushes.

'Let's do it!' I shouted. And if I'd had an engine in that moment, I would have revved it in readiness.

Faye moved off with a war cry and careered past the trail entrance and into the first pool of mud. Her tyres sank into the quagmire almost immediately and the speed she'd gathered was ripped out from underneath them. She wobbled, yelped, ground to a halt and put a foot down in the mud, where it promptly disappeared.

'Eww!' she said, pulling hard to release her foot from the mud vacuum, as I offered moral support by laughing hysterically.

It took us 90 minutes to cover a painstaking three miles. We shoved our bikes through rivers, waded with them through ankle-deep mud, dragged them over tangled roots and lifted them over fallen trees. Things were getting ridiculous, and when things got ridiculous, we knew we had to moderate our frustration with a spattering of sarcasm.

'It's so lovely of us to take our bikes for a walk in the woods, isn't it?!' I shouted at Faye as I negotiated a particularly tricky section of trail.

'We are very kind bike owners! Treating Bernard and Gustavo to a stroll in the fresh air,' she yelled back.

After an hour of doing bicep curl reps with 50-kg worth

of bags and bike, my arm muscles were beginning to tire, but the fun wasn't over yet. We arrived at the pièce de résistance of the trail – a deep gully into which I could only barely fit my bike and its cumbersome baggage. Faye (who had larger wheels and narrower rear bags) managed to wiggle her bike along the bottom of the gully without too much trouble. I observed her technique, as she tip-toed along above the bike on a narrow ledge at the side. I tried to do the same but pretty soon Bernard's bum got stuck. The gully was just too narrow to get him through with the bags on.

'Oh, Bernard,' I sighed.

I looked ahead and considered 'de-bagging' Bernard, but I decided that it was a very long way to carry the panniers. Instead, I opted to get into the gully myself, behind him. In what looked like an event you might see in the World's Strongest Man competition, I lifted Bernard's rear end so that the bags were clear of the top of the gully and steered him forwards, shuffling my feet along behind his back wheel. It was a technique that worked spectacularly well, and I soon reached the end of the gully, exhausted but with bags intact. I looked up at Faye, who was waiting for me, and let out a triumphant cry.

'Rarrrr! Bernard the WARRIORRR! There is no mountain too high, no gully too deep for Bernard! Because he is a WAA-RIII-OOORRR!'

Back on our bikes, we made it out of the forest and onto the shores of the Deserted Lake, a long expanse of jade-coloured water that stretched towards green mountains into the distance. It was a grey afternoon and the clouds had formed a blanket across the sky. It really was a surreal place – so quiet and so calm. It had likely remained unchanged for hundreds of years, as the footprint of civilisation was only faintly visible. I spotted a small red-brick building set back from the shore-line, which I gathered must be Argentinian border control. Looking past it, I was disappointed to glimpse a boat pulling away from the dock.

'There goes our ride,' said Faye.

'Oh, bugger. I'm sure there'll be another one soon,' I said.

It was starting to rain again and the wind was whipping across the waters of the lake, so we kept moving and head-ed into the small immigration building to get our passports stamped. As we were being stamped into Argentina, I casually enquired when the next boat was leaving.

'Five thirty p.m.,' said the border guard, smiling.

I looked at my watch, which read 11.30 a.m. Oh dear.

'Can we stay in here?' I asked the guard.

'No, you must wait by the dock,' he said.

At the dock we found a small open-fronted shed, which had a quad bike in it and some other bits and bobs. There was nothing for it but to spend the next six hours huddled in the shed. I checked the temperature on my watch and shud-dered – it read 5°C. Faye unpacked her sleeping bag, climbed into it and took a nap on the cold concrete floor. I pulled on all my clothes and decided to barricade myself in next to the quad-bike trailer in a bid to stay warm. The wind and rain continued and, over the course of the afternoon, the temperature plummeted. We both leapt up every now and then, dancing around the shed in the hope of getting some blood back into our fingers and toes. As we danced, we willed, with all our might, a boat to appear through the early evening mist and transport us across the Deserted Lake.

***

A day later, we were warm and dry once again and sitting on comfortable beds in a hostel in the town of El Chaltén. After crossing the Deserted Lake, we'd camped just the other side of it, in a patch of dense forest, with the noise of rain rattling on our tents. That morning, as we'd begun our ride into El Chaltén, I couldn't seem to get my left foot to warm up. The sun hadn't yet hit the Diablo Valley and so it felt baltic on the road to town. I could see my breath on the air and my nose began to tingle in protest. When the jagged snow-capped peak of the famous Mount Fitz Roy came into view for the first time, Faye understandably stopped to take pictures. I, by contrast, couldn't focus on anything beyond the searing pain in my left foot. I zoomed past her, pounding on the pedals, desperate to bring my feet back to life.

'Sorry, mate, I've got to keep moving! My toes are freezing – will you send me those snaps of the mountain? You'll catch me up!' I shouted as I passed. When we made it into town at midday my toes were still numb, but I thought nothing more of it until later that afternoon.

'Um, Faye, I'm worried I might have gone crazy.'

'Huh? Why?' said Faye absent-mindedly from the bed adjacent to mine.

'Well, my toes are itchy. They were itchy in the tent last night, and they're itching now.'

'What kind of itchy?' Faye enquired.

'Like a stingy, burny kind of itchy…'

'Get your sock off then, let's have a look.'

I removed my left sock.

'Woah!' said Faye, leaning in to get a closer look. 'Mate, that is not good.'

Staring back at us were four puffy, red, swollen toes. The skin was all shiny and only my big toe seemed to have escaped the podgy plight. What was up with them, I wondered. Had I been bitten? Was it an allergic reaction to something?

I thought back over the previous day's events: wading through icy rivers, six hours spent shivering at the dockside ferry shack, then another night camped in the cold and wet. Evidently, my toes had taken a battering. There was no hope of playing 'this little piggy went to market', because all the piggies were ice blocks.

After much consultation with Dr. Google, and a phone call to my mum (aka Dr. Sue, Medicine Woman) I breathed a sigh of relief that I was not suffering from terminal, degenerative neuropathy (which is where Google had led me) but, instead, it was just a good old-fashioned case of chilblains. 'Chilblains?!' I sat back and exclaimed. I didn't even know they were real. Chilblains are the kind of thing your Nan tells you you're going to get when you warm up your cold hands too quickly.

'Ooh, don't put your hands next to the gas fire, young Anna, you'll get chilblains,' my nanny Rose would say. Nanny was right. The myth is real, and chilblains were bloody painful.

The shame in all of this was that we had just rolled into the hiking destination in Argentinian Patagonia. El Chaltén is famous for its uber-accessible one-day hikes, the most famous of all being the hike to Laguna de los Tres, right at the foot of the Mount Fitz Roy massif. Mount Fitz Roy and its neighbours are a set of jagged peaks that are synonymous with Patagonia. They're often used in adverts for the region and their profile is the logo for the Patagonia clothing brand.

As part of our mission to add some extra spice to this final month of cycling, we'd planned to take a day off the bikes and hike up to Laguna de los Tres. But now, as I looked at my toes, I sighed. In my google session, I'd learned that chilblains happen as a result of damaged blood vessels. The best way to heal them is to keep that part of your body warm for a few weeks. I wasn't sure how possible that would be on the ride down to Ushuaia but, for the next few days at least, I needed to be sensible.

'Don't suppose we'll be going to see Mount Fitz Roy tomorrow then,' I said solemnly.

'Don't suppose we are. Sorry, mate,' Faye said.

'You can always head up there without me?' I said, gesturing towards the mountain.

'Nah. I'm happy chilling out. I'll just have to pop back here one day,' Faye grinned.

My toes were a mess but, on the plus side, unplanned R & R was always welcome. After cycling 700 miles along the Carretera Austral, with just one day off the bikes in the two weeks since leaving Puerto Montt, my body craved stillness. So, for the next two days, we decided to hang out in El Chaltén and just… be still. It was a small, dusty town, with a laid-back vibe, and no more than half a mile from one end to the other. The next significant town was El Calafate, over 230 miles away, so El Chaltén was a key location for tourists to fill up on supplies, in between exploring the nearby mountains. While in town, I mostly slept, drank coffee in quirky local cafes and ate as many vegetables as humanly possible. Vegetables are the food of the gods, after all. Faye slept less than me, and swapped coffee intake for downing as many submarino hot chocolates as she could. By the third morning at the hostel, we were rested and ready to leave. We had packed up, checked out and were now standing astride our bikes in the street outside the hostel. I took one last look at Mount Fitz Roy in the distance. It'd rained on and off over the past few days but the weather had cleared up. The sky was blue, the sun was shining and there were just a few clouds gathered around Fitz Roy's main peak.

'I'm gutted we didn't make it up there. It's such a nice day today,' I said.

'It is,' said Faye. Then there was a long pause before she said… 'We could hike it today?'

'Could we?' I asked.

'Well, I mean – if your toes are okay? We could just stay one more day?' Faye said.

I thought for a moment. I knew that recovery from chilblains should take weeks, but I also knew that I would likely never be here again. This could be my only shot to meet Mr Fitz Roy himself and besides… my feet felt fine. I mean I could feel them, which was a revelation in itself.

'My toes are GREAT!' I exclaimed.

'Really? Are you sure?' Faye said.

'Yes. Sod it! Let's do it! Fitz Roy is a GO.'

God, it felt good to throw caution to the wind and change our plans like that. After all, we were still just about on schedule and could afford to lose one more day in the 750 miles left to ride to Ushuaia. After turning the bikes around, we checked back into the hostel. I went and bought a new snuggly pair of extortionately priced merino hiking socks (just to be on the safe side) and, at midday we set off on a mission to Laguna de los Tres and back again.

The trail itself began at a car park just out of town. At the trailhead there was a sign telling us that it was going to be a 14-mile round trip to the lake and back and that we'd encounter 'steep trails which are dangerous in windy conditions.' There was also an estimate of the time it would take us to make the trip.

'Oh look, it says it's a seven to nine-hour hike,' I said, pointing at the large wooden sign.

'Blimey, do we have time to make that?' said Faye, checking her watch.

'Of course, because we'll halve it,' I said, matter-of-factly.

'What do you mean, we'll halve it?' asked Faye, a look of confusion on her face.

'Well, that's what you do, right? You halve the time the sign says, and you aim for that?'

'Do you? Who does that?!'

'Errrm... well, the McNuff family does. I thought that's what everyone did?' I said.

It was then that I realised I'd only ever been on hikes with a member of my own family, or with Jamie (who doesn't really pay attention to what time of day it is, let alone how long a hike takes) or on my own. Ever since I was a kid, on trips to the Alps or the Lake District, whenever we saw a trail sign that told us how long a section would take, my mum would announce that we should try to halve that time. She would then set off at a clip up the mountain with me, my two brothers and my dad following on behind. Water stops were brief; there might be a sanctioned lunch stop at the top; but all in all you just kept moving until you were back down. And if you needed the toilet, then you must nip off the trail, do your business and catch the family back up. I relayed all of this to Faye and she stared at me, eyes wide, before breaking into a broad grin and then full-blown laughter. It dawned on me that halving the sign time was not something all families did.

'Oh my gosh, McNuff, no wonder you are the way you are, if that's how your family hikes pan out!'

'What do you mean? You don't try to beat the time on the sign when you go for walks with the Shepherds?'

'No! We just… go for a walk.'

'Oh. Well then… seeing as it's early afternoon, do you fancy doing it the McNuff way?' I smiled.

'Go on then, that'll get us back before dark at least. But please don't try to kill me along the way,' said Faye.

'I promise. We can even have a lunch stop,' I smiled and, with that, I turned on my heels and set off up the mountain.

After leaving the gravel car park, the dirt trail bobbed and weaved through light forest. Thirty minutes into the hike, we reached the first lookout and stopped to take in the view. Late autumn was dancing through the valley in all her colourful glory. To my left, a forest-covered ridge line sloped down to the valley floor. Where the wind was at its most biting, toward the top of the ridge, the leaves had turned blood red. Lower down they were orange, then yellow, and at the base was a carpet of green, the trees yet to submit to the change of season. Beyond the ridge, set way back in the distance, we could see the greys and whites of the Mount Fitz Roy massif, the tallest of its peaks shrouded in cloud. It looked like the emerald palace in The Wizard of Oz. A different colour, but similar in shape at least. I could well have been Dorothy in that moment, in my ruby-red trainers, following a dusty trail on our very own yellow brick road.

As we hiked, we began to pass more and more people. Presumably, these were the sensible souls who had left town earlier during the day. For once, I actually enjoyed seeing people on the trail. I was using them as targets, picking each of them off one by one, as we raced up the mountain. The abundance of people wasn't the only difference that day. Instead of having to work hard to keep up with Faye (as I often did on the bike), it was now Faye working hard to keep up with me. Granted, I didn't help her out much as I pushed harder and harder, the higher we went. But I was in my element. I was loving the sick burn in my lungs and my legs. That feeling of taking as deep a breath as I could muster and stretching every tiny intercostal muscle around my lungs to its limit. It was hard to do that on the bike because I was always hunched over, holding onto the handlebars. I'd forgotten how good it felt to really open up my lungs and fill them with cold, mountain air.

At one point, I stopped and looked back for Faye. I'd taken a sneaky side route to leapfrog some other trail users and she was now caught behind in a trail traffic jam. After a minute or so, she reached me.

'Sorry, mate…' I said, still breathing hard. 'I got a bit

over-excited there. Isn't this just amazing? Aren't you just loving it?!'

'You're an animal, McNuff! I think I'm going to vomit,' was her only reply.

As we continued the climb over the next hour, Mount Fitz Roy continued to play hide and seek, disappearing and reappearing at intervals. Every time I stopped to catch my breath when it was in view, I was amazed all over again by its towering majesty.

Finally, we reached our destination – Laguna de los Tres. We stopped to gaze at the multiple peaks of the Fitz Roy massif, a set of jagged giant's teeth that dominate the horizon. From where I was standing, it seemed like we might be able to hop from one peak to the next, using them like stepping stones to leap across the sky. Below the main peaks, snow was being cradled by a long, wide shelf, which led into a glacier, snaking down the eastern side of the mountain and stopping just shy of the blue-green Laguna de los Tres itself.

We sat for 20 minutes at the top, snacking on tortilla wraps, cheese and cold cut-up sausages. We were far from alone and we watched as dozens of people perched precariously on rocks, arms up in the air, hoping to capture that perfect Instagram-worthy image. Everyone wanted to claim some of Fitz Roy, they had come for a piece of it. I supposed that we wanted a piece of it too – that's why we were there, after all. But for some reason, I couldn't bring myself to get out my camera out. It felt like we'd be trying to steal a piece of something that wasn't ours to take. Instead, I snapped a picture with my mind.

'Beautiful, isn't it?' I said to Faye.

'So pretty. It's almost unreal.' She replied.

It was late afternoon by the time we left our lunch spot and began the journey back towards town. At first, the going was slow. There were still lots of people on the trail and many bottlenecks on narrow and steep sections. But, after 90 minutes, we found ourselves alone again. Faye was keeping pace now and, in fact, the roles had reversed. She was streaking down the mountain and I was struggling to keep up. At one point she even broke into a run (this was unheard of) – so we ran the final three miles to the foot of the trail. Five hours and 30 minutes after leaving the car park, we were back in town.

I might have pushed Faye so hard on the way up that she almost chundered but it was all very worth it. We ran straight into the first restaurant we could find at the edge of town and wolfed down a gigantic pizza smothered in cheese with (in my case, at least) a big glass of Argentinian Malbec on the side. The toe-piggies were warm and well again, if a little sore, and I was so glad that we'd taken them for a day out at the Mount Fitz Roy market.

Over an ice-cream dessert, we made a vow to actually leave town the following day. It was 750 miles from El Chaltén to Ushuaia and we had two and a half weeks until our flight home. Barring any more major mishaps or holds-ups, we were confident we'd make it on time.

28

Was it Something I Ate?

Distance cycled: 4,810 miles
Metres ascended: 99,826

We'd heard a lot about the vast and desolate Patagonian Steppe. The fact that, in the space of a couple of days, we could visit a glacier, ride through a swampy forest, cross a deserted lake, hike to a snow-capped mountain, and then cross a semi-arid desert was all part of the region's charm. If ever we were in any doubt, Patagonia was a shape-shifter and, with every turn of our wheels, she changed around us.

As we rode away from El Chaltén, the plains stretched out towards a dusty horizon. Impressive mountains had been replaced by small undulations and, thankfully, a straight tarmac road. I was especially grateful for the smooth road because the plains were savaged by 50-mph gusts of wind. With no mountains to shield us, we felt their full force. Despite the wind-battered riding that afternoon, our spirits were high. Traffic was light; we had left most tourists behind in El Chaltén and, once again, it was back to just the two of us, riding one behind the other, listening to episodes of Desert Island Discs and audiobooks.

In the middle of the afternoon, we hit a small hill. The change in pace as my wheels slowed jolted me from my dream-like state. A thought flashed through my mind and I glanced down at the altimeter on my watch, before doing some on-the-spot maths. I watched the metres tick up, slowly… slowly and then at last…

'Faye, Faye!'

'What is it?' Faye shouted from behind me.

'We've done it!'

'Done what?'

'A hundred thousand metres of going upwards on our bikes.'

'Huh?'

'That little bump… That put us over a hundred thousand metres of climbing. That's eleven times the height of Everest.'

'No way!'

'Yes way!' I shouted back.

'Should we just stop here then? Call it a day?' she asked.

'Yeah, I reckon we could probably stop. Call a cab or something from here.' I said.

'No sense in carrying on to Ushuaia really is there?' Said Faye.

'Let's pull over and celebrate though?' I said, and we stopped and got off our bikes.

'Well done, Faye-bomb,' I said, engulfing her in a giant hug.

'Well done, McNuff,' said Faye, giant-hugging me back.

As I stepped out of our hug, I looked down the road ahead and felt a tinge of sadness.

'I'll be sad when this is all over, you know,' I said quietly.

'Me too. It's been epic,' said Faye, looking down the road as well.

We got back on the bikes and set off again, although now we were side by side and the mood was different. We were full of excited chatter and shared triumph at having achieved the seemingly ridiculous goal we'd set ourselves, together, almost a year earlier. We spent the following 30 minutes working out what 100,000 metres was equivalent to, other than 11 times the height of Everest. As it turned out, 100,000 metres of going upwards was like pedalling to the edge of the earth's atmosphere (and back) three times over. I thought that was a pretty cool comparison. It was also the height of 263 Empire State Buildings, and 58,824 average-sized llamas. But, given that we were heading down towards Antarctica (where there were many, many penguins), our favourite comparison was that it was the height of approximately 300,000 little penguins stacked on top of one another. It was the thought of 300,000 penguins standing on one another's shoulders that made me smile for the rest of the afternoon.

That night, we camped on a patch of scrubland off the

side of the road, next to a small lake. The sky turned lilac as the faint outline of the new moon floated in the clouds above the water. From our camp spot, we had an uninterrupted view back towards the mountains, which filled the horizon from west to east. The sky surrounding Fitz Roy and his friends looked calm, the infamous Patagonian winds had died down to no more than a light breeze, and the soft light of dusk had made the now-amber snow-capped peaks appear like a dozen halos over the mountains.

We opted to dine in front of Casa Shepherd and cooked up a delicious, albeit decidedly 'white' dinner of spaghetti, mayonnaise, cold cut-up frankfurters and parmesan cheese. It wasn't cordon bleu cooking, but it was all we could muster from the limited supplies we'd bought in town. El Chaltén might have been great for stunning hikes but it was no mecca for food shopping. Still, after a day of battling the wind, we were both ravenous. We polished off dinner, said goodnight and were asleep by 9 p.m.

At midnight, I was awake again. Why am I awake? What time is it? I thought. Do I need a wee? My stomach made a hideous gurgle and offered up the answer. I felt nauseous. I took a deep breath. This wasn't unusual, after all. Earlier in the trip I had cleverly decided to drink the sunflower oil in a can of tuna (for calorific reasons) and it had produced a similar nauseating sensation. My oil-induced nausea had passed and I was sure this would too.

Alas, 15 minutes later I was out of my tent and in prime

pre-vom mode. I don't know what your body does when you're about to hurl, but my torso starts to shake violently and my mouth fills with saliva. When that happens, I know that I am T-minus one minute from a VOMCANO. And so it began.

On the first ejection, I made a note that I really should learn to chew my food better. By the light of my head torch, I inspected what was lying at my feet and concluded that it looked like a pizza. There were whole bits of spaghetti amid a spattering of red and white. Better still, I seemed to have deposited the pizza ingredients on the ground in a near-perfect circle. Top marks for vom-style. Feeling much better, I concluded that it must have been something I ate that day and returned to my tent, glad the ordeal was over.

But it was far from over: the fun had only just begun. For the following five hours, every hour, I woke up to be sick. On each trip, the amount of food coming out of me decreased, until I had nothing left to give and was hacking up bile. I took to sleeping in all my clothes with my tent open because I was so fed up with getting dressed and opening the tent zips for each round of puke play.

I succumbed to the sickness, accepting that it was just another challenge, and settled into a ritual. Get up. Head torch on. Try to walk in a different direction away from the tent, while pointing the torch at the ground so as to avoid stepping on any of my previous works of art. Get as far away as possible from the tents, so as not to disturb Faye. Eject the evil. Return to the tent to grab 30 minutes of sleep. And... repeat. The ritual was working well, although on the final two visits, things had took a new twist – the evil started coming out of my back end too.

By 7.30 a.m. I was lying in the porch of my tent with the door open, letting the fresh air flow over me, when I heard Faye rustling in her pop-up palace next door.

'Faye, whatever you do, stay away from the area to the right of the tents: it is a hazard zone. There is DANGER all around,' I wailed.

'Ow, mate. I thought I heard you being sick last night. How are you doing?'

'Well, I haven't puked in two hours now, so by all standards, really good.'

'Do you think it was something you ate?' Faye asked.

'I'm not sure… that's definitely what came up, but we ate the same thing last night. Do you feel sick?'

'No, I feel fine,' she said. Faye had the more sensitive stomach of the two of us, so it was unlikely to have been something we'd eaten. I thought for a moment.

'It could have been from water?' I said. My cheeks had grown weary of sucking the water through my filtration bottle, so I'd recently switched to using iodine tablets to sterilise my drinking water instead.

'Yeah. I'm not sure how good those tablets are, you know. Maybe it's that,' Faye replied.

'Or it could be to do with the fact that I've given up washing and am fully feral,' I smiled, acknowledging that every part of my bike and body had reached critical grime level.

Whatever the cause, I was relieved that I had stopped being sick at last and could now think about the next move. We were 125 miles from the town of Esperanza. That was too far to make on an ordinary day, and especially on a day when I had zero energy. I could see from the map that there was a petrol station at a road junction 35 miles away, so we decided to aim for that first. If I could take a short rest there, I could get some fresh water inside me and maybe even some kind of food, and then we could crack on and camp closer to Esperanza. I felt dizzy and swayed as I swung one leg over the cross bar to get back on the bike. Placing my hands on the handlebars, I whispered myself a pep talk. 'Just get through the next few hours, McNuff. Just a few hours and everything will be better.'

'You ready?' called Faye.

'Ready,' I said. And we set off, across the plains and away from the scattergun of vomit.

I hadn't been able to face anything for breakfast, so instead I dined on podcast replays of Radio 4's Desert Island Discs. Interviews with celebrities Tom Hanks, David Walliams and Kathy Burke kept me company as I slogged along the road, tucked in behind Faye to shelter from the ever-growing wind.

We began to pass signs warning us about the strength of the crosswinds. The signs were yellow with a black palm tree in the middle. The palm tree was distorted, bent sideways like a crescent moon as three black lines denoted the direction of the wind. Those signs let us know that we were entering what we had now dubbed a 'gust zone'. And gust it did. We could be cycling happily along, making steady progress and then… wham! A wall of wind would hit on our right and we would be shoved across the road. When that happened, we'd wrestle ourselves back over to the edge of the tarmac and attempt to regain some kind of rhythm before the next wall of wind thundered through.

It was 1 p.m. when we made the petrol station. I let out a sigh as we slumped into the white plastic chairs in the small cafe area inside. In a bid to get something, anything, into my stomach, I had bought a can of full-fat coke. I'm not much one for drinking full-fat coke – it turns my teeth furry – but in times of need, a little of that black magic goes a long way. I took a few sips from the can before putting my head in my arms and onto the table.

'Oh, mate. Are you alright?' Faye asked, a tinge of concern in her voice.

'Not really. But I will be. I think I need a break though,' I mumbled, keeping my head on the table.

'Me too, and I'm not sick! Let's just sit here for an hour or so. See how you feel?' she said.

'Mmm hmmmm,' I said, shutting my eyes.

Truth be told, I felt horrendous. My stomach had calmed down but my head felt like it was on fire and I was starting to shake. I thought about what we'd be riding into that afternoon. If we carried on, not only would we once again be reduced to my snail-like pace but, after leaving the petrol station, the road would take a sharp turn south. Instead of dealing with strong crosswinds, we would be riding directly into a stiff headwind.

I got up from the table to make a trip to the toilet and caught sight of myself in the mirror. I was white as a sheet. When I returned to the table, I found Faye deep in thought, her brow furrowed as she stared at the floor.

'I'm still wondering what made you sick. Maybe it was the dinner? That was a particularly rank meal, after all,' she said.

'I quite liked that meal. Well, until it came back up that is,' I mumbled.

'This is like a game of Cluedo, you know. Or, better still, puke-Cluedo,' Faye smiled.

'Ha, very good, Faye, I like what you did there,' I smiled back, before putting my head on the table again.

Faye continued to commentate, in a faux-posh voice. 'We find our suspect, slumped, lifeless beside a can of Coca-Cola in the petrol station. She is a shell of a woman, but who or what is responsible for her untimely demise? Is it a) Colonel Mayonnaise, in the soup cup, with the spork?'

I raised my head and smiled at my friend's attempt to cheer me up, as she pressed on.

'Perhaps it was suspect B, Master Cloudy Water, in the river, with an iodine tablet? Or no, what's this? Could it be Mrs

Dirty Bits, with the grime, in the nether regions?! Our investigation continues here on the plains of Argenti—'

Faye's spiel was interrupted by the petrol-station attendant, who had moved from his usual position behind the counter and was now standing next to us. I was convinced that he had come over to ask me to leave. It was clear that I wasn't well and perhaps it was company policy to ask anyone who might spread germs in the petrol-station cafe to leave the vicinity.

'Hola Chicas. ¿Tienen carpa?' he asked. (Do you have a tent?)

'Err... sí...' I said, now very confused as to what us having a tent had to do with anything. Perhaps he wanted to check we had somewhere to stay before slinging us out on our ears.

'¡Vamos!' he said, motioning for us to follow him.

I looked at Faye and pulled a confused face. She shrugged and we both followed the attendant out of the petrol station. He led us around the back of the building, to a patch of straw-coloured grass next to the ventilation grate for the cafe kitchen. He explained in Spanish that we were welcome to camp there for the night, free of charge.

This man was a guardian angel in uniformed disguise. It wasn't the most salubrious camping spot but, without a second thought we sacked off the idea of going any further, thanked the man for his kindness and pitched our tents. Faye went back into the petrol station to hang out for the afternoon as I crawled straight into my tent. By 3 p.m. I was well on my way to the land of nod. I intended just to nap for a couple of hours and then emerge for dinner, but aside from waking up once, drenched in sweat at 4 a.m., I slept all the way through until 9 a.m. the following morning.

Once back on the road, I felt better with every hour that passed. I was amazed that it had taken five months for me to pick up a bug, especially given the strain we'd put on our bodies and some of the dodgy water we'd had to drink.

Thankfully, the bug disappeared as quickly as it had arrived, and all the food I ate stayed where it belonged. Over the next few days, I got back up to full meals and full speed. As we pressed on southwards, the crosswinds continued to test us and, just when we thought they couldn't possibly blow any harder, they did. At times I was frightened by the strength of the wind, and I struggled to keep the bike under control, especially down hills and when travelling at speed. Other times I found it exhilarating, being that close to such a force of nature.

We made a one-night stop at a hostel in Puerto Natales, surrounded by fellow travellers who were preparing to go hiking in the nearby Torres del Paine National Park, the most famous park in Patagonia. I had expected to feel pangs of jealousy, but our journey had given me so much that I didn't envy anyone else's experiences. We left Puerto Natales and carried on to Punta Arenas, the last city on the mainland. From there it was a short ride to the ferry across to Tierra del Fuego, the Land of Fire. And way down at the bottom of the Land of Fire was Ushuaia.

Despite the 24-hour bug, we made good time over the week that followed and so we agreed to take a rest day in Punta Arenas. Taking that day off would mean that I could finally pick up the package with our new cycling shorts, which had been sent on from Corina's hostel to a post office in town. It would also allow me to get my follow-up rabies jab at a clinic and for us both to ready ourselves for the final push to the finish line. I couldn't help but feel relieved that we were so close to being done.

We settled into our usual routine in the city. Faye chilled out in our room at the hostel, chatting to friends and family back home, while I did a tour of the local coffee establishments to sample slices of lemon pie. I also tested out their submarinos, Faye's favourite. Should she choose to venture out for one, it would help to know where to get a mean mug of molten-chocolate-infused hot milk.

Unfortunately, Faye never did make it out of the hostel for a submarino. A week after my own bout of digestive disco, it was her turn. I watched as she went through what we assumed was the same bug as I'd picked up in El Chaltén. She came, she puked, she pooed, and we hoped that she would conquer.

Only, it soon became clear that Faye's bug was behaving differently from mine. Twelve hours of sickness passed, as did 24 hours, and two days later Faye was still being violently sick. She was spending much of each day lying in bed, drifting in and out of sleep as I popped back and forth to keep an eye on her. I was starting to get concerned at her lack of ability to keep anything solid down, but I was reassured that she was sipping on water, at least.

In a bid to lift her spirits, on the third evening I returned to the hostel with a gift. I knew from previous tummy issues that Faye could often stomach gummy sweets. I had found some sweets that resembled a meal while out in town – there was a burger, a pizza, some chips and even a bottle of ketchup too. It all fitted neatly in my palm, and I held it out for Faye to see.

'Here. I brought you dinner,' I smiled. 'I know you can't eat much, but it's a full meal.'

'Thanks, mate. I'll try to eat it later,' she said, placing the meal by the side of her bed and turning over to go back to sleep. The gummy dinner was my attempt to get Faye to eat and to cheer her up but, in hindsight, I realised that I hadn't clocked quite how unwell she was. We'd both been ill a few times over the course of the trip, and Faye frequently had stomach issues, so I assumed this would pass. Her ill health was further disguised by the fact that she is never one to cause a fuss. Despite having spent almost six months with her, I found myself facing a dilemma similar to the one I had faced, way back when, when we were leaving La Paz on our way to Uturuncu. When do you trust that your friend knows her own body best, and when do you step in because you believe she's past being able to tell whether or not she's in trouble? I had to trust that Faye knew herself best.

On the third night, I started to get really concerned. Mostly about Faye's ill health, but also about the dwindling time we had to make it to Ushuaia. We'd allowed for one or two slow days, but my 24-hour bug had gobbled those contingency days up. If we didn't leave town soon, we were in danger of missing our flight home from Ushuaia. One morning, I had secretly looked up bus schedules. I didn't want to end the journey that way, but neither of us could afford to move our flights and I wasn't sure Faye would be well enough to cover 280 miles across wind-battered Tierra del Fuego, if and when she got better.

Worse than the threat of a missed flight, Faye now couldn't keep water down. I knew she was in trouble. She'd lost so much liquid that she was waking up in the middle of the night with cramps, shrieking in pain. At lunchtime on the fourth day, I returned to the room and sat on my bed. Faye stirred and sat up. She looked as white as a ghost. Her face was gaunt and there were dark circles under her eyes.

'How you doing?' I asked.

'Pretty much the same,' she rasped.

'Have you eaten anything?'

'No… I can't.'

'Did you manage any water?'

'I did, this morning, I tried – but it all came out. I chucked it straight back up.'

'Oh, Faye,' I said softly.

'I know. I think I need to go to a doctor. Don't worry, I'll take myself down there,' she said quickly.

'You numpty, you are not taking yourself to the doctor! Have you seen yourself? You can barely sit up! I'll come with you.'

So I bundled her into a taxi and we headed to a hospital on the outskirts of town. We had a brief conversation in broken Spanish with the receptionist. In order to get out her debit card to pay for the treatment, Faye had to let go of the countertop and I watched while she reached into her bag and swayed in front of me. She turned white and almost fell over. I put my hands on her back.

'Woah there! Let's keep you upright,' I said.

The poor girl was a wreck. We sat down on the teal-coloured seats in the modest waiting room and within 10 minutes a friendly looking doctor appeared. He had dark hair, an impressive set of eyebrows and a round face that was at least 80% cheeks.

'Fay-ye Shippparrd? Fay-ye Shippparrdd?' He called out to the waiting room.

I helped Faye to her feet and she followed the doctor down the corridor and through a set of double doors. After 30 minutes of flicking through Spanish magazines in the waiting room, I began to wonder how Faye was getting on beyond those doors. Just then, a picture came through to my phone. It was Faye, giving it a big thumbs up, lying on a hospital bed with a drip in her arm. I laughed, then let out a sigh of relief.

She was being looked after. She was going to be okay. Phew.

Another 30 minutes passed before Faye appeared again. She had colour back in her face, she wasn't swaying in the slightest and, best of all, she was smiling.

'Wow. You look better!' I said.

'I feel better,' she replied.

'What happened? I saw the drip. Did they drug you up?'

'Oh yes. They drugged me gooood, McNuff. It was gastroenteritis.'

'Crikey. That's serious, isn't it?' I said, remembering that my brother had gastroenteritis once and I was pretty sure it had resulted in a week off work. 'Was that doctor who took you in nice? He seemed nice,' I continued.

'He was very nice! He even kissed me on each cheek, in the proper friendly Argentinian way. I could have been infectious, but he didn't seem to care.'

'He's got his priorities in order, clearly. Greetings first, gastroenteritis second. What did they put in your arm? Just fluids?'

'Yep, they hooked me up to some fluids and put an antibiotic IV in too. I feel AMAZING,' she smiled.

'Good! I'm so sorry I didn't get you here sooner,' I said, feeling a wave of guilt.

'Don't be an idiot, McNuff! And besides, if I'd come sooner, I might not have got my double cheek smooches from the doctor.'

'Silver linings! Who cares about a touch of gastro when you're getting cheek smooches, after all?'

'Agreed. Right, McNuff, let's get out of here – we've got some cycling to do.'

29

The End of the World

Distance cycled: 5,259 miles
Metres ascended: 102,578

On the windswept plains beyond Punta Arenas, it was freezing. I'm not talking 'oh what a lovely nip in the air' kind of cold. I'm talking the bone-achingly, chilli-vanilli, toe-tingle-tastic kind of freezing. Except, I couldn't actually feel my toes. I hadn't been able to feel them for a few hours now. I'd been asking Faye to stop every 30 minutes so that I could get off the bike and complete some moves to warm them up. These were moves last seen in 1980s aerobics routines. I even threw in a vintage box step and a couple of grapevines for good measure. The roadside aerobics seemed to do the trick, although any passing drivers might have considered us unhinged. Two women, off their bikes, dancing around on the hard shoulder. Faye's toes weren't as cold as mine so she didn't really need to do the aerobics, but she joined in anyway.

After Faye's dalliance with gastroenteritis, we'd spent a few more days in Punta Arenas, getting some food into her and nursing her back to health. As soon as Faye had managed to inhale a submarino (the universal sign that all was right in the world again), we were ready to roll. I was nervous about the remaining 280 miles to Ushuaia, not to mention the fact we only had four days left to do it. But, after some back and forth (and me double-checking for signs of faux bravery), Faye had insisted that she was up for giving it a bash. So we packed our bags, wheeled Bernard and Gustavo onto the final Patagonian ferry and crossed the Straits of Magellan to the island of Tierra del Fuego, Land of Fire.

Now, I'm a sucker for a good place name. Show me a hunk of land with a dramatic title and I'm rooting for it. I desperately want it to live up to the image that my imagination has gone to great lengths to create for it – and Tierra del Fuego was no different. Despite its heat-centric nickname, I knew that the island was famous for frigid temperatures and biting winds, some of which can reach 60 mph and more. During the winter months (which we were now approaching), the temperature averages at a balmy zero degrees. Add the rush of air that rips in from the South Pacific and the island can feel colder still. It was facts like these that left me in awe of the indigenous people who had lived on the island some 8,000 years ago – long before the white man came a-conquering in the early 1500s. Mostly comprised of the Selk'nam, Yamana and Kawésqa tribes, they wore very little clothing but often lit fires to keep them warm, hence the name 'land of fire'.

In a bid to make our flights on time, we were eager to make swift progress across the island. We opted to follow the main tarmac road, which skirted the east coast before curving inland to rejoin the most southerly peaks of the Andes. From the moment we pedalled away from the ferry at the port of Porvenir, I was struck by a landscape that was nothing like the stereotypical images of Patagonia. It was flat and barren, and the ground was covered in brown-yellow grass that stretched out beneath a blanket of grey cloud. There were no trees, no mountains and no buildings between the small towns of San Sebastián and Río Grande. The northern end of the island was a no-frills kind of place. But that was okay because we were in a no-frills kind of mood. Just like people always have done on Tierra del Fuego, we were doing what we could to survive the harsh conditions that surrounded us.

In those last few days, I was more eager than ever to make it to Ushuaia. I tried to keep my mind away from the idea that we might not make it under our own steam, all the while doing my best to ignore the nervous fizz in my belly. Averaging 70 miles a day on the bikes was perfectly doable under normal circumstances, but what happened if Faye got sick again? Her stomach was still grumbling, after all. And what if one of the bikes broke down? How about if a storm blew through? The past few weeks of handing the vom baton between one other, and the energy needed to cope with the uncertainty of it all, had drained us both. I was exhausted and I wanted to be done, and I could tell that Faye felt the same. And yet... I could feel the slow creep of sadness in my bones. Soon, this would all be over. Soon, I wouldn't have to be worrying about sickness and storms and broken bikes. Those thoughts lowered my energy level even further until I had nothing left to give to the adventure. But, somehow, we kept moving across the plains. It was almost as if there were an invisible rope, tied to the front of our bikes, pulling us both toward the finish.

Two days after leaving town, the state of Faye's insides had improved dramatically but the weather had taken a turn for the worse. Old Man Winter had wrapped his steely fingers around Tierra del Fuego, and his grip grew tighter by the day. One morning it started to snow, an event that somehow managed to transform the wind-battered riding from being a slog to being rather awesome. I like extreme weather, after all. Just like with the lightning storms and altitude, there was something about the extreme conditions that reminded me I was alive. To be out there in nature, and so connected to it, was addictive.

In a bid to keep out the cold, I was wearing two pairs of leggings and three tops and I had even 'double buffed' my face (wearing one buff scarf around my neck and one over my cheeks and nose). Double buffing is a drastic measure but, sometimes, one buff just ain't enough. And besides, even a smidge of skin exposed to the cold air was a smidge too much. Despite there not being a scrap of sun in the sky, we'd both also opted to wear our sunglasses. The wind chill around our eyes was too much to take, and the glasses acted as a shield. The result was that we looked like a cross between ninjas and rock stars. On bikes. Who sometimes stop to do roadside aerobics.

The snow had turned the countryside around us into a winter wonderland, although tufts of dark green grass and patches of brown earth were still visible under the dusting of white. We pushed on through the snow, following a patchy tarmac road around the side of a large mountain. I tried to ignore the missing sections of concrete crash barrier at the side of the road, and the drop into the forest below, keeping my gaze fixed ahead, pedalling towards columns of white-grey cloud and a horizon we could barely see.

With 150 miles left to ride to Ushuaia, we had moved away from the coast, beyond the plains, and were back in the foothills of the Andes. I rounded a sharp bend alongside a large lake and gawped at the scene. To my right, I could see three, no four mountains. All four were covered in snow with a strip of dark, blackish brown around their base. They rose and fell like a wall of thundering waves alongside us, the foamy white crests surging onwards, just as we were, towards Ushuaia.

'This is amazing!' I shouted to Faye.

I hadn't expected the scenery to be so dramatic in the final few days, but South America kept dishing up the good stuff, reminding us that, although we were jaded by the adventure, it was still as sharp and shiny as it had always been.

'Look at that one!' Faye shouted, pointing from her bike. I followed her outstretched arm to see that a new mountain had just come into view. It was different from the others and looked like a perfect pyramid, more at home in Egypt than in snowy Patagonia. I remember thinking how wonderful it was that the mountain stood out like that. What a brave bit of rock it was, with its crisp, straight edges slicing through the sky.

On the penultimate day of pedalling, we were in the middle of a roadside aerobics session when a golden-haired dog appeared at the side of the road. He bounded towards us and stopped a couple of metres away, before letting out a bark and beginning to wag his tail. Both of us stood stock-still. I could tell that we were thinking the same thing. We didn't want this dog to come between us and cause another fight. He looked like a friendly pooch, so I decided in a split second that if this dog wanted to run all the remaining 80 miles to Ushuaia beside us, that was fine by me. I was over doing battle with anyone – with stray dogs, and with Faye. Nothing was more important than ending this journey with our friendship intact.

The dog was an odd breed, as stray dogs often are. I wasn't sure if it was possible, but he looked to be part Labrador and part Husky, which made him cuddly, full of energy and fast, complete with piercing blue eyes. We concluded that he must be a new breed of dog called a Huskydor, and we named him Burt. Burt had a faded pink collar, which suggested that he had a home and an owner somewhere, but he seemed intent on coming with us. It was a downhill ride to where we intended to camp for the night, but Burt managed to keep up, bounding alongside us all the way to a camp spot in orange-gold woods, just off the road.

We threw the bikes down and piled on some extra clothes before starting to pitch our tents for the very last time. Faye paused mid-construction, a tent peg in one hand and her groundsheet in the other:

'Anna…' she said.

'Yep?' I stopped wrestling with my own pop-up palace and looked across at her.

'I was just thinking… we've done really well, you know. I don't mean the cycling, I mean… us.'

I smiled. 'Well?! I think 'well' is an understatement! It's not normal, living the way we have, you know? It's enough to drive anyone bananas. And we both still very much like bananas.'

There was a moment of silence.

'I think it's been the best thing, you know? Us two,' Faye continued quietly.

'Me too, Faye, me too,' I replied. We smiled at one another, and then went back to putting up our tents, just as we had done almost every night for the past half a year.

As it turned out, the task of tent-pitching was more of a challenge than usual, what with Burt having joined us. He was a complete pain in the arse, clambering all over us, bouncing between the bikes like a pinball and knocking them over with all his bounding to and fro. The contrast between Burt's energy and our own lethargy was stark. His canine enthusiasm got to be too much even for Faye and, after a couple of attempts at eating dinner together at the edge of the forest, we agreed to seek refuge, zipping ourselves into our own tents to finish eating. Burt continued to try to force entry by running at the tents, leaving muddy paw prints in neat patterns across the green rip-stop material. Eventually, the patter of paws died down. Chancing a peek out of my porch, I spotted him a way off in the forest, presumably hunting for his own dinner.

'Oop. Burt's gone walkabout in the forest,' I called over to Faye from inside my tent.

'Let's hope he goes walkabout all the way home,' she shouted back.

'Let's hope so. How are your toes doing?' I asked.

'They're alright… sort of. Well, actually, they're freezing. How are yours?' asked Faye.

'Oh, mine are fine. I've stuck them in the chickpea water,' I replied.

'You've what?'

'The water I used to cook the chickpeas in… I've put my toes in it and it's warming them up a treat.'

'Are the chickpeas still in there?' she said.

'Eww, no! I ate them. I don't fancy foot-flavoured chickpeas.'

'Well, I'm glad you can feel your toes again,' she said.

'Do you want some?' I asked.

'What, some chickpeas?'

'No, the chickpea water. It's still warm. You could heat your toes up too.'

'Nah, you're alright, McNuff. You keep it. I can't really

move. I'm wearing all my clothes and I'm not sure I'll ever make it out of this sleeping bag again.'

'Right! I'm coming over!' I said. Removing my feet from the pan, I slid them into my shoes and unzipped my tent.

'What?! Why… what are you doing?' Faye shouted, on hearing the sound of the zipper.

'I am delivering you warm chickpea water for your cold toes, Madame. You have no choice. I'm out! Here it comes,' I said, taking a few steps over the stony ground between the two tents and then sliding the pan into Faye's porch.

'Aww. Thanks, mate, you're a star,' she said.

I walked back to my tent. A few moments later, I got confirmation that Faye was now also experiencing the delights of the chickpea saucepan foot spa.

'Oh my gawwd. This is incredible!' she shouted.

The following morning, Burt the Huskydor was back from his exploration in the woods and I found him curled up outside Faye's tent. We packed up and left the camp spot, with Burt running alongside us for 30 minutes, until we passed a small farm. Pulling over, we tracked down a farm worker, who agreed to hold onto Burt just long enough for us to pedal out of reach. This time, even Faye was in agreement that we needed to find a way to leave Burt behind. He might even have had an owner nearby. His pink collar suggested as much, after all. He was all slobber and smiles as we turned away and walked back to our bikes and it was heartbreaking to leave him there.

He strained on a leash towards us as we pulled out of the farm and got back on the road.

'Oh, Burt. I can't look back,' Faye whimpered.

'Me neither. It's for the best,' I said.

'I know. Bye, bye Burt. You were the best Huskydor ever,' said Faye.

As we set off again, tucked into the two-up time-trial formation that had become so familiar over the past six months, I pulled my phone out of the pouch on my handlebars and checked where we were. It was now 45 miles to Ushuaia. Just 45 little miles – we would be there by midday. I thought back to our arrival in La Paz, how we'd struggled to get the bike boxes off the baggage belt and how Faye and I hadn't spent more than a few days together before then. It all seemed so unreal.

We rounded a bend and started up a small incline. The sun was beginning to peek out from behind the clouds, and the patches of ice beside the road glistened as they reflected the sunlight. I checked my phone again. Thirty-five miles to go. My mind began whirring, spinning like a roulette wheel, through all the moments that had led us to this point. I recalled the heat of the Yungas jungle (and the bugs and the bites and the temper tantrums). The thrill of riding down Death Road, arms juddering, hands sore and brakes almost on fire. I could still almost taste the sticky sweet mangos we'd gorged one afternoon by the cool, clear river.

The cold air stung my cheeks and I breathed hard as we neared the top of another climb. It had begun to snow again, but only lightly. I glanced over my shoulder at Faye – she was working just as hard as I was, but she still had a huge grin on her face. She lifted one arm off the bars and gave me a thumbs up. Twenty-five miles to go. Puffing hard, I remembered our failed attempt to make it to the summit of the mighty Uturuncu, Faye sharing her cheese puffs, the company of Andean flamingos, and roadside gifts of baguettes and orange juice.

Fifteen miles to go. It wasn't every day that your friend gets stung by a scorpion. I wouldn't forget that one in a hurry, nor would there be many more opportunities in life for me to go naked cycling. I was pretty sure I'd get arrested if I tried that anywhere other than the salt flats of Bolivia.

Ten miles to go and the roulette wheel of memories stopped on one last scene: the two condors on Route 13. I could still see them if I shut my eyes. How wild and free they had seemed that evening, soaring above the mountains at sunset, harnessing the wind as they managed to stay airborne, side by side, with such grace under even the toughest of conditions.

At long last we rolled down the final hill and into the outskirts of Ushuaia. Pulling our bikes to a halt at a crossroads, we looked up from the road. There was an alpine feel to the town and it was fancier than I'd expected. The shops were a mix of local, functional places, like launderettes and hardware stores, and well-equipped outdoor-clothing shops, with elegant window displays and eye-watering price tags. It was clear that the posh shops were intended for those who were casually dropping by before boarding a ship to Antarctica – that was no cheap package holiday, after all. Faye and I hadn't said anything to one another over the past hour, but we both knew that down on the waterfront there was a big wooden 'Ushuaia' sign. We'd seen others posing with it online. I took a deep breath and exhaled loudly. I turned to Faye and smiled. She smiled back.

'The sign's down there,' I said, pointing down a road toward the water.

'Okay,' Faye said, quietly.

'I suppose we better go and see it? Take a picture 'n' all that?' I said.

'Okay,' said Faye again.

'Or… we could go and get a burger first? One last meal before the finish?'

'Yes! I fancy a burger. And maybe a hot chocolate too?' Faye exclaimed, notably more excited about getting food than the prospect of visiting the sign.

And so we prolonged the journey's end. I'm not entirely sure why, but it was clear that neither of us wanted to be done, not just yet. Time is such a precious thing, after all – it's so often beyond our control. We wanted to hold it captive, if only for an hour or two. We wanted to sit and be with the ending of it all, just a little bit longer.

Two hours later, full of food that was a welcome departure

from instant noodles and packets of mashed potato, we made it down to the waterfront. The sign was beautifully carved, with Ushuaia and the words 'The End of the World' painted in bright colours. With the help of a passing tourist, we posed for a couple of photos before exchanging a hug and wheeling our bikes towards the shore. Leaning Bernard and Gustavo against a railing, we looked out over the wild waters beyond Cape Horn.

Together, we'd cycled 5,539 miles through three countries, making ten border crossings and 103,753 metres of ascent through the Andean mountains. It had been harder than I'd expected, physically and emotionally. I'd been humbled by the altitude, the mountains and Mother Nature in all her guises. I'd been humbled by the fragility of our friendship too but then again, the most precious things in life tend to be delicate and breakable.

As is often the case with giant leaps in life, none of the fears that Faye and I had confessed to one another at the start of the journey came to pass. But they had been replaced with other lessons. Like just how often our stomachs would ache from bouts of belly-busting laughter. And how, in times of struggle, sometimes what we needed from one another were a few words of encouragement. Or, more often than not, all we needed was silence and the comfort of knowing that the other was there.

'I can't believe it's over,' said Faye.

'Me too. Bet you're glad we didn't go on scooters now, eh?'

I said, and Faye laughed.

'I am. But do you know what?'

'What?'

'I'd have stuck it out with you either way, McNuff.' She smiled.

'I know.' I replied.

Epilogue

Sitting in the back of a taxi on the way to Ushuaia Airport, watching the mixture of small city streets and mountains rumble by, I'd been silent for a few minutes. I was deep in thought.

'Faye,' I said, looking at the mass of auburn hair sitting in front of me in the passenger seat of the car.

'Yes, mate?' she said, still looking ahead.

'I've worked out that we only had four proper arguments in the whole journey, you know.'

'Did we? That's not too bad, is it?'

'Not bad at all. Well, I think we had three full arguments and two half ones.'

'Ha! I love that you've categorised them, McNuff. Remind me what they were?'

'Well, there was that one going up Uturuncu…'

'Oh, yeah… we both apologised for that one…'

'Yeah, and then there was the one when you forgot the tracker on Christmas Eve…'

'Oh crikey,' she said sheepishly. 'I was a right dufus. That turned out okay in the end though. And at least we had orange juice and fireworks to make it right.'

'Then there was the one with the dog that chased us.'

We both fell silent and there was a long pause. We knew that was a bad one.

'And the half ones? What were they?' Faye said.

'Oh, well we got a bit tetchy with one another trying to get into Santiago, didn't we?'

'Oh yeah, that was definitely a half one. We managed to pull it back though. And that scary woman offering us biscuits helped us snap out of it,' she laughed. 'So that's three and a half arguments. What was the last half one? I can't think of any more?'

'Err… there was that time we were going to the supermarket in San José de Jáchal. And you wanted to get there before it closed and I was being annoying, walking really slowly because I had a belly full of lemon pie and didn't want to rush.'

'What?! That wasn't an argument. Did we have an argument?'

'No, not exactly. But, well, I was a bit arsey and you went all quiet so I thought we'd had an argument?'

'Err, I must have missed that one, I can't even remember it! I think you were having an argument with yourself, McNuff.'

I smiled. It was settled then. Three and a half arguments in six months of living in one another's pockets. Jeepers. I was proud.

The truth is, cycling up mountains is wonderful. Gasping for oxygen at 5,900 metres high is tougher than I had ever imagined. Dealing with crashes, dog bites, sub-zero temperatures, running out of food, 50-mph crosswinds and gastroenteritis, these are challenges I won't forget in a hurry. But if you ask me what it is that I am most proud of about our journey, it's the way that Faye and I managed our friendship.

Spending 24 hours a day, seven days a week with another person for six months is quite possibly the most dangerous thing you could do to a friendship. It's hard to explain the kind of relationship that develops through that level of intensity. We are far from blind to one another's flaws and cracks and ugly bits. In fact, we've seen everything there is to see (quite literally) on more occasions than I care to remember. There is a hidden strength in the willingness to be fragile in the company of another human, after all. But, at the heart of it all, there is trust, there is respect and there is patience.

On the outside, Faye and I are very different. In certain areas, we couldn't be more different if we tried (take tent cleanliness, for example – I live gleefully in a pigsty, Faye maintains a palace). But, at our core, we have the same stuff – the good stuff. When all we want to do is fly off the handle or sulk, it's that good stuff that keeps us stuck to one another, makes us take a deep breath and pause. It's the good stuff that allows us to tolerate the silence, or to look past the words that are spewing from the other's mouth and to actually listen to what it is that she is trying to say, which usually boils down to 'I'm frightened', 'I'm frustrated' or 'I'm hurt'. In short, our friendship is like a Jammie Dodger biscuit. No one really cares about the biscuity bits around the edge of a Jammie Dodger, after all. Biscuity edges are ten-a-penny, and they break, crumble and turn to dust. But the stuff in the middle, that's what counts. It's the jam that makes a Jammie Dodger special. And Faye and I both have jam in our middles.

***

Since returning home from the Andes, Faye has joined the emergency services and is now a paramedic in her homeland of Cornwall. I'm sure she won't mind me saying that she used the journey to consider what it was that she really wanted to be doing with her life. Deep down, she knew what that was all along, but pre-Andes she couldn't quite muster the confidence to go for it. There is no one in the world better suited to being a paramedic. I know if I had an accident, I'd want Faye to come to the rescue with her caring nature and outstanding sense of humour. The best news is they don't have scorpions in Cornwall, so she won't be called out to any potentially deadly stings. Although I wouldn't be surprised if she offers her patients cheese puffs when they feel low.

Faye was also reunited with her beloved Jack Russell terriers, Mollie and Jack. Jack has since left this earth for his own adventures in doggie heaven and we decided not to tell Mollie about Burt, or Alf, or the dozens of other street dogs we met in the Andes, for fear that she would get jealous. Mollie is now a true adventure dog – Faye has trained her to sit on her shoulders as she rides her bike around the local trails, and they have plans to complete a Land's End to John O'Groats cycle as a dastardly duo one day.

It seems that 140 characters sent via GPS message are not only enough to keep mothers from endless worry but they are also enough to keep the love alive between couples. Jamie got his visa approved and eventually made it to America, completing a 5,500-mile, year-long run across the country in 2018, dressed as his very own alter ego, Adventureman. I flew back and forth to the States that year, dressing up as Wonder Woman each time to run marathons by his side. Thanks to the Andes journey and the adventures that have followed, we've learned that thousands of miles of land and sea are no match for two hearts so full of love.

Writing this book seemed difficult at the outset because I wanted to be honest about the thoughts I had and the actions I took. I could have chosen to romanticise the journey, to always paint myself in a favourable light. Memories are simply stories that we cement in our mind, after all – they are subject to tricks and omissions of the truth. Goodness knows, Faye's account of our time in South America would have some differences. But that's the beauty of any shared adventure. Physically, you are on the same journey, but you can only ever see everything through one set of eyes.

There were times when I was writing this story, in the comfort of a calm cafe at home in Gloucester, that I was embarrassed I had even had those unflattering thoughts. I still am.

In the cold light of day, many of the things whizzing around in my head seemed so very ugly. I would like to be less human in that way, but I am human. And if our Andean adventure taught me anything, it's that thoughts are not actions. It's okay to think certain things, but it's how you act that matters. We can't control our thoughts, after all – they crash into our minds without permission or invitation and wreak havoc. Guilt. Anxiety. Pride. Envy. Confusion. These are giant oaks, deeply rooted in thought alone.

There were times in South America when I doubted Faye. There were times when I blamed her for things that were my own doing. But, as the months wore on, I learned to recognise these for what they were – thoughts. Although they were a part of me, they did not define me. As the ancient Chinese philosophers say, in the presence of these thoughts, we must act 'as if' – even in the moments we are struggling. Struggling to love someone, struggling to find compassion, struggling to think beyond our own needs, we must act 'as if'. As if we love them, as if we can see their good intention, as if we trust them. Then, sure enough, and soon enough, when the red mist drops, our actions are all that will remain. And it's those actions that connect us to one another.

AUTHOR NOTE

Congratulations to you, wonderful reader, on making it to the end of the world! I really hope you enjoyed yourself, riding side by side with Faye and me. You'll likely be feeling rather tired now, but I would be forever grateful if you could persevere like Sally the Saddle sore and head over to Amazon or Good Reads right this very moment and leave a review for the book.

Even if it's just a one sentence comment, your words will make a massive difference. Reviews are a huge boost to independently published authors, like me, who don't have big publishing houses to spread the word for us. It's safe to say that the more reviews up there, the more likely it is that this book will land in other people's laps.

If you'd like to be kept up to date with future book releases and adventure shenanigans, you can join my mailing list at: **annamcnuff.com/McNewsletter**

No Spam, just awesomeness – that's a pinky promise.

And if you'd like to see a selection of the best pictures from the journey – head to: **annamcnuff.com/southamerica**

If social media is more your kind of fandango, you can say hello here:

On Facebook: **'Anna McNuff'**

On Instagram: **@annamcnuff**

On Twitter: **@annamcnuff**

Or if social media is your idea of hell, I can also be found here:

annamcnuff.com

hello@annamcnuff.com

Failing that, send me a pigeon.

THANK YOU'S

It goes without saying that I must start with a massive thank you to my good friend Faye Shepherd of Cornwall, for helping to create memories that will last a lifetime (and for putting up with me for six months). I came home from the Andes a better person because of your patience, kindness and friendship – you truly are one in a million. Let's go climb Aconcagua one day.

A MEGA thanks goes out to my main editor, Debbie Chapman, who always helps me to polish a turd of words into something truly magical. You are my editorial dreamboat. Thanks also to Sophie 'hawk eyes' Martin for the copyedit and for convincing me to remove sections where I wanted to go off on one about the structure of a peanut.

Muchas gracias to my talented friend Hoogie (and Cleo the cat) who agreed to check my attempts at Spanish and make sure all of those lovely accents were where they should be. A big thanks also to my Great Aunt Ann – the last line of adventure memoir defence. Any mistakes left in the book are because I have decided to make up my own rules around grammar and spelling.

Thank you to Kim & Sally at Off Grid for laying this book out so darn beautifully, for whipping me up some maps and nailing the cover design. And thanks to the team at Alpacaly Ever After in the Lake District for taking photos of their lovely llamas for us. Those knobbly knees are rockin' it.

A big thanks to Richard at Oxford Bike Works for providing me with the wonder of wheels that is Bernard the Bike. I hope you agree that he did us both proud on the journey.

Thank you… to YOU. Yes you! And anyone who has ever followed me on social media or bought one of my books. I am able to live a life I adore because of your ongoing support, generosity and good vibes.

Lastly, thanks to my friends, my family and my McMan, Jamie – for making it so darn easy to maintain a relationship while being thousands of miles apart. And for always supporting my love of writing. You are the sausages to my mashed potato.

QUESTIONS FOR YOUR BOOK CLUB

1. What do you think were some of the most significant changes in the relationship between Faye and Anna over the course of the six-month journey?

2. Was there anything in the descriptions of the landscape, wildlife or the people in South America that surprised you?

3. Which section of the journey from La Paz to Ushuaia would you most like to experience for yourself?

4. Anna mentions, on a number of occasions, how she loves to be close to the wildness of Mother Nature and enjoys storms especially. How important is that connection to nature in our modern lives?

5. There were some fears that Anna and Faye discussed at the beginning of the trip. How often do you think that fear prevents us from exploring a more adventurous life?

6. Anna and Faye both experienced disappointment in their journey along the Carretera Austral in Patagonia. Have you ever had an experience of expectation not matching up to reality during your own travels?

7. Anna talks about maintaining her relationship with Jamie while being thousands of miles apart. How easy is it manage our own desires and goals in life, alongside those of the people we love?

8. How does the book deal with the difference between thought and action? Do you think that either of the women could have acted differently in one of the stressful situations?

9. Do you feel that travelling together prevented Anna and Faye from ever feeling lonely? What do think the major differences are between solo travel and a journey with another person?

10. Final (very serious) question – if you had a bike and you took it to the Andes mountains for 6 months, what would you name it?

ANNA MCNUFF: KEYNOTE SPEAKER

Anna has delivered motivational, inspiring and entertaining talks for schools, charities and businesses around the world.

"Anna's ability to instill a sense of self-belief in those watching her speak is second to none. Despite her own astounding achievements – she very much made the talk at our team away day about us instead. Honest, relatable and wonderfully down to earth."

SKY TV

"An incredibly talented speaker. Full of guts, determination, stamina and vision."

BARCLAYS BANK

"Absolutely Fantastic!"

HRH PRINCE EDWARD

"Hugely entertaining with plenty of food for thought. Thank you for not only having great stories to share, but for sharing them in such a compelling way."

GlaxoSmithKline

"Without a doubt the most energetic speaker we have ever had. Thank you for helping our team find the courage to face challenges head on."

MARS

"Anna's inspiring stories made the audience think differently about their own personal and professional challenges – something very well suited with the current challenges facing our industry."

SKODA

"Anna added so much to our sales conference. Her impact extended far beyond the time on stage and it was clear to everyone that she genuinely cared about helping others to think differently, and do more."

EMERSON

For more information about booking Anna to speak:

Go to: **annamcnuff.com/speaking**

Or email **speaking@annamcnuff.com**

ALSO BY ANNA MCNUFF

Anna was never anything like those 'real' runners on telly – all spindly limbs, tiny shorts and split times – but when she read about New Zealand's 3,000-kilometre-long Te Araroa Trail, she began to wonder... perhaps being a 'real' runner was over-rated. Maybe she could just run it anyway?

For anyone who has ever dreamt of taking on a great challenge, but felt too afraid to begin – this story is for you.

ALSO BY ANNA MCNUFF

With no previous experience as a long-distance cyclist, Anna decides to clamber atop a beautiful pink bicycle (named Boudica) and set out on an 11,000-mile journey on her own, through each and every state of the USA.

Dodging floods, blizzards and electrical storms, she pedals side by side with mustangs of the Wild West, through towering redwood forests, past the snow-capped peaks of the Rocky Mountains and on to the volcanos of Hawaii.

A stunning tale of self-discovery, told through the eyes of a woman who couldn't help but wonder if there was more to life, and more to America too.

ALSO BY ANNA MCNUFF

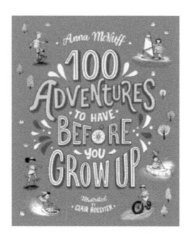

Discover an adventurous life with this energetic guide packed with 100 ideas, big and small.

From building a secret den, to going on a trail run, stargazing in your back garden, visiting a lighthouse and telling midnight ghost stories, every adventure in these pages will get you fired up think creatively and get exploring. No matter where you live or who you are, this book will encourage everyone to fly by the seat of their adventure pants!

ABOUT THE AUTHOR

Anna McNuff is an adventurer, speaker, bestselling author and self-confessed mischief maker. Named by The Guardian as one of the top female adventurers of our time, she is the UK ambassador for Girlguiding, and has run, swum and cycled over 20,000 miles across the globe.

She is best known for her most recent adventure, in which she set off to run 2,620 miles (100 marathons) through Great Britain… in bare feet. Other major journeys include cycling a beautiful pink bicycle through each and every state of the USA and running the length of New Zealand.

Much closer to home, she has also spent a month cycling across Europe directed entirely by social media, run the length of Hadrian's wall dressed as a Roman Soldier, and the length of the Jurassic Coast, dressed as a dinosaur. As you do.

When not off adventuring, Anna can be found curled up with a flat white at a local coffee shop in her home city of Gloucester.

Lightning Source UK Ltd.
Milton Keynes UK
UKHW040221200920
370179UK00003BA/95

9 781999 765859